The Alien's Guidebook Series

I0421921

Ecology of Story

World as Character

Nina Munteanu
M.Sc., R.P. Bio.

PIXL PRESS

Vancouver, Canada

Also in the Guidebook Series

The Fiction Writer: Get Published, Write Now!
The Journal Writer: Finding Your Voice

Other Books by Nina Munteanu

Angel of Chaos

Darwin's Paradox

The Last Summoner

Outer Diverse

Inner Diverse

Metaverse

Collision with Paradise

The Cypol

Natural Selection: A Collection of Short Stories

Water Is…The Meaning of Water

A Diary in the Age of Water

ECOLOGY OF STORY: WORLD AS CHARACTER ©2019 by Nina Munteanu

Edited by Merridy Cox
Book Design by Costi Gurgu
Cover Art by Anne Moody
Interior illustrations by Costi Gurgu

Author Photo by Jane Raptor

ISBN: 9780981163659 (Trade Paperback)
ISBN: 978-0-9811636-3-5 (Hardcover)
ISBN: 978-0-9811636-4-2 (Digital)

Library and Archives Canada Cataloguing in Publication

Title: The ecology of story : world as character / by Nina Munteanu, M.Sc., R.P.Bio.
Names: Munteanu, Nina, author.
Description: Series statement: The alien's guidebook series |
Includes bibliographical references.
Identifiers: Canadiana (print) 20190100990 | Canadiana (ebook) 20190101903 | ISBN 9780981163635 (hardcover) | ISBN 9780981163659 (softcover) | ISBN 9780981163642 (PDF)
Subjects: LCSH: Authorship. | LCSH: Ecology—Authorship. | LCSH: Ecology.
Classification: LCC PN145 .M86 2019 | DDC 808.02—dc23

PRAISE FOR THE FICTION WRITER

"Like the good Doctor's Tardis, *The Fiction Writer* is larger than it appears … Get *Get Published, Write Now!* right now."

—David Merchant, Creative Writing Instructor, Louisiana Tech University

"*The Fiction Writer* is at the top of the required reading list for my Writer's Workshop students. With its engagingly direct, conversational style and easily accessible format, it is a veritable cornucopia of hands-on help for aspiring writers of any age…the quintessential guidebook for the soon-to-be-published."

—Susan McLemore, Writing Instructor, Glynn Academy

"I'm thoroughly enjoying the book and even learning a thing or two!"

—Robert J. Sawyer,
Hugo and Nebula Award-winning author of *Quantum Night*

"As important a tool as your laptop or your pen."

—Cathi Urbonas, Halifax writer

The Fiction Writer "has become my writing bible."

—Carina Burns, author of *The Syrian Jewelry Box*

"I highly recommend this book for any writer wishing to get published."

—Marie Bilodeau, author of *Destiny's Blood*

"Nina Munteanu's *The Fiction Writer* gets to the point, quickly. It is a digest of all the how-to's of writing fiction. Although aimed at the writing student, this is a handy book for the emerging or mature writer as well, as it is a great resource to refresh one's memory on every aspect of the writing process."

—Shane Joseph, author of *Milltown*

"*The Fiction Writer: Get Published, Write Now!* is an excellent tool for all writers, beginners or professionals.It is the most practical book on publishing that I've ever read, and I've read them all! Not only is each chapter packed with advice for writers at every level of the publishing process, but the text is highly readable and even entertaining. The clear format, the direct style and the playful layout keep the large volume of information from ever becoming dry or boring."

—Lucia Gorea, author of *Vlad the Impaler* and
Writing Instructor, University of British Columbia

"Good writing is good writing, and Munteanu has worked hard to provide a guidebook that shows exactly how to achieve that result. Highly recommended!"

—Sherry D. Ramsay, *The Scriptorium*

"High energy writer and teacher of writing Nina Munteanu is an upbeat coach for new and published writers seeking to refresh their art. She relates tales from her own experiences to personalize her frank and helpful advice on getting published. I particularly liked how she focuses on writing good stuff, though. Her light-hearted "alien's perspective" complete with cartoon character combines with her sense of humor and cheerful tone to make the book a positive experience. Short sections. Snappy chat."

—Lynda Williams, author of *Okal Rel* Series.

"Nina Munteanu's *The Fiction Writer* is the book I wish I had 15 years ago. Writers young and old can find ways to improve their work, with the book's fun, easy to read format."

— Theresa Vinson, book seller

CONTENTS

Two … What Is Adaptation?

For Doina

INTRODUCTION

When I was twelve years old, I wrote the CEO of a juice company, exhorting them to make their bottles reusable or at the very least to recycle them; this was long before recycling became common practice in municipalities, homes and businesses. The CEO invited me to a meeting, and was clearly startled that I was just a kid. That day I realized how words on a page can empower, compel and transform.

When I grew up, I became a limnologist, researching freshwater lakes and rivers in western Canada. I zoomed around in a boat, took water and sediment samples, examined organisms and wrote reports on how everything worked—or didn't—along with my recommendations for action.

I've been telling stories since I was five. In the several decades that followed, I've written dozens of stories, mostly speculative eco-fiction: flash fiction, short stories, novellas and novels. As part of my career as a writer, I began coaching writers to publication. I've been doing that for twenty years. I also teach writing at the University of Toronto and at George Brown College. In 2009, I started my writing guide series with *The Fiction Writer: Get Published, Write Now!* I followed in 2013 with *The Journal Writer: Finding Your Voice* on journaling and writing memoirs.

In the decades of coaching and teaching, I noticed one recurring challenge with the writers I was helping: a lack of integration of place in meaningful story and the use of metaphor to achieve this. That's why this third book in my writing guide series focuses on place and its role in story.

The Ecology of Story: World as Character appears in two parts: Part 1, Ecology; and Part 2, Story.

Part 1 will benefit all writers and genres of writing, but particularly those writing in speculative, science fiction and fantasy genres, who must build worlds that are different from our own but remain grounded in science to provide a compelling sense of reality. This is where ecology—the study of place and relationships—is most useful. However, *all* writers will benefit from Part 1, given that all stories are set somewhere. The heart of every story is place; the relationship of place to character, premise, and theme makes knowledge of ecology very useful—given that it is the study of relationships and consequence. Ecology allows a writer to imagine and create anything they wish to populate their world and achieve a sense of realism by providing a realistic process and relationship—all based on biological logic. Ecology provides a source for metaphor—the writer's most potent tool. For a writer to provide truly meaningful setting, atmosphere, place in their story, she must avoid stereotyping or misrepresenting her environment. This will undermine the very purpose of subtext and metaphor of subtle connections. Which brings me to Part 2 ...

Part 2 focuses on place in story, and its obvious and less obvious connection to premise, theme, and character. When a writer is mindful of place in story and not only *accurately portrays environment* but treats it as a character, then her story will resonate with multilayers of meaning. In this section, I begin with meaningful world-building and how it best connects to theme. I then look at place and setting as character through different lenses and metaphoric associations. Throughout, I provide examples of works by authors who have created vivid settings and described memorable places. As with Part 1, I provide a few case studies with in-depth analysis of how place, character and story resonated.

I largely cite two books of mine, which deal with the science and ecology of aquatic environments and limnology. One is non-fiction and the other is fiction.

Water Is... The Meaning of Water (Pixl Press, 2016) has been described by various reviewers as a biography of water. This non-fiction "documentary" of water and humanity is an excellent resource for writers wishing to increase the legitimacy of their world-building and who wish to know more about water in all its aspects. Written in chapters that describe twelve different perspectives on water (e.g., magic, life, vibration, story, and wisdom to name a few), the book draws on my knowledge of limnology and ecology from over twenty-five years as a working scientist.

A Diary in the Age of Water (Inanna Publications, due 2020) is a work of eco-fiction that chronicles the lives of four generations of women and their relationship with water during a period of severe water crisis in Canada. Part of the story is told through the diary of a limnologist during the crisis, with perspectives on ecology and social responsibility.

Both works provide accurate portrayal of often bizarre aspects of environment as a way to illuminate relationship. Which is what all story is about.

Story is place. And place is character.

PART 1: ECOLOGY

16 ONE . . . What is Ecology?

The highest function of ecology is understanding consequences
—Frank Herbert, *Dune*

Ecology is the study of relationships and change. As a scientific discipline, ecology looks at how components of an environment (animate and inanimate) relate through a wide range of consequence, from species adaptations and ecological succession to climate change and evolution.

The word ecology (*ökologie*) was first created in 1886 by German scientist Ernst Haeckel and finds its roots in the Greek term *oikos* (home). The concept of ecology came much earlier with Johann Wolfgang von Goethe, Friedrich Wilhelm Joseph von Schelling, and Alexander von Humboldt, who all embraced *naturphilosophie* to comprehend Nature in its totality. *Naturphilosophie* espoused an organic and dynamic worldview as an alternative to the atomist and mechanist outlook that prevailed at the time. In a world and time when Enlightenment thinkers and scientists predicated their observations on a premise of a static unchanging Nature that functioned like a machine (recall this was prior to Darwin publishing *On the Origin of Species* in 1859), Humboldt argued that Nature's one constant was change. Humboldt proved that species change with circumstance—such as altitude or climate—in a process he described as *Bildungsbereich* or "education." According to biographer Andrea Wulf, *Bildungsbereich* was a force that shaped the formation of bodies. Every living organism, from humans to mould, have this formative drive.[1]

During his journey through South America, Humboldt focused not so much on finding new isolated facts like his contemporaries were doing, but in elucidating their connections. Seeing South America with the eyes Goethe had given him, Humboldt formulated a new vision of nature depicted in his *Naturgemälde*—a "painting of nature" that implied a sense of unity or wholeness. Humboldt's 1807 *Essay on the Geography of Plants*, which he dedicated to his friend Goethe, promoted an entirely different perspective of nature than his contemporaries. Humboldt wrote, "Nature is a living whole," that interacts like a single organism with certain keystone species that are essential for that interconnected web to flourish.[1] This maverick notion would later reemerge over a century later as the *Gaia Hypothesis* of Margulis and Lovelock (see Section 1.17).

Diverging from the focus on classification and taxonomy, Humboldt grouped plants into zones and regions, based on climate and geography.[1] He had invented what would a century later be known as a *biogeoclimatic zone*—a region with a relatively uniform macroclimate and characterized by specific ecological properties such as energy flow, vegetation communities, and soils. Humboldt was the world's first ecologist.

Today, **ecologists** study the structure and function of systems through the interactions and the evolution of all things—animate and inanimate—from individuals and populations to communities, ecosystems and the entire biosphere (Figure 1). Like good storytellers, ecologists focus on the movement of energy and matter through these systems. Ecologists explore how everything relates, adapts and shares: from action and reaction to motivation and decision. We do this by looking at food webs, trophic levels, population dynamics, and evolving paradigms.

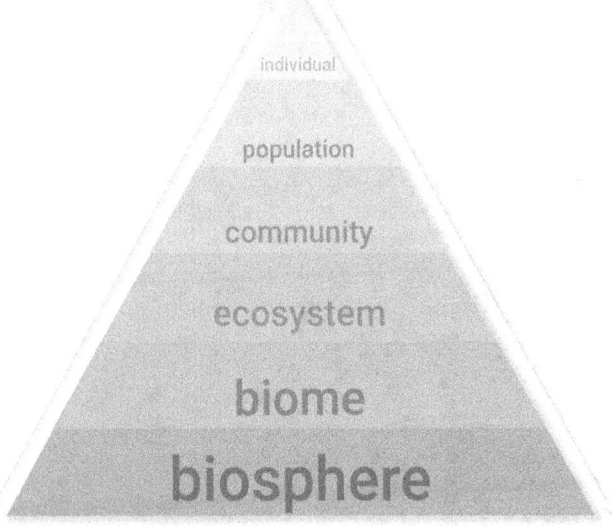

Figure 1 — Ecological Pyramid of systems
Illustration by Costi Gurgu
The pyramid shows their hierarchy from simple to complex, and individual to global. The pyramid also indicates the interactive energy flow of these systems through fractal relationship.

Ecologists acknowledge the inter-connectedness of everything; no organism or system operates in isolation. Just as the writer looks at the scene—not the sentence or word—as the smallest building block of a story, the ecologist looks at the community, not the individual. Take a tree for example. "A tree is not a forest," writes Peter Wohlleben, author of *The Hidden Life of Trees*. "On its own a tree cannot establish a consistent climate. It is at the mercy of the wind

18 and weather. But together, many trees create an ecosystem that moderates extremes of heat and cold, stores a great deal of water, and generates a great deal of humidity."[4] It is the overall effect, created by a collection of individuals, that creates an environment that promotes individual success. In fact, a single tree is not so much an individual as a "community," given the nitrogen-fixing algae, moss, bacteria and symbiotic fungi that populate it.[4]

Ecology embraces quantum science over classic science. The Newtonian model of classic science is mechanistic and applies a reductionist approach, investigating the parts of a whole to determine separate and overall functionality. For instance, in classic science an organism may be described as being controlled by a brain and its nervous system, with energy applied according to the second law of thermodynamics. The neo-Darwinian model would add a competitive random nature to the functions of life systems. Quantum theory applies a holistic approach to describe the whole as an inter-communication of all its parts. The quantum approach acknowledges cooperation and reciprocity, local freedom and cohesion, as part of an indivisible whole. According to the late physicist David Bohm, quantum theory embraces the role of wholeness and process, linked to movement. According to Bohm, everything is in what he calls *universal flux* (a state of process or becoming), a dynamic wholeness-in-motion in which everything moves together in an interconnected process: "undivided wholeness in flowing movement." In the example of the brain, quantum science may describe it as a coherent network like a hologram, connected and operating as both whole and part, every part containing all the information possessed by the whole. This is why people may continue to perform well even after suffering major brain damage.[2]

1.1 FRACTAL ECOLOGY & STORY

Science and technology are generally presented in literature through premise or plot—impacting the journeys of various characters. Ecology—like setting—manifests and integrates more in theme, embedding in the very nature of those characters. This is because, while most of the hard sciences study the nature and behaviour of "phenomena", ecology concerns itself with the consequences of these phenomena and the impact of these behaviours. Most hard sciences—whether phenomenological or epistemological—focus on "what" and "how" things are put together; ecology focuses on "why" and the journey. Like good storytellers, ecologists look for "meaning." And, as with good story, ecologists find meaning through movement and relationship: collision, avoidance, attraction, change, transformation, epiphany.

To better understand the meaning of these relationships and movements, ecologists apply spatial and temporal scaling in a fractal perspective—from simple to complex, from local to global, and from small to large or epic scale. First introduced by Mandelbrot in 1975, *fractals* display self-similarity at progressively smaller or larger scales. Fractals are a scale-related repetition of overall complexity, but not necessarily of the pattern itself. Examples include coastlines, landscapes, habitats, soils, plant root systems, paths of foraging animals, and much more.[2] Fractals describe partly random or chaotic phenomena such as crystal growth, fluid turbulence, and galaxy formation. Ecological processes associated with fractal geometry include how populations disperse and forage, the spread of disease, habitat and niche diversity, complexity and heterogeneity of habitats, how species compete and coexist, evolutionary rates, and ecosystem stability.[3] Parts as wholes; wholes as parts.

In describing an oak tree, journalist and author Lynda V. Mapes writes in her book, *Witness Tree*:

> *The big oak dominates its space … but it also supports a vast web of life and relies in turn on a menagerie of helpers, aboveground and below. With its crown in the wind and its roots in the teeming soil, the big oak connects earth and sky, and many millions of beings, and is home to each and to all. It is just one tree, and yet a whole world unto itself.*[5]

The phenomenon of the oak tree is similar to achieving depth in story through using metaphor and integrating theme. As with large, so the small; as with small, so the large. Hermes Trismegistus—the syncretism of the Greek god Hermes and the Egyptian, Thoth—wrote:

> *As above, so below, as within, so without, as the universe, so the soul …*
> *That which is Below corresponds to that which is Above, and that which is Above corresponds to that which is Below, to accomplish the miracle of the One Thing.*

1.2 ECOSYSTEMS & HABITATS

Ecosystems are systems of living and nonliving things linked through nutrient cycles and energy/matter flow. These are sometimes described as food webs, but encompass more than what we normally think of as "food". Examples include:

- *Aquatic ecosystems,* such as lakes and ponds, rivers, bogs, muskegs, marshes, swamps, fens, estuaries, and oceans

- *Terrestrial ecosystems,* such as forests, grasslands, chaparrals, deserts, and tundra

Aquatic freshwater ecosystems are studied by scientists from many fields such as limnology, hydrology, aquatic ecology, benthic ecology, and so on. As a *limnologist,* I study all aspects of freshwater structure and function, encompassing the disciplines of chemistry, biology, and physics. Limnologists don't restrict their focus to water: we also consider the surrounding land —its geology, biology, and land-use—and air (climate) as important influences of the water ecosystem.

Every ecosystem is made up of many *habitats* where organisms feed and take shelter. For instance, the varied habitats that make up a stream ecosystem can include rocks, fallen logs and branches, rootwads, overhanging banks, gravel and sand, leaf litter, and the moving water itself. These habitats can exist in pools, riffles, glides and shoals or in turbulent eddies. Habitats, in turn, are made up of micro-habitats (e.g., the underside of a stream rock vs. the side that faces the current). Some organisms—such as *caddisfly larvae*—make their own habitat in streams. The caddisfly constructs a home from material nearby, whether it is tiny pebbles of *Glossosoma*—a stone-building caddisfly living in a riffle—or the delicate leaf litter of a *Banksiola* caddisfly that lives in a quiet backwater shoal.

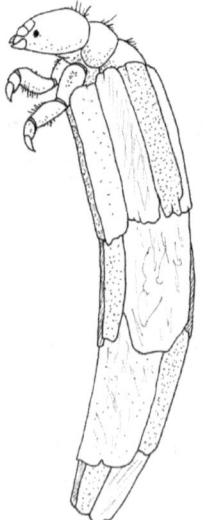

Figure 2 —Drawing of a caddisfly larva

Drawing of a caddisfly larva, Agrypina sp. (Phryganeidae) that builds its case of plant material from its immediate environment.

Illustration by Kerste Voute and Nina Munteanu

Organisms can be creative in adapting to an environment. The ribbon kelp (*Alaria marginata*) of the north Pacific coast finds a way to anchor its holdfast in a shifting sandy seafloor by using the hard casing of a benthic tubeworm, the northern feather duster worm (Sabellidae). The kelp population, in turn, provides an ecosystem for many other organisms to grow, including the provision of food for the tubeworm. Ecologist Matthew Bracken describes this ecological relationship as a *facilitation cascade*, in which one species facilitates the survival of a second, which in turn enhances the environment for a variety of other species, including the original.[6] This is more than simple *symbiosis*, a mutually beneficial relationship (discussed in Chapter Two), given that it involves an entire community (see my discussion of Trophic Cascade, below).

"Ecosystems are complex cycles of recirculating energy matter, and relationships," writes Milton M.R. Freeman, of the University of Alberta. Between the scientist's approach to knowing what is happening and that of the "tradition-based resource user" (or indigenous person), Freeman suggests that the key difference is epistemological: "the scientist is concerned with causality, with understanding an essentially linear process of cause and effect ... but the forager lives in a world, not of linear causal events, but of constantly reforming multi-dimensional interacting cycles, where nothing is simply a cause or an effect, but all factors are influences impacting other elements of the system-as-a-whole. Linear approaches to analysis cannot be applied to cyclical systems ... Nowhere does the Cartesian model of modern science fail so completely and utterly as in trying to explain the workings of natural ecosystems.

—Nina Munteanu, *Water Is... The Meaning of Water*[2]

A *keystone species* is an organism that helps define an ecosystem. Without this keystone species, the ecosystem would alter greatly or cease to exist.[1] This is because keystone species have low functional redundancy: no other species can fill its ecological niche (function). The ecosystem would radically change and, in doing so, may be more vulnerable to invasive species. An example of a keystone species that help define an ecosystem is the Ochre Sea Star (*Pisaster ochraceus*) that ensures a healthy population of seaweeds and associated community of sea urchins, sea snails, limpets, and bivalves. Other examples include the sea otter (that maintains the kelp forest by keeping the sea urchin in check), the African elephant (that maintains the savanna by feeding on shrubs and small trees), the coral (foundation species that play a major role in the creation and maintenance of the reef habitat), and termites, beavers and

22   trees (ecosystem engineers that modify, create, and maintain habitats through their extensive network and influence on the water cycle, ground quality and air quality).

1.3 ECOTONES

Ecotones are areas where two or more ecosystems overlap. In my book *Water Is...* I define an ecotone as the transition zone between two overlapping systems. Ecotones are essentially where two communities exchange information and integrate. They typically support varied and rich communities, representing a boiling pot of two colliding worlds: An estuary—where fresh water meets salt water. The edge of a forest with a meadow. The marshy shoreline of a lake or pond. The transition between Arctic tundra and boreal forest in northern Canada. Edge communities on the boundary between land and sea—such as mangroves, seagrass meadows and tidal wetlands—are called blue carbon ecosystems. Known for their unmatched ability to capture CO_2 from the atmosphere and store it in the ground, these *blue carbon* ecosystems store carbon forty times faster than *green carbon* (e.g., forest) ecosystems.

The increased biodiversity within an ecotone is called the *edge effect*, where greater genetic diversity creates a gene-flow "bridge" from one population to another. Ecotones also provide a "buffer-zone" that helps protect neighbouring ecosystems from potential environmental damage. Wetlands—as ecotones—can efficiently filter and absorb organic matter, excessive nutrients and toxic contaminants in rain, storm water runoff and river inflows. Marsh plants take up the contaminants—as food—and bury them in the soil or transform them into a form that is no longer harmful.[2]

Ecotones are a fitting metaphor for life—and story—given that the big choices we face usually involve a collision of ideas, beliefs, lifestyles or worldviews: these often prove to enrich our lives the most for having gone through them. Evolution (any significant change) doesn't happen within a stable system; adaptation and growth occur only when stable systems come together, disturb the equilibrium, and create opportunity. Good social examples include a close friendship or a marriage in which the process of "I" and "you" becomes a dynamic "we" (the ecotone) through exchange and reciprocation. A version of Bernard Shaw's quote by the Missouri Pacific Agriculture Development Bulletin reads: "You have an idea. I have an idea. We swap. Now, you have two ideas and so do I. Both are richer.

What you gave you have. What you got I did not lose. This is cooperation."
This is ecotone.

—Nina Munteanu, *Water Is... The Meaning of Water*[2]

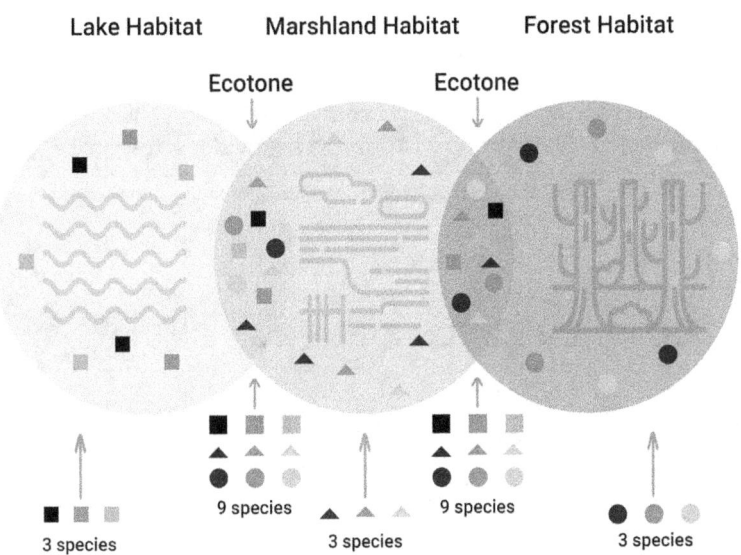

Lake Habitat   **Marshland Habitat**   **Forest Habitat**

Ecotone   Ecotone

9 species   9 species

3 species   3 species   3 species

Figure 3 — Sketch of an ecotone where two ecosystems overlap

Sketch of an ecotone where two ecosystems overlap; the marsh represents the ecotone where forested land and open lake overlap. Open marsh also has ecotones where it overlaps with forest and open lake. Typically, a higher diversity exists in ecotones.

Illustration by Costi Gurgu

Ecotones are places where lines are crossed and barriers breached. Where new opportunities arise. Sometimes from calamity. Sometimes from tragedy. Sometimes from serendipity.

1.4 ECOLOGICAL NICHE

Every aspect of an ecosystem has a role to play in that system. That role is called a *niche* (or job). One of the lion's jobs is to hunt and eat prey; just as the gazelle's job is not only to survive by grazing and make more of itself but to get captured and eaten as food for the lion. This simplified example supports the notion that each niche encompasses a whole as a fractal part of another whole. Parts of wholes and the whole of parts are interrelated and expressed in a choreographed dance of life, death and rebirth. The lion's story is tied to the story of the gazelle, in turn tied to its ecosystem. Each tells a different story—but, taken together, both tell a greater story. (I discuss niche further in the next section and in Section 1.13: Creative Destruction. Niche is further explored in Chapter Two, Section 2.6, through adaptations, resource allocation, and life strategies.)

1.5 TROPHIC LEVELS & ENERGY CYCLES

Decades ago, at university, I learned in my ecology and limnology courses that all inanimate and animate things on Earth are interconnected and interdependent. Nature and her ecosystems flow in a dynamic and sustainable network of relationships and succession. Systems generally operate through a closed loop of natural creative–destruction: from birth, growth and production to senescence, and decay; and from recycling to redistribution, reclaiming, and rebirth. The yin–yang closed circle of the Ouroboros. And, these are all connected through movement.

Energy from the sun cycles through various *trophic levels* from producer to consumer to destroyer, leading back to producer. The word trophic comes from the Greek, *trophē*, which refers to food. The movement of the sun's energy through the various trophic levels is commonly depicted as an *ecological pyramid* or trophic/energy pyramid that shows the biomass or bio-productivity flow of a given ecosystem.

Producers or *autotrophs* first capture the sun's energy, which flows to consumers or *heterotrophs* (heterotrophic herbivores, carnivores, and omnivores) and ultimately destroyers or *saprotrophs*. Energy is typically lost with each trophic transfer until the predator near the top of the pyramid is only receiving a small fraction of the original energy. Every trophic level transfers some energy to scavengers, detritivores, and decomposers (destroyers) that break down dead organisms and transform nutrients to a form that plants can use, completing the cycle of life–energy. This last relationship—though critical—is often neglected in many ecological and energy pyramids.

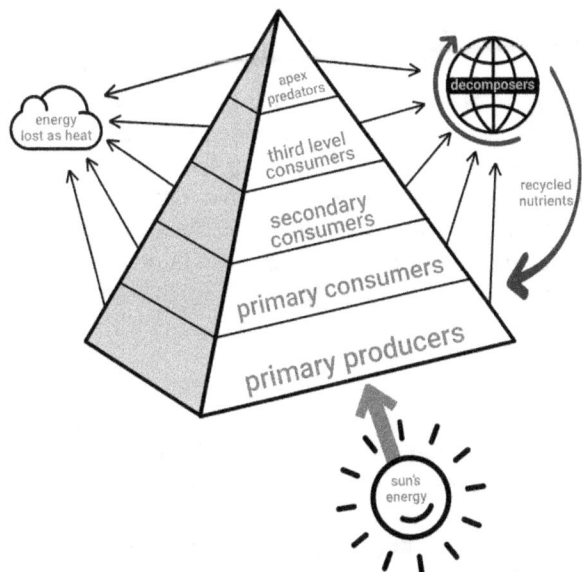

**Figure 4 —
Energy Pyramid**

Energy Pyramid, showing the cycling through various trophic levels of sun's energy from primary producers to apex predator. Energy is lost as heat at each trophic level; decomposers recycle energy as nutrients through the trophic levels.

**Illustration by
Costi Gurgu**

1.5.1 Nature & the Laws of Thermodynamics

While the pyramid representation accurately depicts the loss of energy to each trophic level with distance from the sun's energy, it does not portray the cyclical nature of energy (nutrient) exchange through trophic levels. The simplified pyramid neglects the presence of coherent behaviour and what ultimately allows Nature to defy the first and second law of thermodynamics not only by conserving but sometimes by creating energy and promoting evolution.

The *first law of thermodynamics* expresses the universal law of conservation of energy and identifies heat transfer as a form of energy transfer. The *second law* expresses the universal law of increasing entropy (a classic example of increasing entropy is ice melting). That water behaves coherently, like a self-organized fractal organism, is a concept that remains unaccepted by most scientists.[2] However, biophysicist Mae-Wan Ho and other scientists argue that water has quantum characteristics: water stores information, self-organizes, self-purifies, and demonstrates properties of an organism. Ho argues that

26 these quantum characteristics reflect water's two states (low density and high density) and these two states, which toggle within a stable non-equilibrium, defy the second law of thermodynamics.[2,7,8]

1.5.2 Individual Trophic Levels

Primary producers (autotrophic organisms, such as plants and algae) comprise the bulk of life on the planet. Without primary producers, nothing on the planet would survive. They form the foundation of the energy pyramid; this makes sense, given the loss of energy as organisms move farther from this trophic level. Terrestrial and ocean plants use sunlight and carbon dioxide to make food through *photosynthesis* and produce oxygen as a by-product. Ironically, it is not the largest of these—the trees—which produce the most oxygen and sequester the most carbon dioxide: it is the smallest, the drifting ocean phytoplankton, no more than several microns in size.

Phytoplankton are microscopic floating organisms (photosynthesizing single-celled plants, bacteria, and Protista) that drift in the ocean and make up the bulk of photosynthetic life on the planet. These tiny creatures are comprised mostly of diatoms, dinoflagellates, and cyanophyta (blue-green algae/bacteria); they provide half of the world's oxygen and absorb from thirty to fifty percent of the atmosphere's carbon. The world's boreal forests and rainforests contribute about thirty to forty percent of the world's oxygen production and sequester from a quarter to a third of the atmosphere's carbon.

Consumers (heterotrophic and saprotrophic organisms incapable of photosynthesis) make up the rest of the food–energy pyramid. Carnivores, herbivores, and parasites feed on living organic matter; however, most consumers feed on dead or decaying organic matter. Scavengers, detritivores, saprotrophs, and decomposers feed on dead and decaying organisms and their particles.

Carnivores are predators that occupy the apex level of the energy pyramid; examples include lions, wolves, killer whales, bears, hawks, and eagles. Carnivores feed on live biomass—such as *herbivores* that graze on primary producers. Herbivore examples include invertebrates, mice, squirrels, deer, sheep, and giraffes). Because carnivores occupy a high trophic level and must expend more energy to capture their food, their population biomass comprises a small fraction of their prey population. The hunting strategy of the carnivore reflects this. Strategies vary from the short and solitary high-speed chase of a cheetah to the long endurance chase of a pack of African wild dogs.[9] In their 2007 study, entitled *"The Costs of Carnivory,"* Carbone, Teacher & Rowcliffe analysed the balance between energy intake and expenditure across a range of species; they predict that mammalian carnivores should have a maximum body mass of one ton. Mammalian carnivores are relatively small compared with the largest terrestrial herbivorous mammals, such as the extinct *Indricothere*, which weighed around fifteen tons. The largest currently existing mammalian carnivore—the polar bear—weighs around half a ton; the largest known extinct carnivores, such as the short-faced bear, weighed around one ton. The authors suggest that because large carnivores rely heavily on abundant large prey, the largest modern mammalian carnivores are rare and vulnerable to extinction.[10]

Scavengers consume dead plants, animals, or carrion and break down the organic materials into smaller particles; these are, in turn, consumed and broken down by detritivores and decomposers. In short, scavengers recycle the waste of others. Examples of scavengers include hyenas, coyotes, leopards, turkey vultures, carrion beetles, wasps, and flies. Many predators (that kill and feed on living organisms) also opportunistically practise scavenging behaviour when living prey is scarce or unobtainable.

Detritivores speed up decay of organisms by feeding on larger particles of dead organic matter—debris and solid residues called *detritus*. Typical examples include worms, millipedes, woodlice, dung flies and slugs. The activity of detritivores increases material available to decomposers. Detritivores differ from fungal saprotrophs by their mode of feeding: they directly ingest non-living organic matter or detritus, such as the macroscopic swallowing of detritus by the earthworm.

Saprotrophs (*saprophytes* for plant-like organisms and *saprozoites* for animal-like organisms) get their energy from living on or in dead and decaying organic matter. This includes decaying pieces of plants or animals. More specifically, saprotrophs (such as fungi) secrete digestive enzymes into the dead / decaying matter to absorb the soluble organic nutrients. The process—called *lysotrophic nutrition*—occurs through microscopic lysis of detritus.

Decomposers effectively close the loop by breaking down the organic matter of dead animals and plants on a microscopic level and returning them to the soil in a form that plants can use; they do this by transforming organic nutrients into their inorganic form. Without decomposers, plants would not get essential nutrients, and dead matter and waste would accumulate. Examples of decomposers include bacteria and fungi. *Nitrogen fixation* is practiced by bacteria and some blue-green algae that take gaseous nitrogen from the air

28   and turn it into ammonia, nitrate and nitrite for plants to use. Some leguminous plants (e.g., pea, bean) form a symbiotic relationship with nitrogen-fixing *Rhyzobium* bacteria that live in the plant's root nodules.

Parasites typically grow on the body of another organism from which they
get nutrients and shelter. While many parasites are a nuisance to their host
plant or animal, they usually do not kill them. Examples range in style and
effect, based on the need of the parasite: these range from the physical parasitism of the common flea that feeds on the blood of a cat to the social parasitism
of the brown-headed cowbird (*Molothrus ater*) that lays its eggs in another
bird's nest to avoid raising its own young.

Social parasitism is a kind of arms-race coevolution in which the parasite
exploits the host social system. The cuckoo bird (Cuculidae) exerts what is
known as the *cuckoo strategy* of laying eggs in the nests of host birds with
eggs similar to theirs. While young host birds develop feeding calls that their
parents can distinguish from the cuckoo offspring, the young cuckoos—or
brood parasite—soon learn to copy.[11]
Contrasting with the cuckoo's specialist technique, the cowbird lays its
eggs in the nests of one hundred forty different species. The cowbird egg looks
nothing like the host eggs, which should make it easier for the host bird to distinguish it and discard the cowbird egg. So, why doesn't it? The term "cuckoo
mafia" (after the famous cuckoo) describes the cowbird's strategy that impos-
es reciprocity on its host to raise its young.[11,12]

> If the host bird ejects the cowbird's eggs from the nest, the cowbird destroys
> the host's entire clutch. Running its lifecycle strategy like a mafia extortion
> racket, the cowbird ensures allegiance of its host through retaliation. The
> host birds tolerate the additional work of raising the parasite in their nest
> to avoid endangering the lives of their own offspring. This only works if
> the cowbird is both present and swift in its retaliation; otherwise the host
> bird that quickly removes the parasite egg from its nest will be at an advan-
> tage over its more compliant cohorts. Other defences against the cowbird's
> mafia behaviour include avoiding the parasite in the first place. They can
> select nesting sites that are difficult to parasitize, start incubation early to
> prevent invader eggs being placed there, and nest in aggregations for better
> group-defence.

> But it never ends: hosts and parasites compete against each other in an evo-
> lutionary race. Each strategy is met with a counter-strategy. Arne Traulsen
> at the Max Planck Institute in Plön says, "There is no optimal behaviour
> in such host-parasite relations. Neither party can outsmart the other on a

permanent basis."[11] *They are forever locked in a tense covenant, so long as both exist.*

—Nina Munteanu, *A Diary in the Age of Water*

Parasitoids spend a significant portion of their life history attached to or within a single host organism. Parasitoids differ from typical parasites in that they ultimately kill the host. Most insect parasitoids are from the Hymenoptera and include braconid and ichneumon wasps, and flies. In many species, eggs are laid within the bodies of other organisms (most commonly other insects) and the eggs hatch and feed on the internal organs of the host. Initially, the parasitoid larvae feed on non-essential organs without killing the host. Eventually, the larvae either feed on the vital organs, killing the host—or pupate within the host and then emerge as adults, killing the host. A **hyperparasitoid**, in turn, feeds off a parasite or parasitoid.[12]

A female Glyptapanteles *wasp pounces on an unsuspecting caterpillar and drills into its flesh with its ovipositor. Then she injects some eighty eggs into the living caterpillar. The eggs hatch into larvae that feed on the caterpillar's fluids, then gnaw through its skin and exit en masse, using their last moult as sutures. The caterpillar, which miraculously survives this invasion and egression—rare for a parasitoid, which usually eats its host empty—becomes a slave bodyguard to the maturing larvae. It wards off predators, including hyperparasitoid wasps, until it drops dead from starvation. This bizarre phenomenon happens because one or two larvae sacrifice themselves: they remain inside the host to control its mind with a cocktail of chemicals—to protect their siblings. Here's the thing, though: the defending caterpillars in fact somehow attract the hyperparasitoid wasps, which will eventually inject the* Glyptapanteles *pupae with their own eggs.*[13] *What goes around comes around.*

—Nina Munteanu, *A Diary in the Age of Water*

1.5.3 Host–Parasite Co-Evolution

Coevolution of host and parasite may eventually lead to a different kind of relationship. Most parasite–host relationships have coevolved and are linked through life-cycles. For instance, the common house flea evolved a life cycle that matches the house cat's behaviour and place of residence.

In the case of **endosymbiosis**, the parasitic relationship has evolved into a

30   symbiotic relationship, in which both host cell and parasite-turned-organelle benefit each other.[2] (This phenomenon is described in more detail below, in the Nature's Journey and Creative Destruction sections, and in Chapter Two.)

1.5.4 Trophic Cascades

A *trophic cascade* describes a cascade of effect as a top predator exerts indirect control on species at all lower trophic levels. For example, when predators suppress the abundance or alter the behaviour of their prey, the next lower trophic level is released from predation; this cascades down more trophic levels, ultimately maintaining a balanced and functioning ecosystem.

An excellent example of a cascading ecological interaction was observed in Yellowstone National Park in the western United States when *gray wolves* were reintroduced into the park in 1995 after seventy years of absence. In the 1920s, the local extinction of the park's population of gray wolves (*Canis lupus*) through hunting caused an increase in the population of elk (*Cervus elaphus*). This drastically reduced the abundance of numerous plants—especially aspens, willows, and grasses—eaten by the elk. Overgrazing by the elk destroyed the terrestrial habitats of the valleys and gorges and increased erosion, which impacted the aquatic habitats and ultimately reduced biodiversity. Numbers and kinds of songbirds, raptors, beavers, muskrats, ducks, fish, reptiles and amphibians were suppressed. The reintroduced wolves dramatically reversed of this trend with the reduction of their primary prey, the elk. The shrubs and trees grew back because fewer elk were feeding on them, but also because the elk congregated less in open areas to get away from the wolves. This led to less trampling in the streams and river banks. Newly vegetated banks stabilized and improved the morphology of the rivers. Less erosion improved water quality and enhanced aquatic macrobenthos (mostly aquatic insects) that fed more fish that fed more bears—ultimately promoting a healthier and more biodiverse ecosystem.[14]

1.6 NATURE'S ARCHETYPES & METAPHORS

Psychology mavens suggest that the existence of *archetypes* can only be deduced indirectly through story, art, myths, or dreams. This is because an archetype is linked to a universal (subconscious) understanding that is often best expressed through metaphor, icon and symbol. Carl Jung understood archetypes as patterns and images that originate from and are shared within the collective unconscious (e.g., mother archetype or mentor archetype). Archetypes are the psychic counterpart of *instinct*.

Instinctive behaviour (behaviour in the absence of learning) expresses an innate inclination toward a complex behaviour or pattern.[15] Newly hatched sea turtles automatically move on the beach toward the ocean; honeybees communicate by dancing in the direction of a food source without prior instruction; a marsupial, once born, climbs into its mother's pouch. Imprinting is another instinctive behaviour. Shaking water off fur is an instinctive action. Other examples of instinct include animal fighting, animal courtship behaviour, internal escape functions, and building nests.

Psychologist Michael McCollough argues that environment plays a key role in human behaviors, such as forgiveness and revenge. He theorizes that various social environments cause either forgiveness or revenge to prevail. McCollough relates his theory to game theory. In a tit-for-tat strategy, cooperation and retaliation are comparable to forgiveness and revenge. The choice between the two can be beneficial or detrimental, depending on what the game partner (or organism) chooses. The brain's limbic system processes external stimuli related to emotions, social activity, and motivation; these then propagate an instinctual behavioural response. Examples include maternal care, aggression, defense, and social hierarchy; these behaviours are influenced by sensory input, such as sight, sound, touch, and smell.[16]

Given their relationship to the "story" of a whole system, trophic levels may correspond loosely to archetype in story. We already use some of these in classic *stereotyping*, based on habits and general qualities we've (often erroneously and ignorantly) assigned to representative species. For instance, *pigs* are associated with slovenly behaviour, *sharks* with sociopathic predation, *horses* with unquestioning service, *foxes* with clever and crafty manipulation, and *sheep* with gullibility. George Orwell used animal stereotypes to create archetypal characters in his allegorical satire, *Animal Farm*.

Scholar and mythologist Joseph Campbell drew on Jung's archetypes to provide seven main archetypes in the mythic *hero's journey* (discussed in more detail below and in Part 2). These include: hero, herald, threshold guardian, mentor, shape-shifter, trickster, and shadow. One can identify sub-archetypes within each generalized archetype. The *hero*, for instance, can assume any one or combination of the following: magician, sage, innocent, warrior, outlaw, jester, lover, explorer, ruler, creator, destroyer.[2,17] The list is, in fact, endless and depends on the nature of the story.

Nature's archetypes in story express metaphorically and literally through functions and niches. An example is the strong solitary oak versus a young social stand of beech. The oak honestly comes by its iconic symbol of solitary strength, resistance, and knowledge. Oak wood is very dense (about 0.75 g/cm³), provid-

32   ing great strength and hardness. Its wood resists insect and fungal attack because of its high tannin content. Its bark is strong and coarse, easily withstanding outer wounds, such as lightning strikes. "Whereas beeches last barely more than two hundred years outside the cozy atmosphere of their native forests, oaks growing near old farmyards or out in pastures easily live for more than five hundred," writes forester Peter Wohlleben in *The Hidden Life of Trees*[4] "Even severely damaged [oak] trees with major branches broken off can grow replacement crowns and live for a few hundred years longer … a storm-battered beech is able to hang on for no more than a couple of decades." The oak's thick outer bark is rough and robust compared with the smooth skin of the beech. Wohlleben recites an old German saying: *Was schert es eine Eiche, wenn sich ein Wild-schwein in ihr scheuert?* which roughly translates to: "It's no skin off an old oak's back, if a wild boar wants to use its bark as a scratching post."[4] Oaks are made of stern stuff, says Wohlleben, who found them growing in places no other tree would. The advantage of this hardscrabble existence is the lack of competition from other trees, such as the successfully competitive beech tree.

When provided with more ideal conditions, the beech out-competes the oak in the race for more light through achieving a higher crown. The beech is particularly social in its growth; older trees share nutrients via their root systems with younger saplings; surrounding beeches pump sugar to a stump to keep it alive; beech trees even practice a kind of "socialism versus capitalism" by synchronizing their photosynthesis—"equalizing between the strong and the weak and ensuring that all are equally successful."[4] Whoever has an abundance of sugar shares; whoever is in need of sugar receives from others. The beech epitomizes the opposite of neoliberal capitalism by growing together in community, sharing nutrients and water that are "optimally divided among them so that each tree can grow into the best tree it can be."[4]

The beech also buddies up with the maple to form a climax northern hardwood forest. How the two species—American beech (*Fagus grandifolia*) and sugar maple (*Acer saccharum*)—maintain co-dominance without competitively excluding the other is achieved through differing sensitivities to disturbances and through **allelopathy**, a phytotoxic chemical interference of beech—mostly through leaf leachate—that slightly suppresses sugar maple seedling growth and ensures a balanced hierarchy.[18]

The black walnut (*Juglans nigra*) is well known for exerting dominance using juglone in its leaves, buds, roots and nut hulls to suppress other plants from seeding and germinating nearby.[4,21]

Metaphoric "roles" may provide an allegorical association with a major character in something as simple as a name: the solitary strong-minded shepherd Gabriel Oak in Thomas Hardy's *Far from the Madding Crowd*. Gabriel Oak not only embodies the metaphoric characteristics of an oak; he is also, like the oak, strongly connected to the land. The metaphor may carry through into a

character's very nature and journey: in Barbara Kingsolver's *Flight Behaviour*, 33
Dellarobia Turnbow reflects the title on several layers, from her own "flight"
to her discovery and connection with the flight of the monarch and its plight
with climate change.

The subject of Nature archetypes, niches and symbols in story is further
examined in Part 2: Story.

1.7 NATURE'S CYCLES

Trophic levels cycle the sun's energy through interactions that range from
cooperative altruism to hostile takeovers. Energy and matter flow continually
from: birth to growth and production to death and decay—then recycling, redistribution, reclaiming and rebirth. The yin-yang closed circle of the Ouroboros interprets Nature's "intent" in defying the second law of thermodynamics:
not only conserving energy, but sometimes creating energy and promoting
evolution.[2]

Natural cycles include the carbon, nitrogen, phosphorus, oxygen and water cycles, among many others. Cycles in Nature encompass change within
sameness and these are ubiquitous in the universe. Water, for instance, is continually changing and flowing; yet it has remained the same for eons—not
increasing or decreasing from the time dinosaurs quenched their thirst in Triassic swamps to this morning's rain falling on the roof of your home. Water is
both constant and changing, a paradox of complexity.[2]

1.8 WATER CYCLE

Water circulates around the planet through the *hydrological cycle*: precipitation, evaporation, transpiration, freezing, melting and condensation. Water
and energy circulate in a never-ending global process that flows from clouds
to land, to the ocean, and back to the clouds. Income from precipitation, surface influents, and groundwater sources is balanced by outflow from surface
effluents, seepage to ground water and evapo-transpiration. Limnologists
use the term *watershed* or *catchment basin* to describe the area of land defined
by topography that collects surface material (and ground-water) associated

34 with pooled surface water, such as a river, lake, or sea. Each income and loss vary seasonally and geographically; these are governed by climate, watershed characteristics, and the morphology of water bodies.[2]

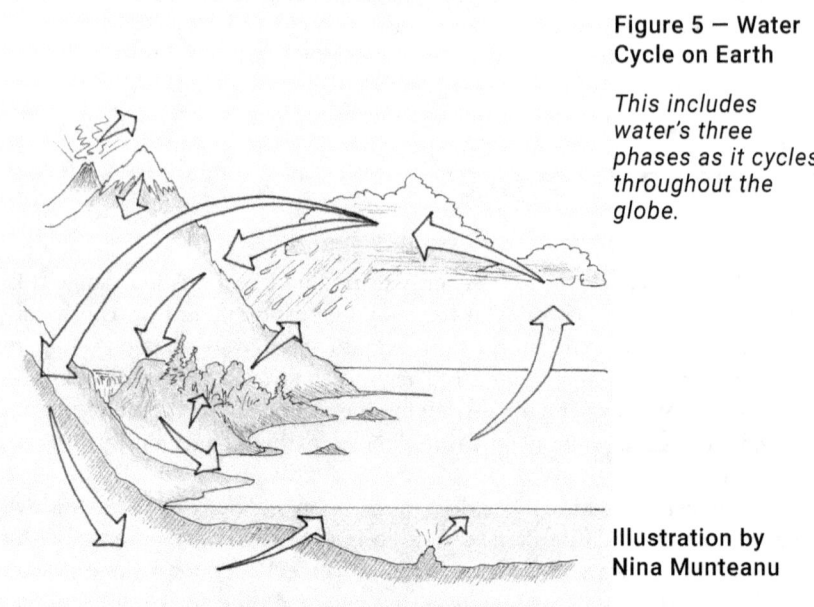

Figure 5 — Water Cycle on Earth

This includes water's three phases as it cycles throughout the globe.

Illustration by Nina Munteanu

"The hydrological cycle emphasizes the dynamic nature of the Earth's environment," Philip Ball shares in his book *H₂O: A Biography of Water*. "Water," he adds, "is the lubricant for biochemical cycling."[19]

"Water circulates around the globe," Japanese researcher Masaru Emoto shares in *The Secret Life of Water*, "flowing through our bodies and spreading to the rest of the world. If we were capable of reading this information contained in the memory of water, we would read a story of epic proportions."[20]

1.9 GLOBAL ECOLOGY

In her book *The Global Forest*, Diana Beresford Kroeger tells us that:

A functioning forest is a complex form of life. It is interconnected by its own flora and driven by the mammals, the amphibians and insects in it. It is kept in place by fungi, algae, lichens, bacteria, viruses, and bacteriophages. The primogenitors of the forests are trees. They communicate by carbon-coded calls and mass-market themselves by infrasound. The atmosphere links forests into the heavens and the great oceans. The human family is both caught and held in that web of life.[21]

Around the time that I started teaching at the University of Victoria, Dr. Tom Reimchen and his team of UVic students had begun ground-breaking investigations of the Pacific Northwest salmon run that eventually involved bears, trees and salmon.

Along the Pacific Northwest, millions of chum, pink, Chinook, sockeye, and coho salmon return from the Pacific Ocean to the stream of their birthplace to create a new generation of salmon. The salmon must find the right stream and battle upstream, sometimes against raging currents and dodging hungry bears, to the pebble-bed (called a *redd*) where they lay and fertilize their eggs. Task complete, the exhausted salmon then die—completing their cycle of life at almost the same place where they were born several years before—their carcasses providing a nutrient-rich fertilizer for the aquatic and terrestrial ecosystems.[2]

Reimchen and others reported a link between the open ocean and the forests that involved bears, trees, and salmon. Links extend from the estuaries and small streams that fringe the coastlines, through to the headwaters of major rivers that penetrate far into the continents.[22,23] Researchers observed that when bears catch salmon, they typically haul them into the nearby line of trees to feast. In their need to fatten up for the long winter hibernation, bears focus on the protein-rich eggs and brain matter of the fish and leave the rest of the carcass to rot in the forest. Using a marker protein, researchers showed that the fish carcasses provide fertilizer for nearby trees and other plants.[22,23] This occurs through mutualistic cooperation with a microbe that breaks down decaying fish carcasses into a form digestible by the trees—in exchange for tree sugar.

The research revealed an intriguing relationship among the bears, rivers, trees, microbes and salmon: the bears depend on the salmon as a source of food, on the river to deliver the salmon, and on the trees to provide cover; the salmon rely on the river to transport them to where they need to spawn,

36   on a good tree canopy to keep the river cool for healthy egg production, and on a predator (the bear) to cull the weaker fish and ensure a healthy future stock; the trees—and their associated microbes—benefit from the bears and the salmon for delivering fertilizer for their healthy growth and, in turn, provide a supportive environment for the bear, the river and the salmon. Unsurprisingly, tree sugars ebbed and flowed with the salmon run.[2]

Some suggest that there is evidence—though unsubstantiated— that the trees along the river increase their sugar levels in *anticipation* of the size and time of the salmon run—while the salmon are still hundreds of miles away in the ocean. This suggests a kind of interspecies communication.[2]

Katsuhiko Matsunaga, a marine chemist at the Hokkaido University, discovered that "leaves falling into streams and rivers leach acids into the ocean that stimulate the growth of plankton, the first and foremost building block in the food chain."[4] There are more fish because of the forest. Higher yields of fish and oysters resulted from increased leaf litter. Ecologists have known this for some time. Since the 1980s, stream ecologists have stressed the importance of *allochthonous* (from outside) input of fine and coarse particulate organic material in providing energy and nutrients to all life in the stream.[24]

1.10 ECOLOGY, PHENOLOGY & CLIMATE CHANGE

Phenology is the study of the timing of cyclical and seasonal natural phenomena related to climate. Dating back thousands of years, phenology is one of the oldest branches of environmental science. Examples include animal migrations, spring flowering, autumn seed formation, and winter cold hardening. As temperatures warm in spring, buds form on plants; as temperatures cool in the fall, deciduous trees and shrubs drop their leaves and go dormant. The word phenology comes from the Greek words *phaino* (to show or appear) and *logos* (to study)—it literally means "the science of appearance."

Latitudes and altitudes affect the timing of seasonal events. A sugar maple tree in Kentucky may bud weeks before one in Ontario, Canada.

In *Witness Tree*, Lynda V. Mapes tells us that, "Seasonal changes in Nature are among the most readily observable clues to the biological effects of global climate change, as warming temperatures reset the seasonal clock."[5] Mapes tells us that:

Trees demonstrate the agency of the stationary. They are rooted in place and
shaped by events around them: the growth of neighbouring trees, prevailing
winds, weather. But they are not passive. Trees manipulate their environ-
ment, exuding chemicals to deter pests and call in predators. They make soil,
alter the hydrological cycle, climate, atmosphere, and habitat. Trees move,
breathe, operate a whole-body circulatory system, eat, have sex, communi-
cate, expel waste, socialize, wage war, compete, cooperate, and create.[5]

Changes in the timing of phases of a plant's life cycle—called *phenophases*—
are affected by temperature, rainfall, and day length (photoperiod).

The amount of warming is not the same around the world. Again, latitude
and altitude play a role. The Arctic, for example, is warming more quickly
than elsewhere in the world. One of the impacts of changing *phenophases* is
that insect pollinators that have co-evolved with plants may become out of
sync. An insect may still be in a larval stage when the flower blossoms, and
unable to fly from flower to flower to transport pollen. Without pollination,
the unfertilized flower will not produce fruit. Like dominoes lined up, plants
and insects will also affect other wildlife that depend on some product of the
plant and insect interaction.

1.10.1 Natural Navigation & Reading Nature's Signs

In a TEDx talk, January 14, 2019, Tristan Gooley (author of *How to Read Nature*) spoke about using Nature as a guide in navigation. "It all starts with the
senses," says Gooley. He showed as an example a tree in a field and pointed
out that its silhouette was not symmetrical, according to the direction of the
midday sun: in the northern hemisphere, a tree will normally extend more
branches to the south, toward the predominant sunlight. Even the leaves "are
being sculpted by the sun," says Gooley, which Mapes reiterated about the
oak tree she studied. The sun leaves (on the south or higher up) are smaller,
lighter and thicker; the more shaded leaves (on the north or lower down) are
darker, larger and thinner.[5] Many of us know that moss grows predominantly
on the north, more shaded side of a tree in the northern hemisphere; this is
based on less evaporation and higher water retention on that side.

When mapping one's journey through a forest, Gooley gives the example
of stinging nettles (*Urtica dioica*) that prefer nutrient-rich soil with high phos-
phates. Such soils are often associated with human activity, making stinging
nettles a reliable sign of human activity. If you see stinging nettles in a forest,
chances are, there is a human settlement nearby. Another example is the birch
tree, described by Gooley as not growing in the heart of woodlands; birches
(*Betula*) are "a colonizing tree that grow on the edge" of a forest and can there-

fore guide you to the edge of the woods. "Everything in Nature is a clue and a sign," given that "everything is connected," says Gooley, who uses these interconnected pieces of evidence to successfully navigate the wilderness.

1.11 NATURE & SUCCESSION

All communities of living and non-living things form with the seeds of change inside them.

Ecological succession, the gradual process of change within an ecosystem over time, is driven by inevitable disturbance—whether from within or without. The colonization of a barren habitat after a fire or flood—which can take months to years—are good examples of primary succession, which involves movement from simple to complex. Colonization and development bring opportunity through change, leading to a more complex ecosystem; the complexity itself leads to death and decay and a reversion to simplicity.

Lake succession follows a natural progression over millennia. For instance, a lake initially formed by glacial scouring experiences erosion and nutrient inputs until a marsh or bog is formed. As shrubs and trees invade from the edges, the lake is eventually obliterated.

An oligotrophic lake is basically a young lake. Still immature and undeveloped, an oligotrophic lake often displays a rugged, untamed beauty. An oligotrophic lake hungers for the stuff of life. Sediments from incoming rivers slowly feed it with dissolved nutrients and particulate organic matter. Detritus and associated microbes slowly seed the lake. Phytoplankton eventually flourish and become food for zooplankton and fish. The shores then gradually slide and fill, as does the very bottom. Deltas form and macrophytes colonize the shallows. Birds bring in more creatures. And so on. Succession is the engine of destiny and trophic status, its shibboleth.

As Nature tames the unruly lake over time, one thing replaces another. As a lake undergoes its natural succession from oligotrophic to a highly productive **eutrophic lake***, its beauty mellows and it surrenders to the complexities of destiny. Minimalism yields to a baroque richness that, in turn, heralds extinction. The lake shrinks to a swamp then buries itself under a meadow.[12]*

—Nina Munteanu, *A Diary in the Age of Water*

1.12 NATURE EVOLVING

Ecologist C.S. Holling suggested that instability in Nature maintains the structure and general patterns of **ecosystem behaviour**; in other words, Nature "learns" and accommodates over time through disturbance and change. Change ensures continued robustness and vitality.[25,26,27]

One example is the all-female species of bdelloid rotifer, *Philodina*, that has thrived for over 40 million years by adopting **parthenogenesis** (asexual reproduction) and an ecological attraction to environmental disaster. When disaster hits—in the form of radiation, freezing or desiccation—the bdelloid goes dormant to ride out the unfavourable condition. Disaster and dormancy are central to a bdelloid's evolutionary success. The mechanism for resistance and recovery is the same and involves repair during dormancy. As bdelloid mothers repair their DNA, they incorporate environmental feedback through **horizontal gene transfer** (HGT) and gene conversion. HGT is the movement of genetic material between different organisms that does not involve vertical transmission of DNA from parent to offspring through reproduction. Transfer of genetic material occurs through various mechanisms including gene transfer agents called *jumping genes* (transposons)—mobile DNA segments that may pick up a resistant gene and insert it into a chromosome. As the bdelloids patch up their broken genes, they inadvertently stitch in genes from some other organism, introducing variability—and environmentally acquired resilience—in their robust population. Up to twenty percent of a bdelloid's genome is made of foreign genes that it stole from the environment. Even humans contain some foreign genes (about one percent).[28,29,30,31,32,33]

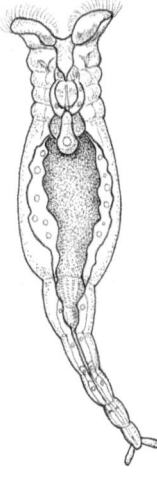

Figure 6 —
Drawing of the bdelloid rotifer *Philodina* sp.

Illustration by Nina Munteanu

1.13 CREATIVE DESTRUCTION

Some time ago, I conducted a limnological study in central British Columbia of a lake affected by both naturally occurring and human-related landslides.[34] The initial challenge involved the elucidation of human-related impact to determine necessary actions toward, costs of, and responsibilities for habitat restoration and compensation. However, the human-related impact was entwined within the ecosystem's own evolutionary tendency and natural succession. The question of what was already naturally occurring and what was exacerbated by humanity's interference remained unresolved. In a world of "who's to blame and therefore, who pays," these are key questions continually debated among government regulators, various stakeholders, and their environmental consultants. The definition and realizable benchmark for what constitutes *pristine* is complex, providing the dilemma: to what level of "natural" can we conceivably and reasonably "restore" the environment? When we do not always recognize "natural change," assigning responsibility and action becomes an insurmountable challenge; one in which most environmental scientists find themselves deferring to politics.[2]

Amid the political and social debate of who was responsible for what, I ran across the ground-breaking papers of C.S. Holling on the ecological model of **creative destruction**.[23,24,25] Economist Joseph Schumpeter introduced the term in 1942 to describe the process of industrial transformation that accompanies radical innovation. According to Schumpeter's view of capitalism, innovative entry into the market by entrepreneurs sustained long-term economic growth, even as it destroyed the value of established companies that enjoyed some degree of monopoly power. Xerox, for example, saw profits fall and its dominance vanish as rivals drew customers away when they launched improved designs or cut manufacturing costs. In the same way, ecologists describe the seral stages of plant colonization as part of ecological succession: pioneer opportunist species that initially monopolize the landscape (e.g., fireweed) give way to increased diversity and niche partitioning, as other species move in. And create something altogether new. Creative destruction is a matter of scale.[2]

Holling's model recognized ecosystem behaviour as non-linear, self-organizing and continually adapting through cycles of change, from expansion and prosperity to creative destruction and reorganization. He described ecosystems as naturally evolving through four phases: exploitation, conservation, creative destruction, and mobilization.[27]

Illustration by Costi Gurgu

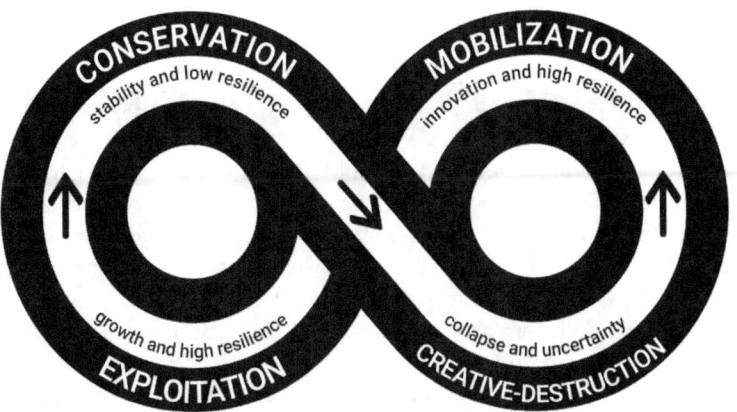

Figure 7 — Schematic of C.S. Holling's ecological model of creative destruction.

The model shows the closed loop of four phases: exploitation, conservation, creative-destruction, and mobilization—leading back to exploitation.

In the *exploitation* phase new opportunities are realized through rapid colonization of new ground and competition. Then, natural forces of *conservation* (e.g., nurturing, consolidating) eventually lead to a vulnerable system (e.g., an old growth forest), as stabilizing factors lose strength and the ecosystem evolves from having few interrelationships to having many. The result is often an abrupt change that both destroys the ecosystem and creates opportunity (*creative destruction*) through fire, storms, pests, or senescence. *Mobilization* of bound, stored "capital" (e.g., carbon, nutrients, and energy) through physicochemical and biological processes (e.g., decomposition and mineralization) completes the dynamic cycle of a functional ecosystem. Then the exploitation phase begins again.[25,26,27]

An example of Nature evolving—essentially from a competitive to a cooperative paradigm—is provided by evolutionary microbiologist Lynn Margulus who endured over twenty years of censure from the scientific community on her theory of **endosymbiosis**. Margulis theorized that the eukaryotic cell arose from the symbiotic cooperation of single-celled organisms, which at its root suggested a world driven much more by *cooperation* than *competition*.[35,36] In a world dominated by competition and "survival of the fittest," Margulis was a hero on a journey.

1.14 HERO'S JOURNEY

In *The Hero of a Thousand Faces*, Joseph Campbell describes a twelve-step *hero's journey* within a three-act play of transformation, influenced by six major archetypes (herald, mentor, threshold guardian, trickster, shadow, and shape-shifter) and motivated by key triggers. Our hero starts her journey in Act 1—in the Ordinary World. She eventually *separates* from the Ordinary World in Act 2, and enters the Special World, where she *transforms* through many challenges. In Act 3, she *returns* to the Ordinary World, changed, with her gift, an elixir. The hero's journey involves—in fact requires—that the hero stray from the good path to learn the value of that good path. To transcend, one must learn and appreciate: one must grow to master oneself and one's journey in the world.[37]

Evolutionary biologist and futurist Elisabet Sahtouris shares an allegory (attributed to Mark Twain, though never verified) of a youth who leaves home for his own adventures and returns surprised that his father has gained considerable wisdom in his absence. "We smile," says Sahtouris. "It is the son who has changed ... A youth cannot perceive the wisdom gained by experience until he becomes experienced himself."[38] This is the quintessential hero's journey of change. It recapitulates a river's journey of maturation: leaving its source to gain "wisdom" in its youthful turbulence, transitioning to a deep quiescence, and returning "home" to the oceans. According to Sahtouris, humanity now stands on the brink of maturity, still in adolescent crisis, but just mature enough to seek ancient wisdom for guidance.

In the chapter "Water Is Story" of my book *Water Is...*, I summarize the twelve steps of Campbell's three-act Hero's Journey applied to water, Nature, and humanity. (Steps of this story and their triggers or tipping points follow below and are further discussed in Part 2: Story.)

1.15 NATURE'S JOURNEY

Sahtouris tells a remarkable story of nearly four billion years of *evolution* that follows a three-act maturation cycle from individuation to fierce competition and finally to mature collaboration and peaceful interdependence. According to Sahtouris, this narrative is punctuated by key tipping points, in which a major evolutionary change avoided a potentially competitive situation and instead embraced a cooperative.[2,38]

The first tipping point, says Sahtouris, was the evolution of nucleated cells as giant bacterial cooperatives. In her 1981 book *Symbiosis in Cell Evolution*, Lynn Margulis argued that eukaryotic cells evolved through a symbiotic union of primitive prokaryotic cells in a process she called **symbiogenesis** (or endosymbiosis).[35] Her evolutionary theory posited that primitive cells gained entry into host cells as undigested prey or as internal parasites, after which the "arrangement" became mutually beneficial to both partners (chloroplasts derived from cyanobacteria and mitochondria from bacteria are two examples). The theory challenged Neo-Darwinism by arguing that inherited variation—significant in evolution—does not come mainly from random mutations, but that new tissues, organs, and even species evolve primarily "through the long-lasting intimacy of strangers." The fusion of symbiosis followed by natural selection leads to increasingly complex levels of individuality, Margulis argued. She contended that evolution proceeds ultimately through *cooperation*, not *competition*: "Life did not take over the globe by combat, but by networking." As far as "survival of the fittest goes," says Margulis, it is a "capitalistic, competitive, cost–benefit interpretation of Darwin." Even banks and sports teams must cooperate to compete. Margulis saw natural selection as "neither the source of heritable novelty nor the entire evolutionary process."[36]

Co-evolution (a kind of cooperation by default) is now an established theme in the biology of virus–host relationships. These relationships include the complex interaction between arboviruses and their vector mosquitoes, the malaria-causing plasmodium and humans, and the hantavirus and deer mice. Virologist Frank Ryan states that "today ... every monkey, baboon, chimpanzee and gorilla is carrying at least ten different species of symbiotic viruses."[2] The notion of discrete life forms with genetic integrity is outmoded. Amid co-evolved symbiotic cooperatives through epigenetics and horizontal gene transfer, a particular life form is best described as a community of interacting and evolving life forms. *Epigenetics* studies heritable changes in organisms caused by modifications of gene expression, rather than alteration of the genetic code itself. *Horizontal gene transfer*, on the other hand, describes the actual movement of genetic material across organisms.[30,39] I talk more about these in Chapter Two, What Is Adaptation.

The second tipping point, says Sahtouris, heralded the evolution of multicelled creatures. Eric Libby and William C. Ratcli discuss why unicellular life evolved into multicellular life some 600 million years ago, despite the obvious successes of "unicellularity." The answer is cooperation; cells benefitted more from working together than they did from living alone.[40]

Humanity crossed a third tipping point when tribes built the first city cooperatives to worship and trade, says Sahtouris. Cities, like the nucleated cells, became new entities that needed to evolve from youthful competition to mature cooperation. Now, after thousands of years of national and corporate em-

44 pire-building, we have reached a tipping point in planetary exploitation, "where enmities are more expensive in all respects than friendly collaboration."[38]

Sahtouris is describing the evolutionary strategies of populations (including humans) from an r-selected to a K-selected life-cycle approach. Coined by ecologists MacArthur and Wilson, and discussed by Pianka, r (for rate) and K (for *Konstante* or constant) define *life-cycle strategies* of populations that reflect an unstable and young density-independent environment (r-selected) to a maturing more stable and density-dependent one (K-selected).[41]

Pianka describes *r-selected* strategists as generally small individuals, of short life-expectancy and early maturation, and producing many offspring in an uncrowded world. Examples include annual plants, most insects, and small rodents. Parents make little investment, except to distribute widely, in the offspring.

K-selected or equilibrium individuals are generally larger, longer lived, take longer to mature and produce few offspring; parents invest time and energy into nurturing their offspring to maturity in an often-crowded world. Examples include large mammals, such as humans, and large plants, as found in a climax forest. The K-selected strategy runs on a successive gradient of maturity, from initially competitive to ultimately cooperative.

Competition is a natural adaptive remnant of uncertainty and insecurity; it forms the basis of a capitalist economy that encourages monopolization and hostile takeovers. Competition results from an initial antagonistic reaction to a perception of limited resources. It is a natural reaction based on distrust of both the environment and of the "other": these are both aspects of "self" separated from "self."

The greed for more than is sustainable reflects a fear of failure and a sense of being separate, which ultimately perpetuates actions dominated by self-interest in what is described by Garrett Hardin in 1968 as *the Tragedy of the Commons*. Hardin argued that humans were fundamentally self-interested and at war with one another and, because of this, unregulated social space would result in over-exploitation and ultimate destruction of natural resources. Neoliberal capitalists and new-colonial development agencies embraced the term to justify privatizing everything. More appropriately termed "the Tragedy of the Enclosures," this movement, based on the insecurity of greed, allowed enclosures and Nature privatization to subdue and transform "valueless chaotic ecosystems" into a surplus of power and production.

1.15.1 Prisoner's Dilemma versus Tit-for-Tat

In Chapter Three of *The Origins of Virtue: Human Instincts and the Evolution of Cooperation*, Matt Ridley recounts the tale of Tosca, the heroine of Puccini's opera of the same name.[42] She is faced with a terrible dilemma. Her lover Cavaradossi is condemned to death by police chief Scarpia, but she is offered a deal: if Tosca will sleep with Scarpia, he will save her lover's life by telling the firing squad to use blanks. Tosca decides to deceive Scarpia by agreeing to his request, then stabbing him dead after he has given the order to use blanks. But Scarpia chose to deceive Tosca too: the firing squad does not use blanks and Cavaradossi dies. Tosca commits suicide and they all end up dead.

Tosca and Scarpia were playing the most famous game in all of game theory: *the prisoner's dilemma*, which applies to any conflict between self-interest and the common good. Both would have benefited if they'd stuck to their bargain: Tosca would have saved her lover's life and Scarpia would have slept with her. But as individuals, each could have benefitted even more if he or she deceived the other into keeping his/her side of the bargain but did not keep his/her own: Tosca would have saved her lover *and* kept her virtue; Scarpia would have gotten lucky *and* rid himself of his enemy.

What's interesting is that in single encounters of the prisoner's dilemma, the outcome is usually driven by selfishness and distrust. Players are usually encouraged to defect and deceive out of self-interest; just like Tosca tried and failed to do. The outcome is entirely different when the game is played more than once. Game theorists found that frequent repetition of the encounter encouraged cooperation. With "the shadow of the future" held over each player, a new game emerged, *Tit-for-Tat*, which relied on the consequence of reciprocity. In the system described by Tit-for-Tat, the long-term reward of cooperation outweighs the short-term reward of defection.

1.15.2 Reciprocal Altruism & Creative Cooperation

The phenomenon of Tit-for-Tat is what Matt Ridley calls *reciprocal altruism* and apparently humans are particularly well suited to it, being gregarious and choosing to live in a society where repeated encounters promote cooperation.[42] Reciprocity permeates our language and our lives: "dept, obligation, favour, bargain, contract, exchange, deal…" Simpler life forms also engage in reciprocal altruism, as Lynn Margulis pointed out in her discussions of endosymbiosis and evolution through cooperation. Margulis suggested that cellular evolution was based on "cooperation" rather than simple "competition" between viruses or bacteria infecting a host cell.[35] This co-evolutionary behaviour runs counter to the traditional route of natural selection and contradicts the ruthless selfishness of Darwinian thinking. Such an evolving relationship between two different species of life, living together in mutual benefit is actually common in Nature. For instance, the ecological "home" of a simple virus is the genome of any potential host, and scientists have remained

46 baffled by the overwhelming evidence for *accommodation*: a virus, initially very aggressive, may exhibit less aggression toward an evolution of partnership.

Co-evolution was first proposed by Ehrlich and Raven in 1964 to explain the parallel evolution of butterflies (caterpillars) and their host plants.[43] Virologist Frank Ryan calls it "a wonderful marriage in Nature—a partnership in which the definition of predator and prey blurs, until it seems to metamorphose to something altogether different."[44]

"Why," asks Frank Ryan, "is co-evolution [and its partner, symbiosis] such a common pattern in Nature?" Ryan coined the term *genomic intelligence* to explain the form of intelligence exerted by viruses and the capacity of the genome to be both receptive and responsive to Nature. Genomic intelligence drives an incredible interaction between the genetic template and Nature that governs even viruses.

Symbiosis and natural selection need not be viewed as mutually contradictory. Russian biologists Andrei Famintsyn and Konstantine Merezhkovskii invented the term *symbiogenesis* to explain the fantastic synthesis of new living organisms from symbiotic unions. Citing the evolution of mitochondria or chloroplasts within a primitive host cell to form the more complex eukaryotic cell (as originally theorized by Lynn Margulis), Ryan noted that "it would be hard to imagine how the step-by-step gradualism of natural selection could have resulted in this brazenly passionate intercourse of life!"[44]

In my speculative novel, *Darwin's Paradox*, one of the characters, Gaia, brings up a grizzly example of reciprocal altruism to demonstrate a point to Julie Crane, the main character.[45] Gaia's story centres on vampire bats. These delightful creatures spend their days in hollow trees and nights in search of large animals whose blood they quietly sip from small cuts they've surreptitiously made. Bats don't usually return sated, many times failing to get their fill or to find prey at all. However, when a bat does get a meal, it usually drinks more than it needs and the surplus is typically donated to another bat by generously regurgitating some blood. Why donate at all? Bats live for a long time and roost together; they also typically groom each other and can tell if someone has a distended belly of unshared blood. A bat that has donated blood in the past will receive blood from the previous receiver; a bat that has refused to donate blood will be refused, in turn. Tit-for-Tat. A bat that cheats is soon detected and ostracized and will likely starve to death. Reciprocity rules the roost.

Competition naturally gives way to *creative cooperation*, as trust in both "self" and the "other" develops and is encouraged through continued interaction.[2] "Communities with many co-operators and altruists do better than groups dominated by narrow and selfish thinking,"[46] writes Alain Ruche, strategist for the Secretary General of the European Union External Service. Ruche adds that a biological predisposition to cooperate appears to be independent of culture, relying instead on other factors, such as "the long-lasting intimacy of strangers."[2,46]

1.16 ECOLOGY EVOLVING

"It must be deeply understood that the term 'evolution,' which is not used by Charles Darwin—he called the process 'descent with modification'—is Anglo-Saxon. It is very much a British–American 'take' on the history of life, traditionally limited to anglophones," said biologist Lynn Margulis in an interview with *Scoop News* in 2009. "Most English-speaking scientists think in hushed hagiographic terms when they mention Charles Darwin, comparable to English thought about physics before Einstein, when Newton was the only game in town. It's a very English nationalist phenomenon, especially as Darwin was later interpreted."[36]

Riane Eisler, author of *The Chalice & the Blade* writes about the ancient Bronze Age culture of Minoan Crete, a society that embraced a gylanic life-model (a social system based on equality of men and women in social and government practice) within an increasingly warlike *androcratic* and patriarchic world.[47] "The whole of life was pervaded by an ardent faith in the goddess Nature, the source of all creation and harmony," writes Eisler, who notes that a "recognition of our oneness with all of Nature" lay at the heart of both Neolithic and Cretan *pantheism*. Cretan art reflected a society in which power was not equated with dominance, destruction and oppression. I think it no coincidence that gender equality and harmony is linked to the pantheistic value of Nature. The appreciation of beauty, grace and harmony are "feminine" characteristics that ambitious, warlike, and highly competitive exploitive hegemonies have no time to cultivate.

Today, the Khasi people of Cherrapunji, in Megahalya, India—possibly the wettest place on Earth—demonstrate an adaptation to the rhythms of extreme abundance and scarcity in a monsoon ecosystem. The wet monsoon, bringing in from 1,000 mm to 4,000 mm of rain in a monsoon month, lasts only three months in the summer, averaging 12,000 mm of rain in a year. The rest of the year, the area faces drought. People adapted by using ground water during times of drought and living within the limits provided by their environment.[2]

An example of their sustainable lifestyle with Nature are the living root bridges that the Cherrapunji have trained over the many swift-flowing rivers and streams of the Khasi Hills. The roots of the rubber tree (*Ficus elastica*) can run over a hundred feet long. They are very strong and gain strength as they age and grow, becoming fully functional as bridges in ten to fifteen years. Some ancient root bridges used daily by the people of the Cherrapunji villages are well over five hundred years old.[2]

The First Nations people of North America continue to maintain a connected existence with Nature, recognizing and embracing Nature as a spirit and guide in their lives. The First Nations, Inuit and Métis people consider the natural world "home." They connect with the Earth as their Mother and take a position of respect, stewardship and gratitude. Indigenous peoples consider themselves caretakers of Mother Earth and respect her gifts of water, air, and fire. Over millennia, writes June Kaminsky, scholar of First Nations pedagogy, the First Nations and Inuit people developed intricate knowledge and understanding of the natural world:

> *First Nations and Inuit people see their relationship with each other and with the Earth as an interconnected web of life, which manifests as a complex ecosystem of relationships. Balance and holistic harmony are essential tenets of this knowledge and subsequent cultural practices. Embedded, too, is a keen belief in both adaptability and change; but change that further promotes balance and harmony, not change that creates distress, death, and the depletion of the Earth's populations and resources.*[2,48]

Another North American example of a society that lives sustainably is the town of Bolinas, California, whose citizens have vowed to live within the carrying capacity of their watershed. They did this by stopping housing development when the limits were reached.[2,49]

Eisler adds,

> *Increasingly, the work of modern ecologists indicates that this earlier quality of mind, in our time often associated with some types of Eastern spirituality, was far advanced beyond today's environmentally destructive ideology. In fact, it foreshadows new scientific theories that all the living matter of earth, together with the atmosphere, oceans, and soil and the universe forms one complex and inter-connected "life" system.*

Quite fittingly, Lovelock and Margulis called this the **Gaia Hypothesis**— Gaia being one of the ancient Greek names of the Goddess of the Earth.[2, 50]

1.17 THE GAIA HYPOTHESIS

When James Lovelock and Lynn Margulis hypothesized in the 1970s that living organisms actively modified their environment to keep the Earth habitable, they were following in the footsteps of James Hutton (the father of modern geology), who in 1785 imagined the planet as a kind of metaphoric "super-organism."[50,51] Lovelock and Margulis' Gaia Hypothesis hinged on sulphur and its essential role in living things. The concept of *feedback mechanisms* lies at the heart of it. Changes in external conditions trigger responses in the system that counteract the imposed changes. Living organisms regulate global environmental change through behaviour that creates a dynamic equilibrium of sorts. I compare this to the homeostatic behaviour of organisms at the cellular and tissue level. In fact, biochemists have applied Gaia-like rationale to the study of human biochemistry, such as the body's impressive ability to regulate glucose production to demand.

The Gaia Hypothesis attracted hostile criticism from the traditional scientific community. They claimed that it contravened Darwinian evolution, required organisms to "know" and have "purpose," and ridiculed its associated New Age overtones. Richard Dawkins, one of the science community's chief objectors, criticized the hypothesis on the grounds that it demanded global altruism among organisms—a feature that counters natural selection, according to those same scientists. It is interesting to note that Dawkins had similarly dismissed Margulis' theory of endosymbiosis (which posited that cells evolved through cooperation)—itself a challenge to both the neo-Darwinist concept of natural selection and Dawkin's concept of the "selfish gene"—only to retract his criticism later, when Margulis' theory was proven fact.

The systems of Gaia are complex, from the tiniest cell to the complex planet itself. Weather, for instance, is a "chaotic system" that displays a fractal structure and a range of chaotic behaviour on many scales. Temperature, air pressure, wind speed and humidity are all sensitive to initial conditions and interrelated on multiple scales that include major influences by life forms (trees, for instance) and are best examined through chaos theory.[2,50,51]

Brian Arthur, professor at Stanford University, shares that the complex approach is totally Taoist. In Taoism there is no inherent order.[52] The Universe in Taoism is perceived as vast and amorphous. The elements always stay the same, yet they are always arranging themselves. It's like a kaleidoscope: the world is a mosaic of patterns that change, that partly repeat, but never quite repeat, that are always new and different and yet the same. It is a paradox that embraces strange attractors, stable chaos, and quantum entanglement in a constant flow.

1.18 DEEP ECOLOGY

German poet and polymath Johann Wolfgang von Goethe believed, as did Johannes Kepler, that the Earth is an intelligent organism. Goethe and Kepler are joined by others such as Plutarch, Leonardo da Vinci, and later by Steiner, Lovelock, and Bohm in embracing the concept of Earth evolving as part of a rising consciousness in the cosmos.[2]

Bringing in his artistic appreciation of all things, Goethe's experiential science, known as *phenomenology of Nature*, provided a conceptual method to dialogue with Nature. Along with Friedrich Wilhelm Joseph von Schelling and Georg Wilhelm Friedrich Hegel, Goethe practiced *naturphilosophie* ("nature–philosophy"), an attempt to comprehend Nature in its totality and unity—later explored by Carson, Thoreau, Eisely, and Dillard. Goethean science touched on concepts later developed in ecology, evolutionary science, and quantum mechanics. Goethe's intuitive science provided the seeds of what is now called *deep ecology*, a science-based and intuitive-based worldview that advocates the inherent value of the natural world, whether connected to human utility or not, and one that encompasses the concepts of *holism* (grasping the authentic whole rather than a collection of parts, given that no parts are independent of the whole) and ecological consciousness—with both forming a Unity.

1.19 ECOLOGY OF EVOLUTION

Complex animals are relative newcomers to Earth, writes Douglas Fox in *Nature*. "Since life first emerged more than three billion years ago, single-celled organisms have dominated the planet for most of its history."[54] These organisms thrived in anoxic and low oxygen environments—relying on carbon dioxide and sulphur-containing molecules or iron minerals that act as oxidizing agents to break down food. Much of Earth's microbial biosphere still sustains itself through these anaerobic pathways. The first "game changer" came in the Cambrian Period, some 541 million years ago, in what is called the *Great Oxygen Event*—an event responsible for the extinction of many anaerobic species but also responsible for creating a new paradigm and *biodiversification* in what is called the **Cambrian Explosion**.

Scientists have documented that since the **Great Oxygen Event** (responsible for its own extinction event), life on the planet has experienced five *mass* *extinctions*—three during the Paleozoic Era, one during the Mesozoic Era, and one that signalled the beginning of the Cenozoic, our era, some 65 million years ago (mya). The first mass extinction of the Ordovician–Silurian (439 mya) wiped out eighty-six percent of life. The Late Devonian mass extinction (364 mya) removed seventy-five percent of species. The Permian-Triassic mass extinction (251 mya) removed ninety percent. The Triassic–Jurassic mass extinction of the Mesozoic (199–214 mya) removed eighty percent of species. At the end of the Cretaceous Period (65 mya) seventy-six percent of species were destroyed. Other major extinction events also occurred, perhaps not as massive in scale, but observable over the millennia. Reasons for these massive extinctions include volcanic eruptions, asteroid collisions, and sea level falls or rises—all affecting rapid climate change. Oxygen levels also appear to have played a major role in these events. In all cases, an *extinction event* was followed by an explosion of *biodiversification*.

1.19.1 Paleozoic Era (541 to 252 million years ago)

Until the onset of the Cambrian Period (541 million years ago) in what's called the **Cambrian Explosion** (the Ediacaran and Cambrian periods together ran from about 635 million to 485 million years ago), a slimy sheet of microbes covered the Ediacaran sea floor. This diverse blanket of "enigmatic animals whose bodies resembled thick, quilted pillows" dominated the ocean floor. Most were stationary, says Douglas Fox in *Scientific American*. "But a few meandered blindly over the slime, grazing on microbes."[54] Animal life at this point was simple. And, there were no predators.

Within several million years, Fox says, this simple ecosystem gave way to a burst of evolutionary innovation toward complex form and activity, including the iconic trilobite. Mobile animals appeared with new designs—from legs and compound eyes to feathery gills and tooth-rimmed jaws. Animals developed shells of calcium and exoskeletons.

Many paleontologists postulate that an increase in oxygen over an ecological threshold—from three percent to over ten percent of current oxygen levels—triggered life to speed up. Large animals had emerged during the Ediacaran period, but they were slow or immobile. They didn't eat each other. According to Guy Narbonne, a paleontologist at Queen's University in Kingston, Canada, they were mostly soft-bodied and immobile, sedentary forms that absorbed nutrients through their skin.[54,55]

Shortly after oxygen levels increased beyond a certain threshold, Ediacaran organisms, such as *Dickinsonia* and *Chaniodiscus*, went extinct. That gave rise to complex Cambrian forms, such as arthropods *Anomalocaris* and *Marrella* and chordates such as *Pikaia*—all predators that consumed other animals.

52 All a result of photosynthesis in cyanobacteria, leading to a small but significant rise in oxygen levels.

The change in grazing style contributed to a change in the ocean floor microbial mat. Previously forming a continuous "plastic wrap" sheet, which ensured that sediments remain largely anoxic (and off limits to animals), the mat started to break up in the Cambrian. This allowed animals to burrow into the sediments and create habitat. Animals now had access to previously untapped nutrients and a refuge from predators.

A mass extinction event that ended the Cambrian Period 488 mya was related to a sudden depression in oxygen. Then, *the Great Ordovician Biodiversification Event* (GOBE) that followed 470 mya was caused by a host of environmental triggers, including geological activity, sea level rise, and increased oxygen in the oceans. Small moss-like plants colonized new rock surfaces. The increase in this carbon sink—possibly along with the uplift of the Appalachians—caused a short but severe ice age 444 mya that lowered sea levels; newly exposed silicate rock may have sucked CO_2 out of the atmosphere, further chilling the planet and causing another extinction event. *The Ordovician–Silurian Extinction Event* wiped out eighty-six percent of marine life.[53]

The climate gradually warmed in the Silurian Period and sea levels fell—possibly due to more landmass uplifting—creating another minor extinction event at the end of the Silurian. In the Devonian Period 419–358 mya, vertebrates flourished in the oceans and trees formed the first complex terrestrial ecosystems. During the Middle Devonian the first tetrapods (proto-amphibians) emerged. *The Late Devonian Extinctions*, 375–358 mya, were caused by lowering oxygen in the seas, which some postulate was indirectly caused by the release of nutrients from the landmass, triggering algal blooms and anaerobic sea bottoms.[53]

During the Carboniferous Period (358–298 mya), oxygen levels increased again, along with an increased humid and warm climate, which produced extensive swamps and forests. High oxygen levels encouraged the growth of large arthropods and tetrapods that could now lay their shell-protected eggs on land. Continental drift formed the giant land mass Pangaea; reduced humidity and temperatures wiped out the giant carboniferous forests 305 mya, known as *the Carboniferous Rainforest Collapse*. By 290 mya, much of Pangaea was desert and mountains and glaciers.

During the Permian Period (298–251 mya), the climate got hotter and drier, as ancient mammals and reptiles coped with harsh conditions.

1.19.2 Mesozoic Era (248 to 65 million years ago)

The Great Dying at the end of the Permian Period of the Paleozoic Era wiped out ninety percent of all life on Earth. Ninety-six percent of sea life and seven out of ten species of land life went extinct in the space of just a few thousand years. The latest notion on the *Permian–Triassic Extinction* is that it was a several-fold calamity: the Siberian Traps volcanic eruptions released huge amounts of carbon dioxide, methane, and sulphur that acidified the seas, created acid rain and resulted in global warming. The oceans became so anoxic that anaerobic sulphur-reducing organisms took over and emitted massive amounts of toxic hydrogen sulphide. At the height of the Permian extinction—some 252 million years ago—carbon was released at a rate of 2.4 gigatons per year into the atmosphere.[53] Just for our reference, we are currently increasing our carbon input into the atmosphere by about 10 gigatons annually. The World Wildlife Fund recently reported that the Earth has lost half of its wildlife in the past forty years due to human consumption and habitat destruction.[57]

1.19.3 Cenozoic Era (66 mya to present day)

About 66 million years ago, *the Cretaceous–Paleogene large-scale extinction*— also known as *the Cretaceous-Tertiary extinction*—wiped out seventy-six percent of animal and plant species over a geologically short period of time. This also marked the end of the Cretaceous-Tertiary Period and the Mesozoic Era. Scientists suggest that volcanic activity and climate change, together with an asteroid impact, wiped out the ammonites of the seas and all remaining dinosaurs on land.[53]

The Tertiary Period of the Cenozoic Era saw the continents finally coming into place and the climate stabilized to its present-day state.

The Holocene Extinction, otherwise referred to as the *Sixth Extinction* or *Anthropocene Extinction,* is the ongoing extinction event of species during the current Anthropocene Epoch—resulting from a combination of human destruction of habitat and the unprecedented rapid climate change precipitated by human activity. We are experiencing the largest period of species extinction in the last 60 million years. The background (pre-human) rate of species extinction was one to five species annually. Scientists estimate that we are now losing species at 1,000 to 10,000 times that rate, with over dozens of species going extinct every day. Because of habitat destruction and deforestation, many species will disappear before we can learn about them or the benefits they bring to our eco-systems and our planet.[56] *The Guardian* recently reported that the Earth has lost sixty percent of its wildlife numbers in the past forty years due to human consumption, habitat destruction, and climate change.[57] A recent study has shown that insect populations—important as food for birds and for pollination of many plants—have decreased by more than seventy percent worldwide, over the past thirty years.[58]

TWO . . . What Is Adaptation?

We must always change, renew, rejuvenate ourselves; otherwise, we harden.
—Johann Wolfgang von Goethe

Ecologists want to know why an organism lives and grows in one place as opposed to another. The answers help us to determine what motivates organisms, how they interact and evolve with their environment.

Some questions we ask about an organism and its habitat include:

- **How does it obtain its food and shelter there?**
- **Is a particular nutrient limiting its growth and/or numbers?**
- **Is something else limiting it?**
- **What is its relationship with other organisms?**
- **Does it reproduce there (or elsewhere), why and how?**
- **Is it absent from parts of the site and why?**
- **How and when do young disperse?**
- **What causes the death of the organism?**

The answers to these questions lie in an organism's *adaptation* to its environment. Adaptation manifests at all levels, from the microscopic physiology of a single organism to the social behaviour of a population or community. Organisms in Nature may adapt to their environment by generalising or specialising. This concept of resource use is called *niche breadth*. (I talk more about it in Section 2.6, below.)

Generalists (e.g., racoon, rat, housefly, cockroach, and oak—species that grow in a wide variety of habitats) are often ubiquitous because they can tolerate and exploit a broad set of conditions, including suboptimal conditions. *Specialists* (e.g., koala, orchid mantis, sword-billed hummingbird, and skunk cabbage) have developed better tools to exploit a narrower set of environmental conditions, overtaking the generalist—but only in optimal conditions. Specialists often show narrow tolerances to some factor, such as temperature, air pressure, radiation, air and water quality, to name just a few.[59,60] When suboptimal conditions arrive, the specialist is the first to go. It is noteworthy that adaptation is a two-way street that involves response and effect, from morphology to behaviour. *Ecological niche* is essentially a species–environment interaction resulting from both impacts and requirements of a species.[61,62]

Specialists with known requirements are often used as **sentinel species** or *indicator species* by ecologists wishing to characterize changes in an environment. Sentinel species are early warning indicators of an ecosystem's perturbation. For instance, a stream supporting the growth of many species of healthy mayfly, stonefly and caddisfly nymphs is certain to be well-oxygenated and unpolluted—given that these immature flies cannot exist in low oxygen and in the presence of contaminants. This group of *benthic invertebrates* is so reliable in its high sensitivity to stream pollution, that aquatic ecologists developed indexes based on their presence or absence to indicate the health of a stream. The **EPT Richness Index** is one of them. EPT stands for Ephemeroptera, Plecoptera, and Trichoptera (i.e., mayfly, stonefly, and caddisfly orders, respectively). The Index is used to calculate the number of taxa of these three orders compared with the total number of taxa. A large percentage of EPT taxa is a strong indicator of high water quality.[63]

The oak tree has successfully existed for 45 million years through co-evolution with the wildlife of the forest; its fossil remains date back to the Eocene Epoch.[5] It isn't rarity or anything unique about the oak that makes it special, says Lynda Mapes in *Wisdom Tree*. The oak is ubiquitous. It is the most common tree in the northern hemisphere and encompasses over six hundred species. The oak grows in an incredibly wide range of habitats from the swamp oak (*Quercus bicolor*) in the wet lowlands of Quebec to the Gary Oak (*Quercus garryana*) clinging to craggy, salty cliffs of Vancouver Island, British Columbia. The reason for this ubiquity lies in generalist adaptation. One example of this is the oak's heat tolerance through variation of leaf shapes on a single tree. Leaves on the oak's sunny south side or on its top are smaller, with deeper scalloping, provide more edge and less blade, to avoid sunburn. Leaves in shaded positions are large and broad, to gather as much light as they can.[5]

The spruce tree (*Picea*) thrives through bitter cold winters of northern Canada, thanks to the stores of essential oils that act like antifreeze in its needles and bark. The yew (*Taxus*), which grows very slowly in the light-poor understorey of a beech forest, has compensated with a root system more extensive than other tree species. The alder tree (*Alnus*) is well-adapted to its swampy environment through a system of air ducts in its roots and cork cells in its lower trunk (acting like breathing holes) that help transport oxygen throughout the tree.[4]

Adaptations of organisms and populations to their environment include: food (energy), predation, competition, cooperation, reproduction, communication, disease (toxicity), weather and climate, and shelter.

Six categories of adaptive strategies, discussed below, include: movement, feeding, reproduction, communication, shelter (from predation and elements), and job (or niche).

2.1 MOVEMENT

Three things to consider in how and why organisms move (or don't move) include: mechanisms, patterns, and intentions. How (and where) organisms move and how much energy they invest in movement depends on how they have adapted and relate to their environment, including why they need to move and whether it's to get food or avoid a predator or to communicate. Is an organism moving to stalk or chase a prey? Elude a predator? Find a mate? Is it attracted to light or sound or smell? Is it so fast—like a hummingbird—that we can barely see it move? Or, is it so slow—like a tree—that we are unable to observe it? Movement is governed by physics and chemistry such as forces of gravity, friction and inertia, the chemical and physical nature of surfaces and textures, and other aspects of materials behaviour. Why, for instance, can a flea jump over eighty times its own height (a height equivalent to a six-foot tall human jumping over a building four hundred eighty feet tall)? Of course, it's related to scale—the mass and size of the object as it relates to gravity (itself a function of the mass and size of the planet). Movement behaviour is determined by a number of things such as bio-mechanics (e.g., propulsion technique), anatomy (e.g., muscle kinetics), and physiology (e.g., energy storage and release).

Perception of movement depends on an organism's visibility: this includes its rate relative to the observer and its size compared to the observer. For instance, that tree—which remains rooted in one place for the duration of its life—is, in fact, constantly moving: its roots grow ever outward, as does its branches. Leaves constantly rustle as the air that carries numerous aerosols and water vapour plays on them. Leaves grow and die. Both conifers and deciduous trees shed leaves—it's just more noticeable in deciduous trees, because they fall *en masse* in autumn.

Leaves of the trembling aspen (*Populus tremuloides*) are particularly susceptible to movement. The flattened leaf stalk, set perpendicular to the surface of the leaf, allows the leaf to flutter more easily at the slightest movement of air—hence the name. In strong winds, the flat petiole permits the leaves to twist easily and reconfigure, providing increased resistance to wind damage. This adaptation is also thought to improve the rate of photosynthesis throughout the tree—either by balancing leaf exposure to sunlight or increasing intake of air, which increases the rate of carbon fixation. Shivering leaves may also deter pests that would otherwise lay eggs on the leaf.

Leaves are also in constant motion on a micro-scale. **Stomata**, tiny pores on the underside of leaves, open and close to help the tree breathe and "sweat," by drawing up water and expelling vapour (through transpiration), along with secondary metabolites in the form of aerosols. The pigments of a leaf's

58 cells also keep moving. *Cytoplasmic streaming* or *cyclosis* is a micro-current in the cell cytoplasm—driven by the energy of photosynthesis—that transports pigments for optimum light exposure and distributes food throughout the cell. Cyclosis efficiently helps move nutrients out of cells in the leaf to the rest of the tree, and ultimately down the tree trunk. Even the tree's "stationary" trunk conceals a busy highway of upward flowing water and solutes through *xylem* and downward flowing sugars through *phloem*.

In short, movement pervades everything on the planet, itself orbiting the sun, which spins as part of the spinning wheel of the Milky Way Galaxy. The entire universe is moving; so, perception of movement is relative.

While individual trees don't perceptively move once they take root, tree populations do *migrate*. Scientists have noted that climate change is directing a succession of tree communities. Across the northeast, maples and birches are migrating north as the climate warms. Parts of New England are developing an oak–pine forest system previously found to the south. Scientists have estimated that the typical natural migration rate for a Canadian tree species is close to ten kilometres over one hundred years.[64] Current predictions using climate modelling, however, show that, to ensure the continued viability of many North American tree species, a migration rate of one hundred fifty kilometres in the next hundred years is needed.[65] A study of the dominant deciduous and mixed woods in the Acadian forests in New England and eastern Canada suggested that sugar maple (*Acer saccharum*), red oak (*Quercus rubra*) and yellow birch (*Betula alleghaniensis*)—a dominant community—would be most affected by climate change.[66] The current decline of the sugar maple in northeastern USA and southeastern Canada is ascribed to increased incidence of extreme weather, acid rain, and increased insect threat. "If there is a young healthy maple out back today," says Ivan J. Fernandez at the School of Forest Resources and Climate Change, University of Maine, "it may live its life out to the fullest. It may not be replaced, however, by another maple."

Sessile organisms remain anchored in one place and rely on the environment to bring them food. For instance, the caddis fly larva *Hydropsyche* anchors on a rock in a stream and lets the current bring food to it. The caddis fly spins a perfect silk net into which tiny insects, algae and other food particles float. The filter-feeding bdelloid rotifer attaches to an underwater surface and spins its two rings of *cilia*. These create a vortex that brings into its tiny mouth food made up of organic detritus, dead bacteria, algae and protozoans.

Many aquatic organisms drift on the current, relying on it to move them. Called *plankton*, these include animals, Protista, plants, and bacteria. They make up over half of organisms that live in the open ocean and move through surface currents or wind. *Phytoplankton* (photosynthetic microscopic organisms) normally concentrate in the surface waters of the *photic zone* (where light penetrates). They also *vertically migrate*, following the rhythms of the sun by changing their buoyancy; this controls how much ultra-violet (UV) radiation and photosynthetic active radiation (PAR) they take in for photosynthesis—too much can damage their DNA; too little can starve them. Freshwater and marine *zooplankton* also vertically migrate every day in a process called *diel vertical migration*, sinking to deep water in the morning and rising as the sun sets—presumably to eat the phytoplankton and elude predators.

Pheromones are chemicals that an animal—particularly an insect—produces and releases into the environment to affect the behaviour or physiology of others (usually of its own species). Pheromones are the reason ants walk in a line; the scent left behind by the leader is followed by the remaining ants. Ants also select foraging routes using statistical distributions of probability. Two factors that affect the ant's movement include: (1) "persistence" (remaining in a straight line without an obstacle); and (2) "reinforcement" (knowledge of which areas have been previously visited—based on a pheromone trail).

The *trap-jaw ant* (*Odontomachus sp.*) uses an additional mechanism to move: its spring-loaded mandibles. Normally used to capture and stun prey at extremely high speeds, the spring-loaded mandible of the trap-jaw ant also allows the ant to jump backward (or even forward) away from danger. Tapping a substrate with its powerful mandible can propel the ant over twenty times its body length. Videos of this fierce-looking tiny insect jumping are stunning.[71]

Dragonfly nymphs use the water they live in to help power sudden movement to hunt or flee a predator. Using gills located inside its anus (where gas exchange occurs), the dragonfly larva can expel water in a sudden jet to propel it in a burst of sudden movement.

Honeybees use vortexes to fly, waggle in elaborate dances to communicate, and use electric fields to move each other. A honeybee flaps and rotates its wings two hundred and forty times a second, creating a vortex that lifts it into the air. They use short wing strokes of less than ninety degrees and a high number of flaps every second to stay aloft. When challenged by difficult conditions, the bees use wider strokes (increasing their wing amplitude) but maintain the same frequency. This stroke pattern is less efficient than the broader wing strokes and slower flapping of fruit flies and other insects, but it allows the bee to generate more lift when it needs to carry a heavy load, such as a cargo of nectar or larvae, and to fly in a straight line, rather than the fanciful flight of the butterfly. Pollen, which the bee collects on its hind legs, is a source of protein for the hive and is needed to feed the baby bees (larvae) to help them grow. The nectar that the bee collects is a sweet, watery substance that the bee processes and then regurgitates into waxy honeycomb cells in the hive. They fan it with their wings to remove excess moisture, and honey is the result. Bees are the only insects in the world that make food that humans can eat. And, honey is the only insect-created food with therapeutic, medicinal, and nutritional value.[2]

60   Upon returning to its hive from a nearby field of flowers, the honeybee starts to dance. It waggles and struts in a figure-eight, conveying the duration and direction of the food source to its hive-mates. In his article in *National Geographic*, March 2013, Ed Yong explains how honeybees move each other with electric fields: "When they return to the hive and walk or dance about, they give off electric fields. Uwe Greggers from the Free University of Berlin showed that they can detect these fields with the tips of their antennae," and this causes them to move.[67] According to Greggers, the waxy cuticle of the bee permits a positive charge build-up of up to 450 volts.

Bumblebees use the sun as a compass. They navigate by polarized light, enabling them to fly the shortest possible route between flowers. Shape, pattern, and colour play a role in the bee's ability to find a particular flower; bees can see visible and ultraviolet light and have precise olfactory receptors. Recent scientific evidence from the University of Nevada shows that bumblebees also detect electric fields that flowers emit and can differentiate between recently visited blooms and fresh ones. Flowers have a slight negative charge relative to the air around them, and bumblebees have a positive charge, due to friction of their body parts in the air. The bees collision with charged particles, from dust to small molecules, tear electrons away from their cuticle—their outer shell—and the bee ends up with a positive charge. That's what helps pollen grains stick to the bee's legs—in the same way that shuffling across a carpet in wool socks creates static. Pollen may actually fly through the air—drawn to the charge on the body of an approaching bee.[2]

Plants use hormones, chemicals and hydraulics to move in response to light, gravity and other signals. Shoots grow. Leaves bend toward light. Flowers open and close, often diurnally. Climbing plants use tendrils or stems to cling to surfaces they climb. Botanist Bernie Hobbs writes in *ABC Science*, "A seedling can make a right-hand turn within hours, a tendril can curl around a stick in minutes, and a Venus fly trap can catch its lunch in under a second."

Phototropism is the movement of plants toward light. In response to light, the plant stem or shoot activates the hormone *auxin* to increase cell growth on the shady side, which bends the plant toward the light. **Gravitropism** (growing toward or away from gravity) also uses auxin. The way it works is based on dense packets of starch called *statoliths* that settle to the bottom of the cell. Their position determines in which direction auxin is released.

Hydraulics are responsible for the rapid movement of the Venus flytrap's sensitive-haired leaves—which can snap shut in 300 milliseconds to catch prey. When the modified "hairs" of the Venus flytrap (*Dionaea muscipula*) are touched, they bend, pushing on the thin-walled cells around their base. This increases the pressure inside, which converts to an electrical signal similar to our own nerve signals. The signal is propagated through the release of chloride ions. The opposing leaves snap shut and the hairs act as a lock.

Water causes most plant movement with changes in **plant turgor** (wilting   61
and swelling); turgor changes occur as potassium ions concentrate in or out
of the cell, directing water to follow. The actions of wilting and swelling act as
levers and create movement that is similar to the extension and contraction of
muscles in our bodies. This wilting/swelling balance—driven by sensors and
a tiny organ called the *pulvinus*—governs all reversible movements in plants:
mimosa leaves closing when touched; stems shifting toward light; flowers
closing and opening diurnally; ivy tendrils curling around a surface. Using
its surrounding thin-walled motor cells—that can quickly expand and shrink
as water rushes in or out with changing potassium ion concentration—the
pulvinus directs movement.

2.1.1 Pattern Recognition

Patterns emerge when circumstances remain the same and we imprint
with **pattern recognition**. If not alert, one can get caught by a scenario that
presents a familiar circumstance yet harbours a deadly difference. When I visited England for the first time, for example, I experienced vehicles moving on
the left side of the road, instead of the right side. As a pedestrian, I had to be
mindful where to look when crossing the street. I'd been in London a week
and had grown dangerously complacent with the familiarity of the streets;
that false confidence almost cost me my life when I was about to cross a busy
street and looked in the wrong direction for oncoming traffic. I was saved by
another pedestrian who seized my arm as I was about to blindly step in front
of a moving car. I'd been fooled by the familiar scenario of street traffic; in
dropping my guard, I'd perilously slid into my old pattern.

Birds search for their dinner using pattern recognition. They select only
one kind of seed until they are all gone and have to learn another seed shape
and size.

2.1.2 Synchronous Movement

I remember sitting as a child next to my father and watching synchronized
swimming events on NBC TV. I thought at the time how beautiful, ridiculous
and wonderful it was all at the same time. I found the swimmers' **synchronicity** magical and attractive; yet, I could imagine the hidden turbulence in the
waters beneath, which produced the flawless synchrony above. Such order!
Such deception! Is this why we like to dance or march in a parade?

In the opening to his compelling book, *Sync: The Emerging Science of Spontaneous Order*, Steven Strogatz describes how every night, along the tidal rivers of Malaysia, thousands of fire flies congregate in the mangroves and flash in unison, without any leader or cue from the environment. "Even our bodies are symphonies of rhythm, kept alive by the relentless, coordinated ring of thousands of pace-maker cells in our hearts ... almost as if Nature has an eerie yearning for order," adds Strogatz. Synchronicity defies the first and second laws of thermodynamics. The first law, for instance, expresses the universal law of conservation of energy and identifies heat transfer as a form of energy transfer. The second law expresses the universal law of increasing entropy. (A classic example of increasing entropy is ice melting.)

Temporary synchronicity, which usually occurs by accident, can be found everywhere (e.g., pigeons startled by a car back firing will take off at the same time). Persistent sync, however, is entirely different. Persistent sync comes easily to human beings and gives us pleasure: we like to dance together, sing in a choir, or play in a band. Strogatz says, "We interpret persistent sync as a sign of intelligence, planning, and choreography. So, when sync occurs among unconscious entities like electrons or cells [or even fire flies], it seems almost miraculous."[2]

Why do they do it? asks the ecologist. We don't know. All we know is that the tendency to synchronize and the existence of spontaneous order pervade our fractal universe, from atoms to animals, and people to planets. Female friends or co-workers eventually find their menstrual cycles synchronizing; sperm swimming side by side toward the egg beat their tails in unison; the tides have locked the moon's spin to its orbit. Strogatz and others suggest that the defining commonality to these sync phenomena is *mathematics*: the mathematics of chaos theory and **self-organization**. This spontaneous emergence of order out of chaos is what Strogatz calls "synchronized chaos" and what I call **stable chaos**. Rhythms of sync abound in humans: heart rhythms, brain waves, menstrual cycles, cell division cycles, waves in the gut, and circadian rhythms—to name a few.

The rhythms of short-term memory, secretion of melatonin, and several other cognitive and physiological functions run in the same phase relationship. Even single-celled algae exhibit circadian rhythms. Theoretical biologist Art Winfree, having discovered an unexpected link between biology and physics, showed that mutual synchronization in biology is analogous to a phase transition (e.g., from liquid to solid).[2]

Volvox, a spherical colony of tiny Protista (called a *coenobium*), is found in freshwater habitats such as ponds, lakes, and rivers. Some 500 to 50,000 algal cells line themselves along the outer boundary of the colony on a sphere of gelatinous glycoprotein. Flagellae face outward as the cells swim in coordinated fashion. Their eyespots near the anterior direct the colony to swim towards light. Volvox individuals work and act like one multicellular organism. Each protist helps propel the entire colony with a synchronized beating of its two flagellae.

2.1.3 Movement & Meaningful Coincidence

Carl Jung created the concept of *synchronicity* in the 1920s to describe events such as "meaningful coincidences," if they occurred with no apparent causal relationship, yet were meaningfully related. In other words, events connected by meaning need not have an explanation through causality. By describing a governing dynamic that underlies the whole of human experience, synchronicity confirmed Jung's concept of archetypes (underlying form in universal patterns and images in the minds of individuals) within the *collective unconscious* (structures of the unconscious mind shared by humanity, populated by instincts and archetypes). The choreography of meaningful coincidences and their gestalt relationships and emerging patterns is the stuff of good stories. As with the fractal whole of ecology, the key lies in meaning.

Synchronicity reflects aspects of self-organization. Examples we are all familiar with include birds in flight and schools of swimming fish. Even sand dunes, like most wave patterns, are self-organized. Whirlpools, from your spiralling bath water to the powerful funnels of tornadoes and hurricanes are self-organized, coherent structures of symmetry.

2.1.4 Fractals & Self-Organized Movement

The concept of *fractal geometry*, developed by Benoit Mandelbrot in 1975, originated in *chaos theory*, both of which show that natural order is not random, given that it generates its own order. It's self-organized.

"Water is a self-organizing system," writes Dr. Paolo Consigli, author of *Water, Pure and Simple*. Water's ability to self-organize generates spontaneous order and synchronicity from disorder through the local self-organizing components within its disordered state. The system creates islands of predictability in a sea of chaotic unpredictability. It's self-creating; that is, it's *autopoietic*.[2]

In 1974, Chilean scientists Francisco Varela, Humberto Maturana, and R. Uribe used the term *autopoiesis* to describe systems that produce themselves in a ceaseless way. Autopoiesis describes the dynamics of a non-equilibrium system that achieves an organized state remaining stable for long periods of time, despite matter and energy continually flowing through it. It is, in fact, this flow that helps maintain the self-organizing aspect of an open autopoietic system. It is both producer and product.

That water behaves coherently, like a self-organized fractal organism, is a concept that remains unaccepted by most scientists. However, Ho and other scientists such as Voeikov and Del Guidice suggest that water has quantum characteristics (e.g., water stores information, self-organizes, self-purifies, and demonstrates properties of an organism). These characteristics reflect water's two states (low density and high density), which toggle within a stable

64 non-equilibrium. The energy dynamics of water defy the second law of thermodynamics.[2,7,8]

2.2 FEEDING

All living things must take in energy (e.g., feed) in some form to subsist. How and what organisms "eat" relies on their trophic nature. *Autotrophs* (primary producers like plants and algae) use the sun's energy and chemical nutrients to subsist. *Heterotrophs* get their energy by consuming plants directly (e.g., herbivores) or indirectly (e.g., carnivores and detrivores).

Virtually all living organisms on Earth are carbon-based and require carbon for their energy, water as a solvent, and DNA or RNA to define and control their form. Carbon comprises close to fifty percent of all dry biomass on Earth; it forms the backbone of complex molecules bonded with other elements, often oxygen and hydrogen (the most common elements in the universe), nitrogen, phosphorus and sulphur. Life on Earth—surrounded by carbon, water, and methane—uses these to live. "But why not cobalt and antimony, or argon and xenon?" asks science journalist Jeffrey Kluger in his article in *Time: The Search for Life in the Universe*.[68] Kluger suggests the possibility that any elements from the periodic table could whip up life-sustaining molecules we can't even contemplate. "We say these chemicals don't exist in Nature, but that's our nature," says astronomer Dimitar Sasselov, the director of Harvard University's Origin of Life Initiative. "If the chemistry is different because the planet is different, would we even know how to look for life there?" What might be a poison here, may very well be a nutrient elsewhere. "Once different conditions are established, life could spiral out in all manner of corkscrew ways, relying on all manner of unlikely ingredients."[68]

2.2.1 Feeding as Source & Consequence of Environmental Change

Some 2.5 billion years ago, during the Precambrian Period, prehistoric multicellular blue-green algae, *Cyanobacteria*, became the first microbe to produce oxygen through *photosynthesis*. They helped create this ecotone and survived because of a specialized cell called the heterocyst.

For a primitive organism, Cyanobacteria are sophisticated revolutionaries that developed big cheats—highly specialized adaptations—at great cost to most other life. Their thick-walled heterocysts are an example.

Heterocysts *apparently originated in the Precambrian some 2.5 billion years ago, when some prehistoric multicellular blue-green alga became the first microbe to produce oxygen through photosynthesis.*

Photosynthesis was the first big cheat. Because the cyanobacteria could exploit a new and almost limitless source of energy—sunlight—they exploded and transformed a reducing anoxic Precambrian Earth of mostly hydrogen, methane and sulphur into an atmosphere rich in oxygen. The Great Oxygen Event brought in a diversity of new oxygen-breathing life on Earth, but not before causing one of the greatest extinction events. Free oxygen is toxic to anaerobic organisms, which were the dominant life forms then. Free oxygen also reduced the greenhouse gas methane. Methane bonded with oxygen to create carbon dioxide and water. Through this process a thinner atmosphere emerged. The Earth began to lose its heat, triggering the longest glaciation period on Earth. It was a game-changer.

Heterocysts are the second big cheat. They're highly specialized and sophisticated independent cells that form "on demand," when nitrogen is scarce. Because the nitrogen-fixing enzyme nitrogenase is sensitive to oxygen, the heterocyst wraps itself in a semi-permeable thick wall to keep out the oxygen to maintain its own anaerobic environment in an aerobic community of cells. The heterocyst gets its organic carbon from its vegetative mates through a pore in its thick wall and its reduced nitrogen is, in turn, transferred to its mates. The big cheat is maintaining an anaerobic inside in an outer aerobic environment. The blue-green algae had found a way to play both games at the same time.

—Nina Munteanu, *A Diary in the Age of Water*[12]

Sulphur-reducing bacteria feed on elemental sulphur by reducing it to hydrogen sulphide—together with the oxidation of acetate, succinate or other organic compounds. Sulphur bacteria thrive where there is no oxygen (*anaerobic*), in places such as oxygen-depleted waters or the mud of fresh and marine waters. Sulphur is the sole energy source for some lithotrophic bacteria and archaea. Reduced sulphur compounds, such as hydrogen sulphide, elemental sulphur, sulphite, thiosulphate, and various polythionates (e.g., tetrathionate), are used by some lithotrophic bacteria and are oxidized by *Acidithiobacillus*.

66   The *amoeba,* a microscopic protozoan, uses its pseudopods to feed on prey such as desmids, other protozoans and bacteria. In a process called *phagocytosis,* the amoeba senses prey that it captures using its streaming cytoplasm (pseudopods) that engulf the prey to form a vacuole (phagosome). The prey (bacteria, Protista, or detritus) is then digested live by lysosome secretion—a rather violent process when viewed under the microscope.

I studied benthic invertebrates (macrobenthos) of streams for over twenty years. Most *macrobenthos* are, in fact, larval forms (called nymphs) of terrestrial insects. In their larval form, they are ferocious predators that stalk and ambush their prey: usually just smaller invertebrates like rotifers, ostracods, daphnia, and copepods. The *Odonata* (dragonflies and damselflies) use a specialized *labium*—a weaponized "lower lip" that shoots out—to grab or impale an unsuspecting prey nearby, then bring it back to its mouth. The labium is powered hydraulically; water is drawn in through the anus in a tight clench to pressure the labium to shoot forward.

Elodea, an aquatic plant, uses *cyclosis* (cytoplasmic streaming) to move its chloroplasts (the pigments that capture and metabolize sun energy into sugars) for efficient use of position in relation to light. The motion is mediated by "motor" proteins that use adenosine triphosphate (ATP) to move one protein in relation to the other. As one protein remains fixed, the other uses it like a ladder to move and drag other materials with it. For instance, actin filaments align inside the cytoplasm like a grid while myosin molecules—attached to the chloroplasts—move along the actin fibers, towing the chloroplasts and sweeping other cytoplasmic material along with them.[69]

2.2.2 When Plants Eat Like Animals

According to Yao-Hua Law in an article for the BBC, carnivory evolved independently at least six times across the plant kingdom.[70] Plants evolved a *carnivorous* habit in nutrient-poor or acidic bogs and rocky slopes. Examples include the common sundew (*Drosera rotundifolia*) in Canada's muskegs, bogs and marshes; the pitcher plant (*Sarracenia purpurea*) in Canada's temperate bogs; the common bladderwort (*Utricularia vulgaris*) in Ontario's bogs and fens; and the well-known Venus flytrap of South Carolina's boggy wetlands. These plants have transformed their leaves into traps that trick, bind, drown, and digest prey.

Aquatic species of bladderwort possess bladders that are usually large enough to feed on substantial prey, such as water fleas (*Daphnia*), nematodes, and even fish fry, mosquito larvae, and young tadpoles. Despite their small size, the traps are extremely sophisticated. The bladder, when "set," is under negative pressure in relation to its environment so that when the trapdoor is mechanically triggered, prey that brush against trigger hairs connected to the trapdoor, along with the water surrounding it, are sucked into the bladder. Once full of water, the bladder door closes again—the whole process taking only ten to fifteen milliseconds.[70]

The sundew attracts an insect to its red glandular hairs that secrete a sticky sweet mucilage; the insect, once trapped in the leaf's tentacles, is dissolved by the plant's enzymes to extract ammonia and other nutrients otherwise collected from the soil. Because of this diversion of energy from harnessing sunlight through photosynthesis, carnivorous plants tend to grow slowly and stay small; the tallest part of the common sundew—the hairy petiole that carries the sticky, insect-eating leaves—is just three to five centimetres tall.[70]

Carnivorous plants have also developed a sophisticated way to prevent their sexual partners (pollinating insects) from becoming their dinner. The sundew (*Drosera auriculata*) of southern Australia uses different scents in its leaves, luring prey insects to eat, and in its flowers, attracting pollinator insects to create more plants. Other species of sundew, whose flowers and leaves grow further apart or appear at different times, also use visual signals and separation to protect pollinators.[70]

2.2.3 Trap-Jaw Ants

Trap-jaw ants (*Odontomachus*) use their **spring-loaded mandibles** to capture or stun prey. The mandibles snap shut at extremely high speeds. Trigger hairs on the face of each mandible connect to neurons that control the latches and release the mandibles.[71]

This reminds me of another adaptation revealed to me during a safari tour I took years ago in Kenya's Serengeti Park. After experiencing a soldier ant swarm one harrowing night, I was told by a local that these soldier ants with huge heads and mandibles bite with a steely grip. They were used by the East African tribal peoples as sutures for wounds. Once an ant clamps on, it doesn't let go. If you pull the ant, only the body snaps off, leaving the head and mandible embedded and locked on—potentially acting as a suture.

2.2.4 Eating "Waste Products"

The waste product of one organism can be the food or nourishment of another. An interesting example is a small Indonesian "cat" called the Asian Palm Civet (*Paradosorus hermaphroditus*), a small viverrid native to South and Southeast Asia. The civet helps maintain tropical forest ecosystems through seed dispersal as they feed on pulpy fruits such as mango, rambutan, and coffee. Upon feasting on ripe coffee cherries, the civet starts to digest and ferment them in its stomach. The cat then poops what's left and farmers collect the poop, clean it, then process and roast the beans. Civet digestive enzymes allegedly remove the acidic taste from the coffee and impart new flavours. The result is **kopi luwak** (cat-poop coffee), an exotic coffee coveted by coffee dilatants and hipsters around the world.

2.2.5 Stealing Food

Kleptoparasitism is essentially parasitism by theft, in which the parasite benefits by stealing something the other organism needs. Kleptoparasitism may occur by unobtrusively stealing collected or stored food. It can also occur through bullying an organism to give up its food they just caught (e.g., an eagle bothering an otter; a Western gull robbing diving birds who have just brought prey to the surface; a hyena robbing a cheetah's kill). The semiaquatic bug (Heteroptera) can steal the catch of the water cricket *Velia caprai*, which often captures very large prey. The little pika (*Ochotona princeps*) that lives on the talus slopes of alpine habitats steals stored hay piles from its neighbours. Kleptoparasitism may apply to more than feeding. For instance, cuckoo bees (*Bombus bohemicus*) lay their eggs on pollen masses made by other bees; chinstrap penguins steal rocks and other nest materials from members of their colony to use in their own nest.

2.3 REPRODUCTION

The highest mandate of most life-forms is to reproduce themselves and continue the species. Reproductive success relies on the fecundity of the individual(s); species continuation relies on a successful adaptive strategy to change. *Reproductive strategies* are as diverse as the biodiversity of this changing planet. Strategies include a range of forms such as: sexual reproduction, cloning, bisexuality, parthenogenesis, self-reproduction (*autopoiesis*), sexual shape-shifting, hermaphroditism and many other bizarre forms and patterns. Strategies have co-evolved with other components of the environment to accommodate cyclical changes and imposed instabilities. Reproductive strategies are aimed at long-term success. The oak tree is a prime example.

According to journalist Lynda Mapes, in her book *Witness Tree*, the red oak won't start flowering until it's over twenty-five years old; it takes another twenty-five years to create a good crop of acorns, which take two years to ripen.[4] Given that the oak is generally shade intolerant, with seedlings faring poorly beneath the thick canopy of the parent tree and forest, the oak has developed ways to disperse its acorns so they can germinate a good distance away. The meat of the acorn is enjoyed by the blue jay, squirrel and other rodents and birds—most of which carry the seed far from the shade of the parent tree. The trick, says Mapes, is to make the acorn "attractive enough to the jays and squirrels that they will pick it up and carry it to a cache—but they can't eat so many that there will be none left to create a new generation of oaks." The oak adopted a "boom or bust" acorn production strategy; they create a bumper crop of acorns only every few years, called *mast years*. Acorn feeders get used to the limited supply; so, during a mast year, there are many more acorns than can feed the animals. This ensures that some acorns will be left to sprout.[4,5]

The beech tree is expected to produce at least thirty thousand beechnuts every five years—now more like every two or three years, due to climate change. The tree is sexually mature at eighty to one hundred and fifty years, depending on light conditions. Given that beeches can grow to four hundred years old, 1.8 million beechnuts are produced in one beech tree's lifetime. "From these," says forester Peter Wohlleben in *The Hidden Life of Trees*, only "one will develop into a full-grown tree ... all the other hopeful embryos are either eaten by animals or broken down into humus by fungi or bacteria."[4] Poplar trees produce far more of their fluffy seeds—some 54 million fluffy seeds annually—but for their extra output, their outcome is no greater than the beech.

Implications of mast year production (usually from a "fat" summer), can influence other aspects of a tree's metabolism. For instance, sugar maples (*Acer saccharum*) develop more watery sap in a spring following a mast year because they used their stored sugars to produce their bumper seeds the previous fall.

2.3.1 Reproduction Co-Evolved with Fire

The *boreal forest* evolved with fire. Fire helps regenerate the forest, consuming dead and decaying vegetation, clearing the way for new growth and converting the burnt vegetation into a nutrient form that can fuel new plants. The jack pine (*Pinus banksiana*) produces resin-filled (*seratonous*) cones that remain closed and dormant until a fire melts the resin. The cone then bursts open and the seeds fall out and sprout in the fire-cleared forest. Together with the aspen, the jack pine is a key pioneer species to recolonize a forest affected by fire. Both trees take advantage of the light to attain some height before more heavily canopied spruce and fir trees outcompete them for light.

2.3.2 Convergent Evolution in Flowering Plants

Seeds disperse in many creative ways. Many types of seed dispersal have symbiotically co-evolved with another organism through what is called *dispersive mutualism*. *Myrmecochory* describes a type of seed dispersal that plants evolved with ants. A plant's *elaiosome* (the fleshy structure attached to the seed) is rich in lipids and proteins. After taking a seed underground, ants consume the elaiosome and dispose of the seed in their waste site, rich in nutrients from ant *frass* (debris, feces and dead bodies), where the seed can germinate. The ants benefit from the food and the plant is effectively planted and fertilized by the ant.

2.3.3. Addiction & the Acacia

The evolutionary alliance between the acacia tree and the ant (*Pseudomyrmex ferrugineus*) that guards it is based on an *addiction* created by the tree. The acacia's nectar is laced with an enzyme—*invertase*—that prevents the ant from eating other sources of sugar. The addiction to acacia nectar with invertase is created by the subversive action of the tree. The ant larvae starts out having the enzyme; but with its first sip its own invertase is disabled by the chitinase enzymes in the nectar of the tree. The tree both disables the ant from being able to use its own invertase and supplies the ant with nectar invertase—creating a dependency.[72]

2.3.4 Evolving Success of Asexual Reproduction

Parthenogenesis is a type of *asexual reproduction* in which offspring develop from unfertilized eggs. It is particularly common in arthropods and rotifers. Parthenogenesis also occurs in some species of fish, amphibians, birds, and reptiles. Parthenogenesis is currently not known in mammals, which rely on *sexual reproduction* and *sexual recombination* to maintain *diversity* for evolutionary robustness and success.

An exemplary case of parthenogenesis is the all-female **bdelloid rotifer** that produce daughters from unfertilized eggs. Bdelloid rotifers practice obligate parthenogenesis (*thelytoky*), which means that this is the only way they reproduce: through uniparental reproduction (only females, produced by only females). The bdelloid rotifer has existed for over 40 million years. Its long-term survival and evolutionary success in the absence of sex is tied to its ability to accommodate and learn from ecological catastrophe. When the environment turns inhospitable, the bdelloid creates protective proteins, called LEA, which act as molecular shields, and then goes dormant. Dormancy lies behind why the bdelloid abandoned sexual reproduction long ago. When the bdelloid comes out of dormancy, she does not need to find a mate to reproduce. This is a great advantage in an unstable and changing environment, where simply looking for a mate requires energy. Bdelloids thrive on disruption. Going into dormancy triggers DNA repair and the unintentional stitching in of foreign genes through *horizontal gene transfer* (HGT). By repairing their DNA and incorporating genes from the environment, bdelloid rotifers adapt to their changing environment. The bdelloid replaced the diversifying role of sex over generations with individual epigenetic-induced gene conversion and HGT over less than a generation. Up to twenty percent of a bdelloid's genome is made of foreign genes that they stole from the environment.[2,12,73]

2.3.5 Sexual Dimorphism, Bisexuality & Transgenderism

Monogonont rotifers respond to unpredictable environments by developing *sexual dimorphism* (a distinct difference in size or appearance between the sexes) and *bisexuality*. For instance, the rotifer *Hydatina senta* reproduces two kinds of females: *amictic* females that reproduce wholly by parthenogenesis; and *mictic* females that reproduce parthenogenetically or bisexually. Rotifer females are always larger than males, and this can range from a subtle difference to the female being up to ten times the size of the male. Triggered by environmental signals (e.g., nutrients, temperature, pH, population density, desiccation), the female produces two kinds of eggs through parthenogenesis: one kind forms mictic females and the other kind develops into degenerate males that cannot even feed themselves. The males survive long enough to produce sperm that fertilize the eggs of the mictic females they copulate with; the fertilized eggs then form resistant amictic zygote females (resting eggs) that can survive desiccation or other environmental perturbations. The zygotes are released and hatch when there is enough water.

BBC's 2018 TV series, *Blue Planet 2*, dramatically demonstrated the sexual fluidity of fish. In the first episode, a ten-year old female kobudai (*Semicossyphus reticulatus*) acted as a *hermaphrodite* by changing into a male in what is known as *sequential hermaphroditism* (a temporal pattern of sex-change). This kind of gender change—going from female to male—is known as *protogynous* (Greek for "female first"). Having previously mated with the current alpha male, she—now a he—battles for dominance and defeats the incumbent to become the new alpha male. By first reproducing as a female, then breeding as a male, the kobudai doubles its reproductive output—maximizing the chances of passing on genes to accommodate environmental change. While the change in the kobudai (or Asian sheepshead wrasse) may take months, the speedy bluehead wrasse female-to-male transformation takes only eight days.[74]

Hermaphroditism is not rare in fish (about five hundred different species in the world are hermaphrodites). Another example of sequential hermaphroditism is the clown fish (Amphiprioninae), who does it in the opposite way—turning from male to female (*protandrous* or "male first"). Because larger clownfish females are more fertile than smaller ones, spreading sperm as a small male and gestating eggs as a larger female is an efficient adaptation. The mangrove killifish practices *simultaneous hermaphroditism* by possessing fully functional male and female genitalia; it self-fertilizes throughout its existence. Other fish—such as the coral-dwelling goby—can shape-shift back and forth depending on environmental triggers.[74]

Demonstrating the extreme gender plasticity of 500 million years of evolution, most fish can switch sex at their embryonic stage when subjected to any number of environmental perturbations such as acidity of the water, parasites, and temperature. One mechanism responsible for sex change in fish comes from the enzyme aromatase, which can alter androgen hormones into estrogenic hormones, changing male gonads into ovaries. Transgender fish may result from the disruption of their endocrine function when exposed to various chemical pollutants. *Endocrine disruptors* interfere in the production, release, transport, and metabolism of natural hormones in the body—hormones responsible for maintaining a balanced developmental process including determination of male versus female or intersex gender, sexual behaviour and even fertility.[12,75]

Leaning on his microscope, Daniel went on, "Wherever there's a sewage treatment plant, pulp and paper mill, or herbicides and pesticides in a stream, you get endocrine disruption, which causes more female or intersex fish populations. Then there's nonylphenols—"

"—Degradation products of surfactants used in commercial and household detergents," I ended for him and leaned against the doorway.

He nodded. "They inhibit breeding in male fish. And herbicides like atrazine—"

"—Create feminized males with female eggs, along with reduced immunity to disease," I finished for him.

I knew all this. Hormonal disruption is global. Environmental toxicologists have been finding it in many aquatic animals like fish, turtles, alligators and frogs. And some terrestrial animals ... even humans ... Was it also causing the steep rise in ambiguous sex in humans? Is Daniel an intersex human? Apparently one in thirty now have bodies that differ notably from standard male or female. Klinefelter [syndrome], androgen insensitivity syndrome, presence of ovotestes, mixed gonadal dysgenesis, and mosaic genetics are all on the rise. Which was he?

*As if he knew what I was thinking, Daniel said dramatically, "The environ-
ment is changing us faster than most think, and it's doing it through epigenetics and HGT."... You get out what you put into the ground. India and
Asia—where endocrine disruptive chemicals are finding their way into the
water—are reporting very low sperm counts in their men as well as higher
incidents of intersex humans. You get out what you put in the water. We are
over two thirds water, after all.*

—Nina Munteanu, *A Diary in the Age of Water*[12]

Other life forms also practice sexual shape-shifting. In the plant world,
jack-in-the-pulpit (*Arisaema triphyllum*)—a small plant that grows on the north
temperate forest floor—is bizarre in both behaviour and looks. Jack's large
hooded and striped flowers appear in shades of green, greenish-white and
purple. The flower features a pouch-shaped *spathe* ("pulpit") and finger-like
central *spadix* ("jack"), which give the plant its common name.

The young jack-in-the-pulpit plant first emerges as a male plant from a
vegetative *cormlet*, putting out male flowers, which produce pollen. As it
grows, the plant switches sex and the larger spadix puts out female flowers,
which produce seeds and a cluster of berries. A more nutrient rich soil or a
brighter area accelerates growth and shortens the transition from male to female. But, if conditions for growth are difficult from lack of nutrients or stress
from drought, the female plant reverts to being a male plant. Its practice of
sequential hermaphroditism ensures that the plant is strong enough to reproduce and produce healthy seeds. Jack is a patient and wise shape-shifter.

2.3.6 Flipping the Switch from Asexual to Sexual

The spherical Protista colony **Volvox** ordinarily grows asexually when the
environment provides optimum conditions. The haploid asexual *V. carteri*
lives in temporary pools of water. The "daughter" colonies—smaller spheres
inside the larger *Volvox* sphere—are called gonads and they grow from the
cells around the equator of the colony. As the pool dries out in the heat of late
summer, the *Volvox* switches to its sexual phase and produces dormant, desic-
cation-resistant zygotes before dying.

2.3.7 Dormant Spores

Several filamentous *cyanophyta* (blue-green algae/bacteria), such as
Anabaena and Nostoc, ride out sub-optimal conditions through the use of

74   *akinetes*—vegetative dormant spores that tolerate desiccation, temperature extremes and nutrient deprivation. During unfavourable conditions, the algal filament releases its akinetes (like broadcasting seed); the akinetes settle and wait for better conditions. An akinete possesses thickened cell walls and stores essential material that allows it to survive years before germinating when conditions become favourable.

2.3.8 Clones & Suckers

A highly successful adaptation of the ***trembling aspen*** (*Populus tremuloides*) tree is its ability to reproduce without putting a lot of energy into making seeds. The aspen does this by growing a spreading mat of roots that send up many stems called "suckers." With good sunlight, a few trees can grow enough suckers to rapidly populate an area—making them an aggressive pioneer species that readily colonizes burned or previously logged areas. The resulting stand is not actually a group of individual trees; it is more like a colony of clones, each an exact genetic replica of all the others. Aspen clones can occupy less than an acre to over a hundred acres, suggesting that it may be the world's most massive living organism. Trees that are almost a hundred years old sprout up from a rhizome mass that may be millennia old. Partly due to its aggressive reproductive capability, but also partly because its bark carries out photosynthesis, trembling aspen is the most widely distributed native North American tree species, capable of growing in greatly diverse regions, environments and communities.

2.4 COMMUNICATION

Communication occurs for various reasons: to attract attention; to exchange information; to direct or maintain behaviour; to create incentive; to show affection; to warn of a threat, and to make a decision.

Communication uses a combination of signals and "language" that often provide overlapping purposes and interpretations. Chemical, physical and biological signals are received and interpreted through the obvious senses of hearing, seeing, smelling, tasting, and touching, as well as the subtler receptors of intuition, electricity, frequency, and wavelength. Wolves mark their territory through scat and urine. Horses rub their noses together, while giraffes put their necks next to each other as displays of affection. Chimps greet each other by touching hands. Cuttlefish distract prey with a hypnotizing display of changing body colours and patterns. Even gravity is communication.

Plants are able to sense the Earth's geomagnetic field. Honeybees communicate with each other using their electric fields. As I mentioned in the section on Movement, bees in flight develop a positive charge and, when they dance and vibrate their wings in the hive, the charge produces a force. The neighbouring bees detect and interpret the electric message, as it actually moves them.

Copepods (tiny zooplankton) of the deep ocean use optical communication in the form of *iridescence* to recognize mates and to elude predators. The tiny ocean floor-dwelling *Sapphirina* copepod (Sea Sapphire) is normally transparent—except when it emits a sudden blue flash. Microscopic layers of crystal plates inside their cells catch light and reflect violet-blue. The deep-sea copepod confuses its predators—one being the ostracod *Gigantocypris*—by effectively discharging a packet of *bioluminescence*. As the flash is delayed like a depth-charge, the copepod slips away, undetected, as the ostracod chases the flashes.

Examples of "strange" communication are the purview of the science fiction writer. It is already the nature of our current world—if you only know where to look. The scope of how Nature communicates—her devices and intentions—embraces the strange to the astonishing. From using infrasound to chemical receptors and sensing magnetic fields. To allelopathy. Aggressive symbiosis. And so much more.

2.4.1 Language of Plants

Plants communicate through visual, electrical, and olfactory signals. They use dyes and fragrant *secondary metabolites* in flowers and fruits to attract pollinators and furry animals that disperse the seeds. Plants often respond defensively to chewing insects by communicating chemical signal cascades within them. Bean, rice, and potato plants form new tissue or produce toxic substances to effectively repel egg-laying pests.

However, because such signals are often too slow—travelling at a third of an inch per minute from leaf and stem to target leaves—the plant also uses olfactory communication to signal adjacent leaves. Neighbouring plants of the same species become unintended beneficiaries of the aromatic warning.[4,76] An example is the umbrella thorn acacia tree in the African savannah. When a giraffe chews on an acacia leaf, the tree creates toxic substances and emits *ethylene gas*. Neighbouring trees of the same species receive the warning and pump out their own toxins in preparation for hungry giraffes.[4]

*Everyone knows about the **primary metabolic compounds** a plant produces to survive: sugars and amino acids. But plants also make secondary metabolites called **allelochemicals** that they use as defences. The volatiles escape into the air to attract, repel or poison an insect or animal. Basil, eucalyptus and pine trees give off obvious volatiles. Over 200,000 secondary metabolites can act as messengers—info-chemical signals—like jasmonic acid and salicylate acid, or as defences, like mustard oil glycosides, terpenes and tannins.*

When a leafminer takes a bite from the leaf of a pea plant, the pea releases hexenol into the air. The aerosol attracts the miner's predator, a parasitic wasp, which eats the leafminer.

—Nina Munteanu, *A Diary in the Age of Water*[12]

The example of the leafminer describes a **tritrophic interaction** shared by other plants; elms, pines and brussels sprouts also use fragrances that call parasitoid wasps. The wasps destroy leaf parasites by using these pests as living incubators for their offspring. These interactions involve three trophic levels within a co-evolved, partly mutualistic relationship: a plant, a herbivore pest, and its natural enemy, a carnivorous predator. The ecological mechanism of indirect plant defence (by enlisting natural enemies as "body guards" against excessive herbivory by pests) may include physical attraction or chemical attraction, such as induced plant volatile chemicals (called *green leaf volatiles*).[12,76]

When attacked by aphids or beetles, the lima bean (*Phaseolus lunatus*), a creeper from Latin America, uses a "sweet call for help" to attract defense troops—a co-evolved species. Pests that nibble on the lima bean leaves trigger nectar production in the plant. The sweet fragrance attracts ants that take on the attackers and suck up the high-calorie treat as their reward.[76]

2.4.2 Listening to Trees

UBC researcher Suzanne Simard, who has published hundreds of papers over thirty years of research, suggests a kind of "intelligence" when she describes the underground world "of infinite biological pathways that connect trees and allow them to communicate" in a forest.[77] This communication allows the forest to behave as if it was a single organism, says Simard. Her early *in situ* experiments showed solid evidence that tree species, such as paper birch (*Betula papyrifera*) and Douglas fir (*Pseudotsuga menziesii*), communicated in a cooperative manner underground through an underground mutualistic-symbiosis involving **mycorrhizae** (from the Greek, "fungus-root"). These trees were conversing in a "cooperative system" using the language of carbon and nitrogen, phosphorus, water, defense signals, *allelochemicals*, and *hormones* via a network of *mycelia*. Fungal threads form a mycelium that infects and colonizes the roots of all the trees and plants. Simard compares this dense network to the Internet, which also has nodes and links—just as does the forest.

Fungal highways link each tree and plant to its community, with busiest nodes called **hub trees** or **mother trees**. Calling them "mother trees" is appropriate, given that they nurture their young in the understorey; they send excess carbon to the understorey trees, which receive less light for photosynthesis. "In a single forest," says Simard, "a mother tree can be connected to hundreds of other trees." These mature trees act as nodal anchors—like major hub sites on the Internet—for tree grouping. According to Simard, they look after their families, nurture seedlings and even share wisdom—information—when they are injured or dying.[77,78]

North temperate trees, such as beech, spruce, and oak, emit saliva-specific pheromones that summon beneficial predators to dispatch insects feeding on them. Elms and pines call on small parasitic wasps that attack leaf-eating caterpillars by laying their eggs inside them.[4,76]

2.4.3 Songs of Nature's Relationships

Recognizing overarching communication in all things through relationship, David George Haskell, author of *The Songs of Trees* writes:

We're all—trees, humans, insects, birds, bacteria—pluralities. Life is embodied network. These living networks are not places of omnibenevolent Oneness. Instead, they are where ecological and evolutionary tensions between cooperation and conflict are negotiated and resolved. These struggles often result not in the evolution of stronger, more disconnected selves but in the dissolution of the self into relationship.

Because life is network, there is no "Nature" or "environment," separate and apart from humans. We are part of the community of life, composed of relationships with "others," so the human/Nature duality that lives near the heart of many philosophies is, from a biological perspective, illusory. We are not, in the words of the folk hymn, wayfaring strangers traveling through this world. Nor are we the estranged creatures of Wordsworth's lyrical ballads, fallen out of Nature into a "stagnant pool" of artifice where we misshape "the beauteous forms of things." Our bodies and minds, our "Science and Art," are as natural and wild as they ever were.

We cannot step outside life's songs. This music made us; it is our nature.

Our ethic must therefore be one of belonging, an imperative made all the more urgent by the many ways that human actions are fraying, rewiring, and severing biological networks worldwide. To listen to trees, Nature's great connectors, is therefore to learn how to inhabit the relationships that give life its source, substance, and beauty.[79]

2.4.4 The Loud Silence of Infrasound

In her book *The Global Forest*, botanist and medical biochemist Diana Beresford-Kroeger suggests that trees use their great size and tensile movement in the air to communicate by *infrasound* (what Beresford-Kroeger calls "silent sound"). Beresford-Kroeger argues that each tree produces a sound as individual as the iris of an eye or fingerprint of a hand.[21]

Known natural sources of infrasound include waterfalls, ocean waves, earthquakes, and atmospheric phenomena such as thunder, lightning and the northern lights.

Infrasound is used by elephants to communicate over long distances. Whales use infrasound—and dolphins, ultrasound—to navigate the oceans. Infrasound propagates as long sound waves at a frequency below 20 Hz, too low in pitch to be heard by the human ear (as opposed to *ultrasounds*, which are inaudible frequencies over 16,000 Hz, like that emitted by bats). The roar of a tiger apparently incorporates infrasonic frequencies. Honeybees in a hive act as a self-organized aggregate when triggered by a storm, by generating an infrasonic alarm signal.

2.4.5 Bioluminescence & Phosphorescence

Bioluminescence—the production and emission of light by a living organism—is widely used by marine vertebrates and invertebrates to attract mates, lure prey, mimic other animals, startle or misdirect predators, as counter-illumination camouflage (used by the firefly squid), and as a "burglar alarm" to point out what is about to eat them to higher trophic predators.

Copepods (tiny zooplankton) of the deep ocean use optical communication in the form of *bioluminscence* to recognize mates and to elude predators. The tiny ocean floor-dwelling *Sapphirina* copepod (Sea Sapphire) is normally transparent—except when it emits a sudden blue flash. Microscopic layers of crystal plates inside their cells catch light and reflect violet-blue. The copepod *Gaussia princeps*, found deeper than one thousand metres in the Sargasso Sea, is another example of a bioluminescent species. Bioluminescent deep-sea copepods confuse their predators—one being the ostracod *Gigantocypris*—by effectively discharging a packet of bioluminescence, whose flash is delayed like a depth-charge; the copepod slips away, undetected, as the ostracod chases the flashes. Speaking of ostracods (seed shrimps), some species in deeper water use glowing vomit to attract mates.

Ninety percent of deep-sea fish and crustaceans that dwell one hundred to one thousand metres deep are capable of bioluminescence.

Flashlight fish hunt and communicate with a flashing Morse code sent out by light pockets that pulse under their eyes. Tubeshoulder fish shoot luminous ink at their attackers. Hatchetfish make themselves appear invisible by generating light on their underbellies to mimic down-welling sunlight; predators prowling below look up to see only a continuous glow.

—*Quanta Magazine*

Most of these shining organisms, *Quanta* writes, require three ingredients: oxygen, a light emitting pigment called *luciferin* (from the Latin word "Lucifer," meaning light-bringing), and an enzyme called luciferase. When luciferin reacts with oxygen it uses *luciferase* to form an excited, unstable compound that emits light when it returns to its lower energy state.

Bioluminescence is not restricted to deep ocean animals. **Dinoflagellates**—phytoplankton of warm coastal surface waters—create *phosphorescence* in the water when they are disturbed, such as in breaking waves or the slide of a paddle through the water's surface. The dinoflagellate uses bioluminescence to draw predators to the creature trying to eat it.

Some bacteria bioluminesce, as do fireflies, glow worms, and some fungi.

2.5 SHELTER

Organisms generally need shelter from predation and from aspects of the environment that may rob them of energy, health, and the ability to successfully reproduce. In its widest context, **shelter** is an aspect of habitat, which includes all environmental conditions an organism needs to survive (e.g., water, food, and space). Shelter protects (against predators and weather), nurtures

80 (offspring) and stores (food and tools). Shelter varies with habitat and the organism's mobility, feeding and other life-strategies. Shelters may be fixed or mobile; permanent, temporary or recurring (e.g., seasonal); singular or plural. They may be part of and created by the environment or part of the organism or of its population or community.

Coyotes create dens in the ground, on hillsides and deep creek beds that allow for easy digging and earthmoving. The elusive roaming *puma* creates temporary nurseries in thickets, rock piles or hollow trees to provide shelter for her kittens. *Bears* may shred bark from trees and pull it into a den to use as nesting material, along with grasses leaves and twigs. Their dens may occupy fallen trees, rock piles and brush piles. Mice, voles and many other rodents may dig extensive burrow systems, often under tree roots, or make a nest beneath a rock. *Squirrels* make leaf nests called *dreys*, typically built of twigs, dry leaves and grass and assembled in the forks of tall trees. Some squirrels are fortunate to inherit a tree cavity den that was created and abandoned by a woodpecker.

This kind of reusability and repurposing of materials is common in Nature. For instance, the tiny *acorn ant* (*Temnothorax* spp.) makes its home year-round in small sticks and nuts such as hickory or a hollowed-out oak acorn. Eighty to one hundred workers and several queens nest in an acorn that has been initially pierced by a parasitic insect (most often a gall wasp). The acorn is then hollowed out by developing parasitic wasp larvae that leave a convenient exit hole for the acorn ant, who then makes the hollowed acorn its home. Considered trophic generalists, *Temnothorax* ants are opportunistic foragers. They are generally found in the mesic forests of the Northern hemisphere at mid-to-high elevations and are common in the mid to northern states of the USA.

The *hermit crab* scavenges an empty mollusc shell to cover its soft abdomen to protect itself from predators. The crab carries around the seashell into which its whole body can retract if necessary. As the crab grows, it must find a larger shell. When properly sized gastropod shells are unavailable, the hermit crab will find whatever it can to protect itself from the heat of the sun and from predators—including tree nut hulls or pieces of beach litter. This practice has increased due to the prevalence of human litter and the depletion of seashells from human collection and changes in habitat.

Termites of the family Termitidae in Africa, Australia and South America are detrivores and *bioturbators* that use feces, digested plant material, wood and soil to build sophisticated networks of underground tunnels and large mounds (some five metres high) to live in. Colonies consist of casts with a queen, a king, soldiers and workers. Some species maintain a "garden" of specialized fungi (*Termitomyces*) that they eat.[80] One study in Brazil revealed four thousand-year-old mounds of extensive bio-engineering by a single insect species—as old as the pyramids of Giza.[81] Termites are considered the most important *soil ecosystem engineers* in the tropics. They provide essential ecosystem services such as: soil loosening, aeration and vertical/horizontal translocation. They cycle nutrients, sequester carbon, increase soil biodiversity and ecological stability, increase water-holding capacity, and reduce erosion—all these ultimately help to regenerate degraded soil and achieve entire ecosystem integrity. "The ability of termites to [live] in harsh environments and to promote water infiltration in crusted soils as a part of soil rehabilitation and vegetation cover regeneration has been strikingly demonstrated in Africa and Asia," write Jouquet and team in the *European Journal of Soil Biology*.[82] The role of termites in water infiltration and runoff relates to the structure and arrangement of their subterranean biogenic structures, which comprise foraging and storage galleries, feeding chambers and communication channels.[82]

The passive cooling system of the mounds created by the termites has even inspired biomimetic energy-efficient building designs. The Eastgate building in Zimbabwe is an example of termite-inspired design, modelled on the self-cooling mounds that maintain the temperature inside to within one degree of 31°C day and night—all year.

Cliff swallow (*Petrochelidon pyrrhonota*) nests are unmistakable: gourd-shaped "bowls" covered with mud pellets, attached to a vertical surface such as a cliff. They often build nests on a bridge over a river or a wall of a building, with a small entrance tunnel. Nests are usually placed very close together and under an overhang to avoid heavy rains, which could be disastrous to mud homes!

The *Alcon blue butterfly* uses true deceit to obtain shelter for its young. The Alcon blue butterfly lets another organism provide shelter and a nurturing environment for its growing caterpillars—without doing anything itself. Acting as a true social parasite, the Alcon exploits the host's social system to raise its young as if they were its own.[12,83,84]

*The Alcon blue butterfly (*Phengaris alcon*) lays its eggs on the marsh gentian; the eggs drop off the plant during their fourth instar and wait on the ground to be discovered by ants. The larvae emit chemicals called allomones that are similar to what ants use to communicate. The ants adopt them and carry them into their nests to their brood chambers; the worker ants feed the caterpillars through regurgitations and devour any ant larvae left unattended. Some ant colonies have slightly changed their larva chemicals to defend against this parasitism, only to have the Alcon adapt, in turn. The ant's progress is lost during interbreeding with colonies who haven't developed a similar defence.*

Once the Alcon pupa hatches, the ants recognize it as an intruder. But it's too late; their bites can't penetrate the loose scales of the new adult butterfly, who escapes unscathed.

Of course, it's not that easy for the butterfly. Before it reaches that invincible stage, the Ichneumon eumeris *wasp smells it out while it's still a caterpillar in the underground nest; the wasp then sprays a pheromone that triggers the ants to attack each other. During the confusion, it enters the nest and injects the unprotected caterpillar with its own eggs. The wasp eggs then hatch and eat the butterfly chrysalis from the inside.*

It's a strange tale of exploitation and subterfuge.

Like mortal pawns trapped in the crossfire of two competing gods, the ants are manipulated by butterfly and wasp in a seductive and devious tango.

—Nina Munteanu, *A Diary in the Age of Water*[12]

2.6 ECOLOGICAL NICHE

Every organism occupies an *ecological niche* (a job or functional role) in an ecosystem. Niche is essentially what the organism does: how it interacts with (and succeeds in) its environment to live and reproduce. As with a human job, the successful occupation of a niche is realized through heuristic learning and evolutionary adaptation. These include: interactions with abiotic factors, such as soil type and climate, and biotic interactions that may include competition or cooperation, predation, parasitism, mutualism, and commensalism.

Niche partitioning (niche segregation or separation) is a strategy used in interactions within or among species that allows them to co-exist—usually by using resources differently. This can occur through spatial allocation (*spatial niche partitioning*) or time allocation (*temporal niche partitioning*). Anole lizards (*Anolis carolinensis*) living in the Caribbean share common food needs; the species avoid competition by occupying different physical locations—an example of spatial niche partitioning. Some live on leaf litter below trees, while others live on branches.

Resource partitioning, in which a limited resource is divided between species through behaviour or morphology reduces competition for the same resource. Some lizard species can co-exist in the same habitat due to their differing sizes. Different types of phytoplankton co-exist based on differing needs for nutrients such as nitrogen, phosphorus, silicon, and light. Finches of the Galapagos Islands co-exist based on differing beak sizes and, therefore, food size. Warblers co-exist by selecting different parts of a tree to nest. In the same

way, copepods (tiny aquatic crustaceans) exploit different parts of an aquatic
ecosystem: barrel-shaped herbivorous *calanoid copepods*, which have very long
antennae, most often live an entirely open pelagic existence; pear-shaped, omnivorous *cyclopoid copepods*, which have short antennae, prefer closed bodies
of water; elongated *harpacticoid copepods*, also having short antennae, settle on
substrates and live a benthic lifestyle as detrivores.

2.6.1 Niche Breadth & Niche Partitioning

Niche breadth describes the concept of resource use and adaptation by
organisms, which can either "specialize" or "generalize." *Specialists* tend to
occupy a narrow niche, able to live only in a narrow range of conditions: diet,
climate, camouflage, etc. *Generalists* are able to survive a wide variety of conditions and changes in the environment: diet, climate, predators, and so on.
    Product strategist Max Olson writes:

> *Specialists thrive when conditions are just right. They fulfill a niche and
> are very effective at competing with other organisms. They have good
> mechanisms for coping with "known" risks. But when the specific condi-
> tions change, they are much more likely to go extinct. Generalists respond
> much better to changes/uncertainty. These species usually survive for very
> long periods because they deal with unanticipated risks better. They have
> very coarse behavior: eat any food available, survive in many climates, use
> a simple mechanism to defend a wide range of predators, etc. But unlike
> specialists they don't maximize their current environment, because they
> don't fill a niche where they could be more successful. It's tough being a gen-
> eralist—there's more competition.[85]*

An environment with more competing species breeds more specialists.
Highly diverse rainforests, old-growth forests, and coral reefs are good examples of environments with high competition and, therefore, many specialists.
Specialists most often demonstrate a highly successful exploitation of a co-
evolved condition and environment. The colourful orchid mantis (*Hymenopus
coronatus*) of the tropical rainforest has appendages like leaves and thrives
only on orchids. The sword-billed hummingbird (*Ensifera ensifera*), with its
longer than body beak, has co-evolved with flowers with very long corollas.
The koala (*Phascolarctos cinereus*) lives almost entirely on the eucalyptus tree,
toxic to most animals.
    Generalists tend to be more ubiquitous and widespread. The cockroach
survives in most climates and requires little water and food. The omnivorous

84 raccoon has a wide diet and tolerates a wide set of conditions—including successful adaptation to human habitation. The rat has adapted to live anywhere but the Arctic, and they are not picky eaters. The horseshoe crab also has a wide diet and can tolerate a wide range of water temperature, low oxygen and desiccation for extended periods. While generalists lag in competition next to specialists, they take advantage of change where the specialist falls short. Change is the specialist's dilemma and the generalist's boon.

Max Olson applies the "specialist's dilemma" to human business: "The advantage of the specialist's strong competitive position [from the niche it occupies] is durable *only as long as the niche itself remains viable. In other words, the more specialized a company's dominance is, the stronger its advantages are*—but the higher the odds of the niche itself eventually disappearing." Such a company is less likely to disappear from competitors than from the niche being completely destroyed and replaced by something else. When this happens partially depends on the "clock speed" of innovation within the industry.[85]

A good example of successful **niche partitioning** is demonstrated by siblings of a family who successfully avoid the tension of competition by choosing exclusive pursuits and interests. In my science fiction trilogy, *The Splintered Universe*, the blenoid—a fictional ferocious desert animal on the planet Upsilon-3—exerts a self-imposed sharing by co-evolving into unique cohorts with different nutrient needs: one cohort produces feces that feed another. This creates a kind of resource-partitioning and an efficient recycling of resources—permitting more animals to occupy a resource-limited area. These different qualities also allow cohort members to better identify their kin.[86]

Individuals of different species—or different cohorts of a species, such as blenoids—compete less with one another (interspecific competition) than individuals of the same species or cohort (intraspecific competition) by consuming slightly different forms of a limiting resource or using the same limiting resource at a different place or time. Species, therefore, limit their own population growth more than they limit that of potential competitors, and resource partitioning acts to promote the long-term coexistence of competing species or groups.

2.7 EVOLUTIONARY STRATEGIES (CO-ADAPTATION & CO-EVOLUTION)

Evolutionary *co-adaptation* and *co-evolution* of life on Earth include a wide range of strategies with various aspects of the environment. Strategies may include antagonistic or mutualistic behaviours and mechanisms.

Some examples of such adaptations include species with the means to blend in to avoid getting eaten, using mimicry or camouflage; species that co-evolve structures that permit specialization to get food and reproduce (e.g., bees and flowers); and species that develop physiological characteristics permitting survival in a harsh environment (see Section 2.9). A wonderful example of *mimicry* is the viceroy butterfly (*Limenitis archippus*) that mimics the appearance of the unpalatable monarch butterfly (*Danaus plexippus*) to avoid predation. Cuttlefish (*Sepiida*) open and close red, yellow and brown pigmented sacs called chromatophores (controlled by the nervous system) as *camouflage*, to blend in with the substrate and to not be seen by a predator. (See more on specialists versus generalists in Section 2.6.)

No species lives in isolation from its environment—which includes other species. *Interspecific interactions* and *intra-specific interactions* are a given. Ecologists have identified five major types of species interactions: predation, competition, mutualism, commensalism and amensalism. Simply put: in predation the interaction is win:lose; in competition it is negative:negative; in mutualism it is win:win; in commensalism it is positive:zero; and in amensalism it is negative:zero. The reason I use "negative" versus "lose" in some cases is because that interaction is usually not final or absolute, resulting in death; they may only involve suppression and in a positive way, such as most examples of *plant allelopathy*.

Despite the popularity of Darwin's survival of the fittest concept that focused on inter-specific competition, Nature's evolutionary changes involve many cooperative processes, such as commensalism and mutualism. *Mutualism* is considered a major driver in the evolution of current biological diversity in the world—including flower forms and co-evolution among groups of species.[87,88] Lynn Margulis demonstrated that some previous antagonistic relationships evolved into mutualistic relationships over millennia; an example is the *chloroplast*, an important organelle that began as a parasite, but which helps plants process energy (see Chapter One, Sections 1.13 and 1.15).

Mutualism describes an ecological interaction between two (or more) species that increases fitness in both, through direct interaction. Examples in which each species benefits include: vascular plants and mycorrhizae, their fungal partners; flowering plants and their pollinating insects; seed dispersal of plants by animals; and the mutually beneficial cooperation of corals with

86 their photosynthetic partner the zooxanthellae, which are protected by the coral. Forester Peter Wohlleben discusses the mutual relationship of the oak tree and the milkcap fungus (*Lactarius quietus*), which grows directly into the soft root hairs of the tree. In exchange for up to a third of the tree's produced sugar and other carbohydrates, the fungus not only doubles the available nitrogen and phosphorus for the tree but also helps direct the tree's root cell growth. The fungus filters out heavy metals, which are more harmful to the tree than to itself and helps ward off intruders, such as harmful bacteria or destructive fungi.[4]

Commensalism is a one-sided symbiosis that describes an association between two organisms in which one benefits and the other is neither harmed nor helped. Egrets and cattle are one example. Other examples include remora fish and sharks, orchids that grow on branches of trees, the monarch butterfly and milkweed plant, burdock seeds that catch a ride on the fur of passing animals, barnacles on whales.

Amensalism describes a kind of passive asymmetrical competition, in which the actions or secretions of one organism negatively affect another, without a clear or exclusionary benefit. One could say that the other is an unfortunate casualty by its presence. A good example of this is the interaction between the Spanish ibex (*Capra pyrenaica*) and weevils (*Timarcha*) which feed on the same type of shrub. The presence of the weevil has virtually no influence on food availability, yet the presence of ibex exerts a notable detrimental effect on weevil numbers by consuming significant quantities of plant matter and ingesting the weevils along with it.

In Chapter One, Section 1.6, I discussed *allelopathy*, a phytotoxic chemical interference exerted by the American beech tree (*Fagus grandifolia*) on its co-dominant sugar maple (*Acer saccharum*). This can be considered a case of amensalism, given that the chemical secreted by the beech slightly suppresses maple seedling growth; however, this suppression establishes a balanced ecosystem in which both species benefit. A healthy hierarchy of complexity in a fully functioning ecosystem is achieved. The black walnut (*Juglans nigra*) also practises amensalism and allelopathy through a cocktail of chemicals that suppress other plants from germinating nearby. These flavonoids, terpenoids, alkaloids, steroids, carbohydrates, and amino acids, as well as juglone are found in the leaves, roots, husks, fruit and bark of the black walnut.[4,21,77]

In the final analysis, it could be argued that amensalistic interactions—particularly those involving suppression—serve the role, like predation, of creating a more balanced and healthier ecosystem with complex biodiversity. In his book *The Hidden Life of Trees*, Peter Wohlleben describes such a role by "mother" trees on their own saplings. "Young trees are so keen on growing quickly that it would be no problem at all for them to grow about eighteen inches taller per season," writes Wohlleben about a beech stand he studied in

Germany. The young beech trees don't grow fast because their mother trees don't let them. The mother trees shade their offspring with a dense canopy that only lets in three percent of the total sunlight, while feeding them via their root system.[4,5,77] The light-deprived saplings are forced to grow more slowly. This slow growth, argues Wohlleben, creates an inner wood with smaller cells and almost no air. This makes the trees flexible, more resistant to breaking in storms and more resistant to harmful fungi.[4]

2.7.1 Symbiosis

Symbiosis, Greek for "companionship," describes a close and long-term interaction between two organisms that may be mutually beneficial (mutualism), beneficial to one with no effect on the other (commensalism), or beneficial to one at the expense of the other (parasitism). Symbiosis is currently recognized as a key selective force behind evolution, strongly driven by cooperation, interaction and mutual dependence among organisms. Many species—perhaps most species—show a long history of interdependent co-evolution.

Symbionts may be of the same or different species. The term was created in 1879 by Heinrich Anton de Bary as "the living together of unlike organisms." When both symbionts depend on the other for survival, the relationship is called *obligatory symbiosis*. An example of obligate symbiosis is the acacia ant (*Pseudomyrmex ferruginea*) that protects the acacia tree from preying insects and from other plants competing for sunlight; the tree, in turn, provides nourishment and shelter for the ant and its larvae.[72] Part of what makes the symbiosis obligate is the dependency created by the acacia on the ant for its particular kind of nectar.

Facultative symbiosis, which is opportunistic, occurs when the symbionts can generally live independently. *Conjunctive symbiosis* describes a symbiosis involving physical attachment, such as lichen, a composite organism that is a partnership of several fungi and an alga or cyanobacterium.[89] *Endosymbiosis* describes a symbiosis in which one partner lives inside the tissues of the other (e.g., nitrogen-fixing bacteria living in root nodules of leguminous plants).

2.7.2 Aggressive Symbiosis

In his book *Virus X*, Dr. Frank Ryan coined the term *aggressive symbiosis* to explain a common form of symbiosis where one or both symbiotic partners demonstrates an aggressive and potentially harmful effect on the other's competitor or potential predator.[90] Examples abound, but a few are worth mentioning. In South American forests, a species of acacia tree produces a waxy berry of protein at the ends of its leaves that provides nourishment for the growing infants of the ant colony residing in the tree. The ants, in turn, not only keep the foliage clear of herbivores and preying insects through a stinging assault, but they make hunting forays into the wilderness of the tree, destroying the growing shoots of potential rivals to the acacia.[91]

In Borneo, a species of rattan cane has developed a symbiotic relationship with a species of ants. The ants make a nest around the cane and drink its sweet sap. The ants, in turn, protect the cane. When a herbivore approaches to feed on the leaves, the ants attack.[90]

When nitrogen levels go too far down, the fungal partner (*Laccaria bicolor*) of the eastern white pine tree (*Pinus strobus*) releases a toxin into the soil that kills any nearby springtails—the tiny and highly common soil invertebrate, *Folsomia candida*. The dead springtails then release nitrogen from their bodies and become fertilizer for both the fungus and the tree.[4,92]

Ryan draws an analogy between this aggressive symbiotic partnership and that of new zoonotic agents of disease. He argues that when it comes to emerging viruses, animals are the cane and ants are the virus.[90]

Viruses commonly form aggressive symbiotic relationships with their hosts. One example is the herpes-B virus, *Herpesvirus saimiri*, and the squirrel monkey (*Saimiri*). The herpes virus passes harmlessly from mother to baby monkey. If a rival species like a marmoset monkey invades their territory, the virus jumps species and wipes out the challenger, inducing fulminant cancers in the invaders. In this way, the virus protects the squirrel monkeys' habitat from invading primates. It is in the squirrel monkeys' evolutionary best interest not to try to purge the virus from their systems, and so the virus can replicate free of immune interference. A similar virus, *Herpesvirus ateles*, protects spider monkeys (*Ateles*) in South American jungles, killing all encroaching monkeys who lack immunity. The spider monkeys pass both the virus and immunity to it from mother to child, benefiting all. This "jungle immune system" protects the inhabitants from invading primate species, even when that invading species is us.[90]

Ryan suggests that Ebola and hantavirus outbreaks follow a similar pattern of aggressive symbiosis. This may explain why Ebola is so virulent. The Ebola virus is so fierce that victims don't make it very far to infect others, suggesting that the virus is an evolutionary failure. However, if the virus is acting as an aggressive symbiont, it may be fulfilling its evolutionary purpose by protecting a host species we haven't yet identified.[90]

Historian William H. McNeill suggested that a form of aggressive symbiosis played a key role in the history of human civilization. "At every level of organization—molecular, cellular, organismic, and social—one confronts equilibrium [symbiotic] patterns. Within such equilibria, any alteration from 'outside' tends to provoke compensatory changes [aggressive symbiosis] throughout the system to minimize overall upheaval." One of a legacy of examples of aggressive symbiosis in history includes smallpox: the Europeans introduced smallpox (symbiotically co-evolved with them) to the Aztecs with devastating results. Other examples of aggressive symbiosis include measles, malaria, and yellow fever.[93]

2.8 COOPERATION & ALTRUISM

In Chapter One (Section 1.15), we explored some evolutionary strategies that lead to co-adapted cooperative systems. Examples include kin selection (roles and castes adopted by individuals for the overall good of the group); reciprocal altruism (e.g., vampire bat); true altruism (inter-species altruism practised by dolphins); group selection (e.g., humans selecting to live within the sustainability of an area); communal feeding (by lions); cooperative parasitism (practised by the green tree frog: small males associate with larger louder ones and feed/mate with his leftovers).

2.8.1 Altruism & Nature's Heroes

Some scientists argue that altruism is an ancient impulse and an empathic instinct; something more primitive than culture and, in fact, considerably more ancient than the human species itself. They posit that altruism is deeply innate, predating the phylogenetic split that occurred six million years ago.

Nineteenth-century scientist Edward Westermarck argued that morality involved both humans and non-human animals and both culture and evolution. Of course, he was met with much skepticism. In 1999, zoologist Brenda Bradley wrote, "Altruism is difficult to explain within traditional models of natural selection, which predict that individuals should exhibit behavioural traits adapted to promoting genetic self-interest." She has a point—so why limit ourselves to a traditional model then? Scientific discoveries are made by stepping outside tradition. It turns out that scientists have been demonstrating for years that cooperation among organisms and communities and acts of pure altruism (i.e., not reciprocal altruism or kin/group selection) are, in fact, more common in Nature than most of us realize. Chimpanzees, unable to swim, have drowned attempting to save the lives of their companions. Human children as young as one year old were observed comforting others. Household pets have also demonstrated a response to distress in people by

90 attempting to comfort them. Valid examples of true animal altruism in the wild do exist. The vervet monkey (*Chlorocebus pygerythrus*) is one example. This species evolved a complex community that fosters the existence of an altruistic individual: *the crier monkey*.[2]

Vervet monkeys travel in groups, and the criers give alarm calls to warn fellow monkeys of the presence of predators, even though by doing so they attract attention to themselves and increase their chance of being attacked. Biologists argue that the group that contains a high proportion of crier monkeys will have a survival advantage over a group containing a lower proportion, thereby encouraging this trait to continue and evolve among individuals. The crier monkey is Nature's hero.

2.8.2 Interspecies Cooperation & Empathy

The 2017 BBC TV series *Blue Planet 2* captured excellent footage in the Great Barrier Reef of the astonishing partnership of an octopus (Cephalopoda) and a grouper fish (Actinoperygii). These two hunters seek the same small fish that dart in and out of the coral and hide in crevices too small for the grouper to reach and hard for the octopus to find. To solve the dilemma, the two have partnered up: after chasing the fish into a crevice, the grouper turns pale to attract the octopus's attention, then—in a show of rudimentary sign language—the grouper stands on its head and wiggles its tail to signal the position of the little fish. The octopus pokes its long tentacle into the crevice, flushing out the prey. Sometimes the octopus gets the fish; other times the grouper does. The grouper is demonstrating forward planning and co-operative hunting with a completely unrelated animal. The BBC team shared that the grouper tries this technique with other species—such as the moray eel, who doesn't understand, even when the grouper nudges it in the right direction. The octopus, however, knows right away.[94]

The dolphin exemplifies interspecies cooperation (i.e., mutualism and altruism). Aubrey Manning writes in *The Daily Mail* of a female dolphin who selflessly saved a beached mother whale and her calf off Mahia Beach in New Zealand. In Laguna, Brazil, bottlenose dolphins (*Tursiops truncates*) pursue a cooperative relationship with fishermen. Local artisanal fishermen rely on the assistance of cooperative dolphins to catch their fish. Researchers found that the most helpful dolphins are also particularly cooperative and social with each other.[2]

Frans De Waal explains that "evolution favours animals that assist each other, if by doing so they achieve long-term benefits of greater value than the benefits derived from going it alone and competing with others."[2] The prevalent phenomenon of altruism is Nature's answer to *the prisoner's dilemma* (a canonical example in game theory, suggesting why two rational individuals might not cooperate, even if it seems in their best interest). See Section 1.15 for more on this.

"Empathy evolved in animals as the main ... mechanism for [individually] directed altruism," said de Waal. De Waal further proposed that the scientific community has become polarized between evolutionary biologists on the one side and, on the other, a discrete group of economists and anthropologists that "has invested heavily in the idea of strong [in-kind] reciprocity," which demands discontinuity between humans and all other animals.[2]

Some scientists argue that altruism is an ancient impulse and an empathic instinct.

What drives an individual to act heroically to sacrifice itself for the greater good of its tribe, species, or community? From the crier monkey to the sterile worker bee to the kamikaze pilot ... Whether mediated by brainwashing or true altruism—these selfless (and sometimes aggressive) acts are prompted by a sense of being part of a common "organism" or part of something greater than oneself. This begs the question of identity and the definition of "self". How far does it go?

Certainly, the stuff of story ...

2.9 EXTREMOPHILES: THRIVING IN EXTREME ENVIRONMENTS

The human physiology needs to meet very restrictive conditions to live comfortably and survive. We need a lot of water (we are made of over seventy percent water). We freeze or cook beyond minus 40 to plus 50 degrees Centigrade in a galaxy that goes from minus 400 at the Moon's south pole to plus 25 million degrees inside the Sun. We faint from lack of oxygen on our tallest mountains. We need a pH balance of 6.5 to 7.5 to stay alive. Ionizing radiation kills us at low concentrations. Many compounds in the wrong amounts are toxic to us. Humanity has developed many strategies to ensure that these necessary parameters are met. Our ingenuity and tools allow us to live in some extreme environments—but we're not extremophiles.

Extremophiles are organisms adapted to thrive in extreme conditions on the planet. The 2001 BBC TV series *Blue Planet* and its 2017 sequel, *Blue Planet 2*, provide exemplary footage of two bizarre ecosystems in which extremophiles thrive: *hot hydrothermal vents* and *cold brine seeps* in the deep ocean floor, both

92   of which contain energy-rich chemicals. Because there is no sunlight, there are no photosynthesizing plants. Instead, bacteria and archaea use *chemosynthesis* to convert minerals and hydrogen sulphide into organics to support a rich and bizarre community.

Hydrothermal vents support a thriving community near these *ephemeral* short-lived hot springs of undersea volcanoes: red-tipped siboglinid tube worms (or beard worms), two metres long; shrimp with eyes on their backs; over three hundred species of gastropods, zoarcid fish, octopus; and many other creatures. These communities are fairly short-lived in the volatile environment of hydrothermal vents. The vents experience extreme and strongly fluctuating temperatures, along with unstable pH, sulphide and oxygen levels.

Cold brine seeps occur over fissures in the sea floor caused by tectonic movement below the surface. A seep leaks hydrogen sulphide, brine, methane and other hydrocarbon-rich fluids from beneath the ocean floor. These stable ecosystems resemble "lakes" of more dense water beneath the less dense ocean above and support chemosynthetic bacteria. "Beaches" of mussels and siboglinid tubeworms surround the brine-rich "lakes" of sodium chloride, magnesium and potassium sulphates. The sulphide-mining tubeworm (*Lamellibrachi luymesi*) may live for over two hundred fifty years in this ecosystem.

California's Mono Lake is an *endorheic lake* (a lake with no outflow), which is extremely salty, alkaline, and anaerobic. Brine shrimp (Artemiidae) are salt-loving and hatch in the trillions every season. Flies in the lake breathe underwater by carrying an air bubble with them. The bacteria of this anaerobic lake use sulphur instead of oxygen to metabolize.

Spain's Rio Tinto contains elevated concentrations of toxic heavy metals and a high acidity resulting from *mining activity*. Acid rock drainage has increased the dissolved iron, giving the river its red colour and feeding certain anaerobic and *acidophilic bacteria*. The river is devoid of life except for these microbes that draw nutrition from dissolved iron and metal sulphides. The high concentration of metal sulphides in the water provide a food source for these *chemolithoautotrophic bacteria* (e.g., *Acidithiobacillus* spp. and *Leptospirillum* spp.). The product of metal sulphide metabolism through oxidization is ferric iron and secretion of acidic liquid—further maintaining the low pH. These organisms protect themselves from the industrial toxins with a biofilm membrane through which they absorb the nutrients they need.[68,95]

Soviet Union's Chernobyl, the nuclear power plant that leaked gamma radiation since its meltdown in 1986, supports no life. However, in 1991, several *radiotrophic* melanin-rich fungi (*Cladosporium*, *Wangiella*, and *Cryptococcus*) were discovered wrapped around the rusting consoles and debris of the reactor. These "black fungi" increased their biomass significantly faster when exposed to gamma radiation five hundred times the background radiation level. The fungi perform *radiosynthesis* by using the pigment melanin to convert

gamma radiation into chemical energy for growth—similar to how plants use   93
chlorophyll to grow. Exposure to radiation triggered the fungi's melanin to
alter its shape, so it was four times better at carrying out a common metabolic
chemical reaction.[68,96]

Chili's Atacama Salt Flats in the *hyperarid region* in the Andes is one of
the driest and oldest deserts on Earth. This desert supports virtually no life,
except for some extremophiles, such as hypolithic algae (chlorophytes and the
cyanobacteria *Chroococcidiopsis*) and halophilic species of Bacteroidetes, Halo-
bacteriales, and Proteobacteria. The photosynthetic microbes survive desiccation under extreme dry conditions by positioning themselves beneath protective salt crust quartz rocks (evaporitic deposits of halite) that transmit the
sunlight necessary for photosynthesis, while conserving precious moisture
provided by a coastal fog. The halite deliquesces to a highly saline solution
in its mineral pores, creating a "wetting event" exploited by the microbes.[68,97]

THREE . . . Two Case Studies

I haven't been everywhere, but it's on my list—Susan Sontag

3.1 THE COSMOPOLITAN BRACKEN FERN

The **bracken fern** (*Pteridium aquilinum*) has been a highly successful life-form for millions of years. It is the only terrestrial fern that dominates large tracts of land outside woodland in temperate climates. Robust and an aggressive competitor, the bracken fern is **cosmopolitan**, living on every continent (except Antarctica) and in a wide range of conditions. Why is it so ubiquitous? Its success comes from its "long game." The bracken fern has evolved several life style strategies to outlive and outcompete its surrounding challenges. These include a varied lifestyle. It has several ways to reproduce and grow to accommodate seasons, drought, and burning; an arrangement with local ants who protect the bracken for its tasty nectar; use of cyanide and ecdysones by its young shoots; release of allelopathic chemicals to help it establish; and tough carcinogenic fronds that contain glass-like silicates to deter predation.

Life Style Strategies: In north temperate climates, the bracken fern is deciduous; it turns red in the fall and dies back, while rhizomes continue growing underground, making it hard to eradicate. Burning encourages bracken growth (only the fronds burn, while the rhizomes remain untouched); in fact, the bracken fern uses ash as a sterilizer (against predatory fungi and insects) for its spore growth.

Reproduction: Bracken fern uses several ways to reproduce. The fern's spores can survive for months in a dry dust-like state, ready to colonize new areas once conditions improve. Once established, the fern spreads in a local area through vegetative reproduction using underground *rhizomes* that spread like a virus to saturate open habitats. The rhizomes contain large carbohydrate and nutrient reserves to keep it going and spreading; the fern can also restrict its water loss better than other ferns, permitting it to grow outside the typical woodland habitat of ferns. Even though spores rarely take hold, once they do, the plant clones itself and spreads quickly. Like the beech tree, the bracken fern releases *allelopathic chemicals* to subdue competing plants nearby, ensuring its establishment.

Protection: Bracken fronds are tough to chew; they are full of tannins, lignins, and silicates, which are like glass. The fern is toxic to plants and animals; fronds, shoots and rhizomes contain a cocktail of indanones, cyanogenic glycosides, and tannins—all direct defences against herbivore attack. The fern's fronds and spores contain a chemical known as *ptaquiloside*, which is *carcinogenic* to predatory mammals. The fern uses an enzyme that destroys thiamine (Vitamin B1). Young fronds are less tough but also produce *hydrogen cyanide*—a quick poison—when they are damaged. Fronds also contain *ecdysones* (insect moulting hormones) that cause uncontrollable rapid moulting in insects.

Competition: Thick and fast-growing fern fronds act like a thick tree canopy, shading out other plants from growing (like a thick hemlock stand.) The fern also creates a large amount of litter that prevents other species from colonizing. Its use of allelopathy additionally prevents other species from encroaching.

Aggressive Symbiosis: Young fronds secrete nectar which attract ants and they, in turn, may defend the bracken fern against attacking herbivores. Although experiments generally do not support this theory, one conducted in South Africa demonstrated that the black cocktail ant (*Crematogaster peringueyi*) rapidly removed the eggs of the moth *Appana cinesigna* before its caterpillars could emerge and feed on the young bracken fronds.

Despite its many uses (e.g., potash fertilizer, heating fuel, roofing, and bedding for animals), the bracken fern is considered a pest. In truth, it is a hardy, versatile adapter to changing environments. And that is what our climate-changing world is fast becoming.

3.2 THE UBIQUITOUS TARDIGRADE

Tardigrades, also known as *water bears* or *moss piglets*, are plump, microscopic invertebrates with eight clawed legs. Fossils of tardigrades date to the Cambrian period, over 500 million years ago. Over nine hundred species are known. These tiny invertebrates (about 0.5 to 1.0 mm long) are found mostly in damp moss and lichen and feed on plant cells, algae and smaller invertebrates, such as rotifers. They are a cosmopolitan group found anywhere from mountain tops of 20,000 metres to ocean depths of 3,000 metres, in Japanese hot springs, and 80 metres under the surface of a glacier.[2]

Tardigrades were first described by the German pastor Johann August Ephraim Goeze in 1773 and given the name Tardigrada, meaning "slow stepper," by the Italian biologist Lazzaro Spallanzani. Tardigrades reproduce asexually (*parthenogenesis*) or sexually. They mostly suck on the fluids of plant cells, animal cells, and bacteria.

Tardigrades survive adverse environmental stresses including:
- high and low temperatures (e.g., -273°C to +151°C)
- freezing and thawing
- changes in salinity
- lack of oxygen
- lack of water
- levels of X-ray radiation 1,000x the lethal human dose
- some toxic chemicals
- boiling alcohol
- low pressure of a vacuum
- high pressure (up to 6x the pressure of the deepest ocean)[2]

Tardigrades respond to adverse environmental stresses through **cryptobiosis**, a process that greatly slows their metabolism. The water bear survives dry periods by shriveling up into a little ball or *tun* and waiting it out. It makes a protective sugar called *trehalose*, which moves into its cells to replace lost water. You could say that the *water bear* turns into a *gummy bear*.

Tardigrades have revived from one hundred years of desiccation. They can do this because the antioxidants they make soak up dangerous chemicals and they can repair damaged DNA from a long-term dry-out. In low oxygen, the tardigrade stretches out, relaxed muscles letting more water and oxygen enter its cells. The tardigrade's cold-resistant *tun* also prevents ice crystals that could damage cell membranes.[2]

Tardigrades survive temperatures, pressures and ionizing radiation not normally found on Earth. All this raises questions of origin and evolutionary adaptation. Why would they evolve such extreme tolerances? Abilities not required in their current habitat or ecosystem? How—and why—have tardigrades developed the ability to survive the vacuum and ionizing radiation of space? Some suggest that it's because they originated there. Others argue that similar conditions may have occurred during their long existence in Earth's volatile history (e.g., in water bodies that freeze or dry up and undergo anoxia). But, how does that explain existing in higher than Earth-like pressures, temperatures and ionizing radiation?

Now, *that's* a story …[2]

PART 2: STORY

ONE . . . What is Story?

I travel, always arriving in the same place—Dejan Stojanovic, *The Shape*

As young girls, my sister and I conjured epic stories of thrilling adventure and discovery from interstellar travel in the far reaches of the Universe, to the exploration of the great Nile and Amazon Rivers of Earth. We'd never been out of Quebec, Canada, let alone on a space voyage; yet, we both shared a vivid idea of the characters of these exotic places.

Without realizing it, we were tracing the story of humanity's great journey.

We are all storytellers. We share our curiosity with great expression; our capacity and need to tell stories is as old as our ancient beginnings. From the Palaeolithic cave paintings of Lascaux to our blogs on the Internet, humanity has left a grand legacy of "story" sharing. Evolutionary biologist and futurist Elisabet Sahtouris tells us that, "whether we create our stories from the revelations of religions or the researches of science, or the inspirations of great artists and writers or the experiences of our own lives, we live by the stories we believe and tell to ourselves and others." This is why stories and storytelling are so powerful and necessary.

But, when does an anecdote become a story? What makes a story a story?

1.1 ANECDOTES vs. STORIES

In her article in *Quartz Magazine*, Lila MacLellan suggests that "we've become masters of telling anecdotes, and terrible at telling our friends real stories." Sometimes people think they are telling a story, but they are really just telling anecdotes, MacLellan reports after interviewing Maggie Cino, senior story producer for *Moth* storytelling series. While "anecdotes just relate facts," Cino explains, stories are "about letting us know that things started one way and ended a different way." Stories create space for movement.[1]

Merriam-Webster defines an *anecdote* as a "short narrative of an interesting, amusing, or biographical incident." Anecdotes serve to incite interest and to illustrate a point. They are often amusing, odd, sad or even tragic; if they are biographical, they often serve to reflect someone's personality, attitude or philosophy. While anecdotes often provide a contextual jumping board to make a point—drawing you in with relevance—they lack the structure of stories. An anecdote is something that happens; a story has a structure that makes it memorable and provides a depth of meaning. *Stories* move with direction; they have a beginning, middle and end. Stories evoke emotional truths. They compel with intrigue then fulfil us with awareness and, sometimes, understanding. The best stories are told through metaphor, those universal truths we all live by. And all good stories weave a premise, theme, plot, character and setting into a tapestry with meaning.

I teach new writers at the University of Toronto and George Brown College how to tell stories. I teach how stories can tell us who we are. Where we've been. And sometimes, where we are going. The stories that stir our hearts come from deep inside, where the personal meets the universal, through symbols or **archetypes** and **metaphor**. Depth psychologist Carl Jung described these shared symbols, metaphors and archetypes as pre-existing forms of the psyche. He drew parallels between synchronicity, relativity theory and quantum mechanics to describe life as an expression of a deeper order. He believed that we are both embedded in a framework of a whole and are the focus of that whole.[2]

Jung was describing a *fractal whole*, which reflects quantum scientist David Bohm's quantum vision of **holomovement**. Jung's concept of embedded whole and a universal collective unconscious was embraced by **Hero's Journey** author and scholar Joseph Campbell, who suggested that these mythic images lie at the depth of the unconscious where humans are no longer distinct individuals, where our minds widen and merge into the mind and memory of humankind—where we are all the same, in Unity. Carl Jung's thesis of the *"collective unconscious"* in fact linked with what Freud called **archaic remnants**: mental forms whose presence cannot be explained by anything in the individual's own life and which seem aboriginal, innate, and the inherited shapes of the human mind. Marie-Louise von Franz, in 1985, identified Jung's hypothesis of the collective unconscious with the ancient idea of an all-extensive world-soul. Writer Sherry Healy suggested that Jung viewed the human mind as linked to "a body of unconscious energy that lives forever."[2]

1.2 STORY PARTS & STORY STRUCTURE

A good story is about something important; attracted by gravity, it has purpose and seeks a destination. A good story goes somewhere; it flows like a river from one place to another. A good story has meaning; its undercurrents run deep across hidden substrates with intrigue. A good story resonates with place; it finds its way home. We've just touched upon the five main components of good story: premise, character on a journey & plot, theme and—what is ultimately at the heart of a story—setting or place.

1.2.1 Story Components

The *premise* of a story is like the anecdote, a starting point of interest. It is an idea that will be dramatized through plot, character and setting. In idea-driven stories, it can often be identified by asking the question: "What if?" For instance, what if time travel was possible?

A *character on a journey* propels the story through meaningful change. Characters provide dramatized meaning to premise through personal representation of global themes. A character takes an issue and through their actions and circumstance in story provide a fractal connection to a larger issue. Characters need to move. They need to "go somewhere." *Archetypes*—ancient patterns of personality (symbols) shared by humanity and connected by our collective unconscious—are metaphoric characters (which includes place) in the universal language of storytelling that help carry the story forward.

The *theme* of a story takes the premise and gives it personal and metaphoric meaning by dramatizing through a character journey. It is often identified by asking the question: "What's at stake?" In taking the time travel premise, a theme of forgiveness may be applied by choosing a character wishing to return to the past to right a wrong, when what they just need to do is forgive others and themselves, not travel to the past at all, and get on with their lives.

In such a story, the *plot* would provide means and obstacles for the character in their journey toward enlightenment. Plot works together with theme to challenge and push a character toward their epiphany and meaningful change. Plot provides obstacles. Challenges. Emotional turning points. Opportunities for learning and change.[3]

The role of *setting* or *place* is often not as clear to writers. Because of this, place and setting may often be neglected and haphazardly tacked on without addressing its role in story; in such a case the story will not resonate with what is often at the heart of the story: a sense of place.[3] In stories where the setting changes (either itself changing such as in a story about the volcanic eruption of Vesuvius impacting Pompeii's community; or by the character's own movements from place to place) it appears easier to include how setting affects characters. However, the effect of place on character when the setting does not change can be equally compelling even if more subtle; the change is still there but lies in the POV character's altered relationship to that place—a reflection of change within them.

1.2.2 Kinds of Stories

According to Orson Scott Card, four major story structures dominate novels. These include: 1) the idea story; 2) the character story; 3) the event story; and 4) the milieu story. All four elements occur in stories, but which one dominates is essentially based on what kind of story the author is writing and their primary focus.[4]

1) The Idea Story

According to Scott Card, idea "stories are about the process of seeking and discovering new information through the eyes of characters who are driven to make the discoveries ... The idea story begins by raising a question; it ends when the question is answered." Most mysteries follow this structure. Scott Card suggests that the writer begin as close to the point where the question is first raised, and end as soon as possible after the question is answered.[4]

2) The Character Story

Character stories focus on the transformation of a character's role in the communities that matter most to her. The story, according to Scott Card, "begins at the moment when the main character becomes so unhappy, impatient or angry in her present role that she begins the process of change; it ends when the character either settles into a new role (happily or not) or gives up the struggle and remains in the old role (happily or not)."[4]

3) The Event Story

"In the event story," says Scott Card, "something is wrong in the fabric of the universe; the world is out of order. In classic literature, this can include the appearance of a monster (*Beowulf*), the "unnatural" murder of a king by his brother (*Hamlet*) or of a guest by his host (*Macbeth*), the breaking of an oath (*Havelock the Dane*), the conquest of a Christian land by the infidel (*King Horn*), the birth of a child portent who some believe ought not to have been born (*Dune*), or the reappearance of a powerful ancient adversary who was thought to be dead (*The Lord of the Rings*). In all cases, a previous order—a "golden age"—has been disrupted and the world is in flux, a dangerous place."[4]

The event story ends, says Scott Card, at the point when a new order is established or, more rarely, when the old order is restored. Most fantasy and much of science fiction use the event story structure, according to Scott Card.[4]

4) The Milieu Story

"The milieu is the world—the planet, the society, the weather, the family, all the elements that come up during your world-creation phase," says Scott Card. "Every story has a milieu, but when a story is structured around one, the milieu is the thing the storyteller cares about most." Gulliver's Travels is

104 a good example. "Gulliver traveled and then compared the societies he found there with the society of England in Swift's own day ... The real story began the moment Gulliver got to the first of the book's strange lands, and it ended when he came home."

"This structure is most common in science fiction and fantasy," says Scott Card, "but it also occurs in other types of novels. James Clavell's *Shogun*, for instance, is a milieu story: It begins when the European hero is stranded in medieval Japan, and it ends when he leaves. He was transformed by his experiences in Japan, but he does not stay—he returns to his world." [4] The observer is transformed by what she sees and then comes back a new person. The closure is in the return.

It is easy to see the role of setting and place in the milieu story; but setting is just as important—though subtle—in the idea, character and event story. In these story types, writing craft techniques such as metaphor, sensual description, and others become crucial in drawing place into story and connecting with character.

1.2.3 Storyboarding & Plot Approach

Given that plot—just like theme, character, and premise—does not exist in isolation, it is relevant to discuss plot approach as it pertains to and makes use of setting and place.

Story components fit together like connective tissue through a structure that tells a compelling narrative. One approach to recognizing this structure is the 3-Act Plot Structure that I discuss in Chapters B, J and P of *The Fiction Writer*. I discuss the "Hero's Journey" plot approach as a 3-Act story structure through character journey that involves *Separation* (Act 1), *Initiation and Transformation* (Act 2), and *the Return with a Gift* (Act 3). This can also be interpreted as *Promise, Movement,* and *Fulfillment*.[3]

It is advantageous to see story as a hero's journey (whether the hero is obvious as in an allegory or subtle as in literary fiction); viewing story this way acknowledges movement and change as two requisites that act together for compelling storytelling. Key concepts are "movement" (plot) and "journey" (character). Setting is the fabric and theme is the thread that stitches plot and character together into meaningful story.

The hero is an agent of change. Joseph Campbell defines the hero as "the champion not of things to become but of things becoming; the dragon to be slain by him is precisely the monster of the status quo; Holdfast the keeper of the past." The hero's task has always been to bring new life to an ailing culture, says Carol S. Pearson, author of *The Hero Within*.[3] The journey acknowledges archetypes in story—main ones being hero, mentor, herald, threshold

guardian, shapeshifter, shadow, and trickster. Embedded within each archetype is a role in moving the story toward its inevitable conclusion. In this way
we see how important world and place are. They too can serve as archetypes
in story, particularly if personified.

1.3 PLACE YOUR STORY

Every story has a few important characters doing important things, each
enacting his or her story. "Put all the stories together and you [have] at their
center a portrait of a place," says acclaimed novelist Richard Russo.[5]

Without a place there is no story. Setting serves multipurpose roles from
helping with plot, determining and describing character to providing metaphoric links to theme. Setting, like the force in *Star Wars*, provides a landscape
that binds everything to weave context and meaning into story. Without setting, characters are simply there, in a vacuum, with no reason to act and, most
importantly, no reason to care.[3,5]

"If you're not writing stories that occur in a specific place," adds Russo,
"you're missing an opportunity to add depth and character to your writing."[5]
Settings effectively depict their characters. The setting and all the objects in it
are described to your reader through your POV characters. This gives you an
excellent opportunity to show the mood, temperament, judgment and bias of
your characters. Humans are creatures "of [their] environment," wrote Robert Louis Stevenson. "[Their] outlook on life will be colored by the setting in
which [they are] placed."[3]

EXERCISE 1: The Psychology of Place #1:
How Characters Relate to Place

1. *Write about a public place from your childhood that inspires powerful emotions. Describe it from as many senses as you can remember. Make a hindsight connection to you in the present, if you can.*

_____
_____
_____
_____
_____
_____
_____
_____
_____
_____

2. *Describe a place through the POV of Character #1 (with a certain mood and temperament); now describe the same place through the eyes of Character #2 (who is different from #1 and has a different mood). Use vivid language and try to bring in as many senses as possible. Now compare.*

3. *Have Character #1 describe a place or object that belongs to Character #2. Is it full of new things or old things? Is it tidy or a mess? Dark or bright? Cluttered or empty? What insights might we get on either character through the description?*

_____
_____
_____
_____
_____
_____
_____
_____
_____

_____

_____

_____

_____

_____

_____

_____

_____

_____

_____

_____

_____

_____

_____

This exercise is adapted from Writing the Breakout Novel Workbook by Donald Maas. In the workbook Maass writes:

> "How many settings are there in your current novel? From how many points of view is each of them seen? Each outlook on each location is an opportunity to enrich your story. In your novel, how many of those opportunities are you taking?"[6]

For follow up work, Maass also suggests figuring out which setting most recurs in your work and in whose point of view it is most often seen. This can provide a sense of "ownership" of a particular landscape or place—and can often help define that character.

TWO . . . What is World?

"That land is a community is the basic concept of ecology, but that land is to be loved and respected is an extension of ethics."—Aldo Leopold

Worlds can express as character, symbol, and premise. Depending on the story genre, expression of the world may range from subtle subtext in romance to more literate representation in eco-fiction. No matter what kind of story you're telling, the setting helps provide its tone and feel. The world and circumstance in which you place your story help to articulate its emotional quality and help define its metaphoric meaning. Every part of a world and place contribute to the story in some way.

2.1 THINGS TO CONSIDER IN A WORLD

When setting your story (e.g., location, time, season, weather) in literary or contemporary fiction, you recreate what is already there; but you give it a unique quality specific to your story. You characterize it with eccentricities and other qualities that make it memorable and relevant to the story plot, theme and characters. You create "atmosphere." Kimberly Appelcline, creative writing instructor at San Francisco State University, describes atmosphere as "the overall 'feeling' to a place: romantic, threatening, welcoming" which depends largely on your word choice and on the narrator. For instance, "a room with 'oppressive low ceilings and blood-red curtains' feels much different to a reader than a room with 'cozy low ceilings and cheerful red curtains.' "[3]

When you build an entire world—such as in fantasy or science fiction—you create far more than atmosphere; you create a civilization, a political structure, a culture, history and *zeitgeist* as backdrop and influence to story.

Consider these epics and the world the author created:

- Jacqueline Carey's *Kushiel's Dart*
- J.R.R. Tolkien's *Lord of the Rings*
- J.K. Rowling's *Harry Potter* series
- Arthur C. Clarke's *Rendezvous with Rama*
- Philip Pullman's *Dark Materials* trilogy
- Larry Niven's *Ringworld*

- Vernor Vinge's *A Fire Upon the Deep*
- Ursula LeGuin's *Left Hand of Darkness* or *Earthsea* series
- Frank Herbert's *Dune* saga
- Paolo Bacigalupi's *Windup Girl*

There is a basis for every single part of a world; all are tied into premise and theme and ultimately to the story's dramatization through character. World informs character; character informs world.

2.1.1 Frank Herbert's Desert Planet

For Herbert, the creation of his desert planet in *Dune* began with an assignment to write an article about the control of sand dunes—pioneered by the U.S. Forest Service pilot project in Florence, Oregon. Herbert realized that, "Sand dunes are like waves in a large body of water, just slower. And the people who treat them as fluid learn to control them."[6] Fluid mechanics, with sand. This would later lead to his creation of an ocean-like desert planet and how the indigenous Fremen of *Dune* succeeded in the desert—while the colonialists didn't. Herbert accumulated folders about the ecology of deserts and studied the indigenous peoples of various deserts. In an interview, Herbert argued that, "You can't just stop with the people who are living in this type of environment: you have to go on to how the environment works on the people and how they work on their environment." Why did some succeed and others not? What were their motives? Their understandings? Their outlooks? How did they impact that environment and how did the environment impact them? Answers to these questions lay embedded in the overarching theme of his book and his belief that humankind inflicts itself on its environment— as an ecologically destructive force and at consequences to itself. The House of Atreides, House of Harkonen, the space Guild and the Imperium. Even the native Fremen. All "forces inflicting themselves on this planet." [7] World informs character; character informs world. In Section 4.2, I discuss in more detail Herbert's effective world building in *Dune*.

2.1.2 Nina Munteanu's Galaxy

The *Splintered Universe* trilogy, set in our universe, takes place over two hundred years after first contact. Beyond light-speed space travel is achieved through crystal and wavelength technology connected to a sentient being's dream-state. Humans have colonized many worlds and interact with a host of alien species, superior to them in many ways. Rhea's journey and character

110   arc are intimately tied to this perception.[8] The world of the trilogy reflects this: a place where humans are a small part of a much larger universe, rich in alien worlds and cultures.

The fractal relationship between global themes and personal themes is revealed through the main character's journey as she improves her self-perception to better perceive her universe.

2.2 CONSTRUCTING A WORLD

World building enhances real physical and social facts by adding the author's imagination to create a civilization, a political structure, a culture and zeitgeist as backdrop and influence to story.

Most fantasy and science fictions novels require major world-building, which involves both real and imagined aspects. Some writers define world-building as the process of constructing an imaginary world, usually associated with a fictional universe. The term was popularized at science fiction workshops during the 1970s, and according to Brian Stableford, author of *Historical Dictionary of Science Fiction*, it describes the development of an imaginary setting that is coherent and possesses a history, geography and ecology that is rich, unique, and resonates with the story's premise.[3]

Things to consider when first building your world include the following:

- **The world** (e.g., on Earth or not) and **what populates in it**
- **Physical and historical features** (global climate & local weather, geography & geology, resources)
- **Ecology & Life forms** (interrelationships in the natural world, including intelligent species)
- **Magic and magicians** (e.g., rules of magic, technology, science)
- **Peoples and customs** (e.g., language, ethics and values, religion)
- **Social organization & structure** (e.g., government, politics, conflicts, fashion, entertainment)
- **Commerce & trade** (e.g., industry, transportation, communication)

2.3 SCIENCE & ART OF WORLD-BUILDING

If a novel is a historical fantasy set on Earth, science is not as critical as historic accuracy; if a novel is set on some probable planet in the *Andromeda Galaxy*, then science becomes an integral part. In both cases the writer needs to do his or her research. In the case of the historical fantasy, world-building will be based on accurate historical information, even if an alternate history is being written. To provide a realistic alternative, one needs to understand the reality. One of the main reasons for this is to provide valid rationale for how the scene—or its alternate—plays out, or doesn't play out. Understanding that world during that time period and circumstance is best shown in the minutiae of ordinary living.

Part of the reason people read historical epics is to learn more about that particular civilization, its environment, and time period. The reader trusts that the writer will give him or her the facts on the world, while taking liberties on the remaining story elements. Similarly, a science fiction reader opens the first book in Larry Niven's *Ringworld* series with the expectation of learning about a made-up world based on accurate principals of science.

A lot of science fiction is written by nonscientists. That said, many science fiction readers— particularly those who enjoy hard science fiction—expect the writer's science to be not only plausible but somewhat proven and the premise to be based upon sound scientific principle. They expect the research to be impeccable because they are expecting to learn something—in science.[3]

You can refer to *The Fiction Writer*, Chapters B and R, for details on doing research to do with world-building.[3]

2.4 TYING WORLD TO THEME AND PLOT

What's important to remember is that the world you build is an integral part of the story. It isn't just a lot of "interesting" detail. The world you build, like a character in your story, plays a role in defining and supporting its theme. The major qualities of your world are, therefore, best derived for plot and thematic reasons—which come from premise and "story". The rest—the details—are things you can find in books and websites or get from experts in your local university. Don't let science intimidate you; but ensure that you get it right by using your resources and verifying your information with an expert. Use your local libraries, universities, colleges, and online resources.

112 Interview scientists, technical people and other writers. That's part of being a writer too. The world you build should reflect aspects of theme. It may subtly or clearly occupy a central role in the story.

The following examples of wholly realized worlds provide good representations of a world intimately tied to its premise and character journey. Paolo Bacigalupi's *Windup Girl* is set in post-climate change Bangkok; Costi Gurgu's *RecipeArium* is set inside a giant swamp monster on an alien planet. In both stories the world strongly drives the story.

2.4.1 Paolo Bacigalupi's World in *Windup Girl*

Paolo Bacigalupi's biopunk science fiction novel *The Windup Girl* occurs in 23rd century post-food crash Thailand after global warming has raised sea levels and carbon fuel sources are depleted.[8] Thailand struggles under the tyrannical boot of ag-biotech multinational giants such as AgriGen, RedStar, and PurCal—predatory companies who have fomented corruption and political strife through their plague-inducing and sterilizing genetic manipulations. The storyline's premise could very easily be described as "what would happen if Monsanto got its way?"

Bacigalupi's story opens in Bangkok, "City of Divine Beings", now below sea level and precariously protected by a giant sea wall and pumps that run on bio-power:

> *It's difficult not to always be aware of those high walls and the pressure of the water beyond. Diffiicult not to think of the City of Divine Beings as anything other than a disaster waiting to happen. But the Thais are stubborn and have fought to keep their revered city of Krug Thep from drowning. With coal-burning pumps and leveed labor and a deep faith in the visionary leadership of their Chakri Dynasty they have so far kept at bay that thing which has swallowed New York and Rangoon, Mumbai and New Orleans.[9]*

Energy storage in this post-oil society is provided by manually-wound springs using cruelly mistreated genehacked *megodonts*—elephant-like slave labor. Biotechnology dominates via international mega-corporations—called calorie companies—that control food production through genehacked seeds. The companies use bioterrorism and economic hitmen to create markets for their products. Plagues have wiped out the natural seed stock, now virtually supplanted by genetically engineered sterile plants and mutant pests such as cibiscosis, blister rust, and genehack weevil. Thailand—one of the economically disadvantaged—has avoided economic subjugation by the foreign calorie companies through some ingenuity and is now targeted by the agri-corporations.

Bacigalupi's opening entwines the clogged and crumbling city of Bangkok 113
and its swarming beggars, slaves and laborors:

> *Overhead, the towers of Bangkok's old Expansion loom, robed in vines and*
> *mold, windows long ago blown out, great bones picked clean. Without air*
> *conditioning or elevators to make them habitable, they stand and blister in*
> *the sun. The black smoke of illegal dung fires wafts from their pores, mark-*
> *ing where Malayan refugees hurriedly scald chapatis and boil* kopi *before*
> *the white shirts can storm the sweltering heights and beat them for their*
> *infringements.*[9]

Later in the novel, Bacigalupi writes of the Sir Francis Drake bar in town
(note the metaphoric use of verbs and nouns):

> *The entire ramshackle structure is scabbed to the outer wall of a wrecked*
> *Expansion tower. A hand-painted sign ... is a recent addition, relative to the*
> *decay and wreckage around it, painted by a handful of farang determined*
> *to name their surroundings. The fools who did the naming long ago disap-*
> *peared up country, either swallowed in the jungle as blister rust rewrites*
> *swept over them, or torn apart in the tangle of war lines over coal and jade.*
> *Still, the sign remains, either because it amuses the owner ... or because no*
> *one can summon the energy to paint over it. In the meantime, it peels in the*
> *heat ... There are other, lower, dives for those sailors who manage to pass*
> *Customs and quarantine and washdown, but it is here, with the snapping*
> *white tablecloths of the Victory [Hotel] on one side of the cobbled street, and*
> *Sir Francis' bamboo slum on the other, where those foreigners who settle in*
> *Bangkok for any length of time eventually sink.*[9]

Anderson Lake is a *farang* (of white race) who owns an AgriGen factory
trying to mass-produce kink-springs—successors to the internal combustion
engine) to store energy. The factory covers for his real mission: to find and exploit the secret Thai seedbank with its wealth of genetic material. Emiko is an
illegal Japanese "windup" (genetically modified human), owned by a Thai sex
club owner, and treated as a sub-human slave. When she meets Lake, he cav-
alierly shares that a refuge in the remnant forests of northern Thailand exists
for people like her (the "New People"); so Emiko embarks on a quest to escape
her bonds and find her own people in the north. But like Bangkok itself, both
protected and trapped by the wall against a sea poised to claim it—a bustling
city of squalor caught up in the clash of new and old—Emiko cannot escape
who and what she is: a gifted modified human—and herald of a sustainable
future—vilified and feared by a humanity obsessed with the road set before it
(and unable—or unwilling—to see another).

Bangkok emerges as a central character in a story that explores the paradoxical juxtaposition and machinations of conflicting dialectics. Anyone who has spent time in Bangkok will recognize the connective tissue that holds together its crumbling remnants with ambitious chic: its dynamic people. Just like the novel's cheshires. Bangkok's cheshires are genetically created "cats" (made by an agri-giant as a "toy") that wiped out the regular cat *Felis domesicus*. As with *Alice in Wonderland*'s Cheshire Cat, these crafty creatures have adapted to Bangkok's unstable environment. The cheshires exemplify the subversion of good intentions gone wrong; they also reflect the paradoxical nature of a shape-shifting city of Thais, Chinese and Malaya refuges—even the *farangs*—who struggle to survive in a place that is both haven and danger:

> *The flicker-shimmer shapes of cheshires twine, yowling and hoping for scraps … The old man's flinch is as hallucinogenic as a cheshire's fade—one moment there, the next gone and doubted … The devil cats flicker closer. Calico and ginger, black as night—all of them fading in and out of view as their bodies take on the colors of their surroundings.*[9]

Bacigalupi's best use of metaphors throughout the novel link with environment and premise. Early on, the character Hok Seng scrambles to answer his boss's hard question: "He bored through the excuses like a genehack weevil."[9] The weevil has been genetically modified by the multinationals into a biological "weapon."

The rivalry between Thailand's Minister of Trade and Minister of the Environment represent the central conflict of the novel, reflecting the current conflict of neo-liberal promotion of globalization and unaccountable exploitation with the forces of sustainability and environmental protection. Given the setting, both are extreme and there appears no middle ground for a balanced existence using responsible and sustainable means. Emiko, who represents that future, is precariously poised.

2.4.2 Costi Gurgu's World in *RecipeArium*

The more original the world is, the more likely that it will resonate with the story's theme. This is well portrayed in Costi Gurgu's novel *RecipeArium* about an alien race seeking a road to the afterlife within the confines of a strange world.[10] The highly sensual world in *RecipeArium* is a huge beast—a *Carami* that lies in a wasteland desert surrounded by a salty ocean—and within which various characters live and thrive. The *phril* Morminiu is a Recipear (one who creates and presents bizarrely sensual recipes that help an individual transcend into the afterlife).

A Course must look so nauseating that a bitter taste comes immediately to your tongue and activates your acidular glands; a jugular spasm should precede the feeling that your stomach is turning and rising in your throat. Only then can you say, "Yes, this so piques my appetite that I could not live one more second without Tasting the Course."[10]

Morminiu travels through the desert from the Southern Swamps to the largest Carami, the Royal Carami where the swallowed Green Kingdom thrives:

... Its body covered a huge area, guarded on one side by a mountain chain with peaks buried in the clouds. On the other side, the behemoth sprawled over a dry wasteland crisscrossed by commercial roads cutting their way to the north. The monster holding the city was like a mountain itself ... Shining green-gray, the Carami's body rose from the murky water of the lake at the lower end of the valley, a mass of moist flesh under which stretched muscles and pulsing veins. Its rear wasn't visible, and what did lie exposed didn't have any definite shape, no symmetry to its form. A bony belt wrapped its body right above the mouths. Tentacles waved in the strong currents of the lake that surrounded it.[10]

In the Green Kingdom, stimulation through the sense of taste is a powerful and complex art form that rules the lives of the male *phrils*. Not only does it bring pleasure, it can change a *phril's* destiny, even guide him into death and beyond. But only if he can afford the services of the artists called Recipears. Without a Recipear, a *phril* will live and die a pagan, with no chance of an afterlife. The female of the species, called *phriliras*, cannot experience RecipeArium; they replace it with their faith in one God. This is a clearly dualistic world from the dimorphic sexes to the class systems of the various kingdoms.

Gurgu begins the novel with the *phril* Morminiu, chased by assassins, as he runs straight into the Carami's slick and toothless mouth, "icy saliva splattered on his head." He loses his posse by running along the beast's bone bridge. Inside, the *phril* finds his way to the palace that "looked like a great wounded beast ... old, heavy and spiky. Age had blackened the bone of the walls, and the windows were stuffed with shells. The entrance was an open maw framed with curved fangs. A pink tongue unfurled down the steps onto the street." Carrying the soul of his RecipeArium master within him, Morminiu comes to the royal Court seeking revenge on his master's enemies and wishing to become the Master Recipear of the Kingdom.

At every turn in this dark fantasy, sensations and flesh invite and repel. The novel takes us on a journey to discover the meaning of love in a boldly imagined world where art is transformative and immortality the destiny of

116 the few. Gurgu uses fantastical settings—from the vast and forgotten lands of the Edge of the World to the corrupt decadence and intrigue of the nobility who dwell inside the monstrous Carami—to explore a metaphoric spiritual transformation, a dialectic quest of duality to realize itself as whole.

2.5 WORLD BUILDER'S DISEASE

"Fantasy writers have a penchant for working up histories of imaginary empires that can run for hundreds of pages, full of maps and chronologies and genealogical trees a yard long," says Ansen Dibell, author of *The Elements of Writing Fiction: Plot*. "Similarly, science fiction writers can fall in love with their hardware and want to show it off," he adds and describes this as a kind of narrative cancer, a "World-Builder's disease."[3,11]

Most world-building writers keep extensive files of background information on their worlds. In some cases, these can be published as companions to the main book series (e.g., J.K. Rowling's books on Quiddich or magical creatures, which most certainly came from her extensive background notes). Dibell's point is that this information doesn't belong in the main book, where it can interfere with the process of storytelling. It becomes "info dump", which is often very static, lacks drama, and proves ultimately boring.[3] This information should, instead, be archived away and used for inspiration in scenes in the novel. Just knowing its details will add colour and a sense of reality to your world without us needing to read the details.

THREE . . . What is Place?

"Tell me the landscape in which you live and I will tell you who you are."—José Ortega y Gasset

3.1 PLACE AS CHARACTER & ARCHETYPE

When portraying several characters, a novelist may often find herself painting a portrait of a place. This is place being "character". Place functions as a catalyst, and molds the more traditional characters that animate a story. Think of any of your favorite books, particularly the epics: *The Wizard of Oz, Tale of Two Cities, Doctor Zhivago, Lord of the Rings, The Odyssey,* etc. In each of these books the central character is the place, which is firmly linked to its main character. How much is Frodo, for instance, an extension of his beloved Shire? They are one in the same. Just as the London of Charles Dickens spawned Scrooge. Or Hardy's Egdon Heath shaped Eustacia Vye in *The Return of the Native.* D.H. Lawrence suggested that the heath was the most important character in Hardy's book:

> *Egdon, whose dark soil was strong and crude and organic as the body of a beast.*

Hardy personified trees as interpreters between Nature and humanity: from the "sobbing breaths" of a fir plantation to the stillness of trees in a quiet fog, standing "in an attitude of intentness, as if they waited longingly for a wind to come and rock them." Trees, meadows, winding brooks and country roads were far more than back-drop for Hardy's world and his stories. Elements of the natural world were characters in their own right that impacted the other characters in a world dominated by nature.

Place ultimately portrays what lies at the heart of the story. Place as character serves as an *archetype* that story characters connect with and navigate in ways that depend on the *theme* of the story. A story's theme is essentially the "so what part" of the story. What is at stake for the character on their journey. Theme is the backbone—the heart—of the story, driving characters to journey through time and place toward some kind of fulfillment. There is no story without theme. And there is no theme without place.

Things to consider about place as character begin with the POV character

118 and how they interact with their environment and how they reflect their place. For instance is that interaction obvious or subtle? Is that environment constant or changing, stable or unstable, predictable, or variable? Is the place controllable or not, understandable or not? Is the relationship emotional, connected to senses such as memory?

I discuss archetypes in detail, particularly as part of the "Hero's Journey" in Chapter J of *The Fiction Writer*.[3] In summary, archetypes are ancient patterns of personality shared universally by humanity (e.g. the "mother" archetype is recognized by all cultures). When place acts as an archetype or symbol in story—particularly when linked to theme—it provides a depth of meaning that resonates through many levels for the reader. From obvious to subtle.

A subtle yet potent example of this is provided by Annie Proulx's novel *The Shipping News*; Proulx uses subtle body language of her protagonist to provide a strong sense of place. The main character, Quoyle, displays a self-conscious gesture of covering his strong native chin with his hand until he leaves New York to his homeland of Newfoundland from where he is descended—a place where he can live a natural and graceful life without apology.[3,12]

In Ray Bradbury's *The Martian Chronicles*, Mars symbolizes a new Eden—though unimagined. Like Bradbury's aboriginal Martians—who are mostly invisible—the planet is a mirror that reflects humanity's best and worst.[13] Who we are, what we are, what we bring with us and what we may become. What we inadvertently do—to others, and finally to ourselves—and how the irony of chance can change everything.

> They came because they were afraid or unafraid, happy or unhappy. There was a reason for each man. They were coming to find something or get something, or to dig up something or bury something. They were coming with small dreams or big dreams or none at all.[13]

The 1970 Bantam book jacket aptly calls *The Martian Chronicles*, "a story of familiar people and familiar passions set against incredible beauties of a new world … A skillful blending of fancy and satire, terror and tenderness, wonder and contempt."

Written in the 1940s, *The Martian Chronicles* drip with a nostalgic atmosphere — shady porches with tinkling pitchers of lemonade, grandfather clocks, chintz-covered sofas. But longing for this comfortable past proves dangerous in every way to Bradbury's characters — the golden-eyed Martians as well as the humans. Starting in the far-flung future of 1999, expedition after expedition leaves Earth to explore Mars. The chameleon-like Martians guard their mysteries well, but soon succumb to the diseases that arrive with the rockets — recapitulating the tragedies that European colonization imposed on our indigenous peoples. Colonists appear on Mars, most of them with ideas

no more lofty than starting a hot-dog stand, and with no respect for the culture they are impacting and an entire people they are destroying. Bradbury
weaves metaphor into the opening when the heat of a rocket ship turned an
Ohio dark winter into summer:

> *Rocket summer. The words passed among the people in the open, airing*
> *houses. Rocket summer. The warm desert air changing the frost patterns on*
> *the windows, erasing the art work. The skis and sleds suddenly useless. The*
> *snow, falling from the cold sky upon the town, turned to a hot rain before it*
> *touched the ground.*
>
> *Rocket summer. People leaned from their dripping porches and watched the*
> *reddening sky. The rocket lay on the launching field, blowing out pink clouds*
> *of fire and even heat. The rocket stood in the cold winter morning, making*
> *summer with every breath of its mighty exhausts. The rocket made climates,*
> *and summer lay for a brief moment on the land...* [13]

What unfolds is a profound and tender analysis of the quiet yet devastating
power humanity can wield unawares. Bradbury paints a multi-layered tapestry of hopes and dreams through metaphor. To Bradbury everything a writer
writes is metaphor. Metaphor is powerful through perspective. It makes the
ordinary strange and the strange ordinary.

In Emmi Itäranta's *Memory of Water*—about a post-climate change world of
sea level rise—water is a powerful archetype, whose secret tea masters guard
with their lives:

> *The story tells that water has a consciousness, that it carries in its memory*
> *everything that's ever happened in this world, from the time before humans*
> *until this moment, which draws itself in its memory even as it passes. Water*
> *understands the movements of the world; it knows when it is sought and*
> *where it is needed. Sometimes a spring or a well dries for no reason, without*
> *explanation. It's as if the water escapes of its own will, withdrawing into*
> *the cover of the earth to look for another channel. Tea masters believe there*
> *are times when water doesn't wish to be found because it knows it will be*
> *chained in ways that are against its nature.* [14]

Water, with its life-giving properties and other strange qualities, has been
used as a powerful metaphor and archetype in many stories: from vast oceans
of mystery, beauty and danger—to the relentless flow of an inland stream.
Margaret Atwood's *The Penelopiad* is just one example:

Water does not resist. Water flows. When you plunge your hand into it, all you feel is a caress. Water is not a solid wall, it will not stop you. But water always goes where it wants to go, and nothing in the end can stand against it. Water is patient. Dripping water wears away a stone. Remember that, my child. Remember you are half water. If you can't go through an obstacle, go around it. Water does.[15]

EXERCISE 2: Premise / Theme & A Character of Your World

1. *Identify a* **PREMISE** *(and its dramatization through character) for your story. A premise is an idea, the "what if" that underpins and sparks the story and its character's journey (e.g., climate change causes the monarch butterflies to change their flight path; main character Dellarobia Turnbow is on her personal flight through the forested hills toward a love affair when she discovers the monarchs, spectacularly congregated and in her way—Flight Behavior by Barbara Kingsolver). Write it down:*

_____

_____

_____

_____

_____

_____

_____

_____

_____

_____

2. *Identify a* **THEME** *for your story. A theme is the "so what" part of the story, what's at stake for the main character and what they must learn/discover/ overcome. (e.g., the main character learns that a connection with Nature [and community] can help direct her flight to be true to herself and help the world). Write it down:*

_____

_____

_____

_____

_____

_____

_____

_____

_____

_____

3.   *Name and describe a* **CHARACTER** *(preferably minor) that personifies some aspect of the ecology of your world (e.g., the Monarch butterfly in* Flight Behavior*):*

_____

_____

_____

_____

_____

_____

_____

_____

4.   *Tie in three (3) ecological traits of that "character" with theme (e.g. predator vs. prey; authotroph vs. saprotroph; r-selected vs. K-selected; in a commensal relationship; uses camouflage to avoid predation; practices temporal niche partitioning).*

Trait	Connection with Theme

In Barbara Kingsolver's Flight Behavior, the Monarch reflects the theme of Dellarobia's journey by being: 1) resilient and responsive to Nature's vicissitudes; 2) unaware of its own beauty; 3) showing its bright colours in a gestalt display of natural being.

EXERCISE 3: Place as Heart of the Story

Pick a story from Table 1 that you've read—or choose a favourite of yours. Link the main character to the place.

Table 1 : Stories With a Strong Setting / Sense of Place

Wizard of Oz	Tale of Two Cities	The Shipping News	Divergent
Doctor Zhivago	Lord of the Rings	The Martian Chronicles	Wuthering Heights
The Water Knife	To Kill a Mockingbird	Gone with the Wind	Dune
Harry Potter series	Return of the Native	The Great Gatsby	The Three Body Problem
Rebecca	The Brothers Karamozov	The Grapes of Wrath	Flight Behaviour
Handmaid's Tale	White Oleander	Barkskins	The Overstory
Neuromancer	The English Patient	The Memory of Water	Angela's Ashes
Year of the Flood	Vanity Fair	The Poisonwood Bible	Outer Diverse
Girl in the Blue Coat	Snow Falling on Cedars	The House of Djinn	Anthill
Nineteen Eighty Four	Affinity	Recipearium	Darwin's Paradox

1. *Explore how the main POV character (or any other character, for that matter) relates to their environment and world; be mindful of the character's changing interaction with a world and its various settings. Use the following as prompts to define setting (and interaction) as:*

- *Interacting through metaphor and archetype (e.g. world as antagonist, trickster, shapeshifter, etc.)*
- *Communicating as environmental force (language)*
- *Obvious or subtle*
- *Controllable or not controllable*
- *Emotionally connected (positive or negative) to character*
- *Understandable or not understandable*
- *Constant or changing, stable or unstable, predictable or variable*

_____

_____

_____

2. *Explore the meaning behind this relationship, particularly to do with the character's journey, and the over-arching theme of the story.*

_____

_____

_____

Donald Maass writes in **Writing the Breakout Novel Workbook**: "The beauty of seeing a locale through a particular perspective is that the point-of-view character cannot be separated from the place. The place comes alive, as does the observer of that place, in ways that would not be possible if described using objective point of view."[6] *The POV character's relationship to place helps identify the transformative elements of their journey. Such transformation is the theme of the story and ultimately portrays the story's heart and soul.*

3.2 PLACE AS METAPHOR

Everything in story is metaphor, Ray Bradbury once told me. That is no more apparent than in setting and place, in which a story is embedded and through which characters move and interact. Metaphor is the subtext that provides subtleties in story, subtleties that evoke mood, anticipation, and memorable scenes. Richard Russo says, "to know the rhythms, the textures, the feel of a place is to know more deeply and truly its people."[4] When you choose your setting, remember that its primary metaphoric role is to help depict theme. This is because place is destiny.

Metaphor provides similarity to two dissimilar things through meaning. In the metaphor "Love danced in her heart" or the simile "his love was like a slow dance", love is equated with the joy of dance. By providing figurative rather than literal description to something, metaphor invites participation through interpretation.

When I write "John's office was a prison," I am efficiently and sparingly suggesting in five words—in what would normally take a paragraph—how John felt about his workplace. The reader would conjure imagery suggested by their knowledge of a prison cell: that John felt trapped, cramped, solitary, stifled, oppressed—even frightened and threatened. Metaphor relies on subtext knowledge. This is why metaphor is so powerful and universally relevant: the reader fully participates—the reader brings in relevance through their personal knowledge and experience and this creates the memorable aspect to the scene.

Russo tells us that place is crucial to human destiny and the formation of human personality. "The more specific and individual things become, the more universal they feel," says Russo.[4] This is not an oxymoron, but an example of the principle of a truism that primarily comes to us in the form of paradox (like all good truisms). Detail provides the color and texture of your story and helps it resonate with a sense of place. This does not necessarily translate into a lot of exposition; but it does require creative choice of words. So, instead of "He took a drag from his cigarette as he drove his sports car along a winding road in the country"; (twenty words) try something like "Vinnie sucked on a Camel as his red Corvette careered the hair-pinned curves of Hell's Gate." (seventeen words).

3.2.1 Place Personified

Personification is powerful metaphor that gives nonhuman things human qualities. It personalizes, energizes and emotionalizes. Place described through personification can illuminate both characters and their environment in compelling ways. By giving an object, place, or animal the qualities of a person, personification provides subtle aspects of mood and links the reader to a cocktail subtext of human feelings and struggles. Personification can connect the reader to "lifeless" objects such as water, soil, rock, the sun, moon, planet, concrete, paper, etc., to map the larger meaning of the story. Putting a character's feelings into the objects around her—as POV character—creates a subtle but deep connection with the reader: "The darkness embraced her"; "The open-throated roar of the river pulled her near."

D.H. Lawrence's creates strong personification of Thomas Hardy's Egdon Heath in *Return of the Native:*

> *...Egdon, whose dark soil was strong and crude and organic as the body of a beast.*

In *The Handmaid's Tale*—a dystopian tale of oppression and intrigue—Margaret Atwood writes:

> *There is something subversive about this garden of Serena's, a sense of buried things bursting upwards, wordlessly, into the light, as if to point, to say: Whatever is silenced will clamour to be heard, though silently ... Light pours down upon it from the sun, true, but also heat rises, from the flowers themselves, you can feel it: like holding your hand an inch above an arm, a shoulder. It breathes, in the warmth, breathing itself in.*[16]

E. Martin Nolan's *Still Point* creates powerful imagery of a storm aftermath through an abandoned old shed and contrasts its loneliness to the half-wild woods nearby:

> *A deserted shed by the road, buckling under its roof, kneels into the tall grass. The woods beyond it hide the river ... I turn back to the half-wild woods. These trees speak to each other, are wild enough for that. They live together, holding the riverbanks in place.*[17]

Cixin Liu's *The Three Body Problem*—set against the backdrop of China's Cultural Revolution—follows Wenji Ye, disillusioned by the massive environmental deforestation in the labour camps she is sent to work:

> *Her company wielded hundreds of chain saws like a swarm of steel locusts, and after they passed, only stumps were left. The fallen Dahurian larch, now bereft of branches, was ready to be taken away by tractor. Ye gently caressed*

the freshly exposed cross section of the felled trunk. She did this often, as though such surfaces were giant wounds, as though she could feel the tree's pain ... The trunk was dragged away. Rocks and stumps in the ground broke the bark in more places, wounding the giant body further. In the spot where it once stood, the weight of the fallen tree being dragged left a deep channel in the layers of decomposing leaves that had accumulated over the years. Water quickly filled the ditch. The rotting leaves made the water appear crimson, like blood.[18]

In *Memory of Water*, Emmi Itäranta personifies this life-giving substance whose very nature is tightly interwoven with her main character. As companion and harbinger, water is portrayed simultaneously as friend and enemy. As giver and taker of life.

Water is the most versatile of all elements ... Water walks with the moon and embraces the earth, and it isn't afraid to die in fire or live in air. When you step into it, it will be as close as your own skin, but if you hit it too hard, it will shatter you ... Death is water's close companion. The two cannot be separated, and neither can be separated from us, for they are what we are ultimately made of: the versatility of water, and the closeness of death. Water has no beginning and no end, but death has both. Death is both. Sometimes death travels hidden in water, and sometimes water will chase death away, but they go together always, in the world and in us. [14]

Personification of natural things provides the reader with an image they can clearly and emotionally relate to and care about. When a point-of-view character does the describing, we get a powerful and intimate indication of their thoughts and feelings—mainly in how they connect to place (often as symbol). When this happens, place and perception entwine in powerful force.

3.2.2 Place as Symbol

"In their simplest form, symbols are anything outward that stands in for anything inward or abstract, such as a mood or an idea," writes Donald Maass in *Writing the Breakout Novel Workbook*.[6] As representations, symbols often serve as markers in a story. They may be a talisman, a totem that inspires a shift or awakening. In story, a symbol—particularly as talisman—may come as a gift to a character in need of inspiration. In the Hero's Journey trope,[3] this is often provided by a mentor archetype. An example in story is the light saber that Obi Wan Kenobi presents to Luke Skywalker to aid him on his journey as a Jedi master. Symbols often reoccur as motif to incite an emotional trigger or turning point for a character.

128   Symbolism in literature provides richness, colour and depth of meaning. Use of symbols helps deepen theme beyond conscious appreciation and into emotional and subconscious levels. Symbolism can be portrayed through figure of speech in which an object or situation has another meaning than its literal meaning. It can also express through the actions and observations of a character, language or event that creates deeper meaning through context.

Maass provides the example of Barbara Kingsolver's *The Poisonwood Bible* to depict superb use of symbol in storytelling:

She is inhumanly alone. And then, all at once, she isn't. A beautiful animal stands on the other side of the water. They look up from their lives, woman and animal, amazed to find themselves in the same place. He freezes, inspecting her with his black-tipped ears. His back is purplish-brown in the dim light, sloping downward from the gentle hump of his shoulders. The forest's shadows fall into lines across his white-striped flanks. His stiff forelegs play out to the sides like stilts, for he's been caught in the act of reaching down for water. Without taking his eyes from her, he twitches a little at the knee, then the shoulder, where a fly devils him. Finally he surrenders his surprise, looks away, and drinks. She can feel the touch of his long, curled tongue on the water's skin, as if he were lapping from her hand. His head bobs gently, nodding small, velvet horns lit white from behind like new leaves.

It lasted just a moment, whatever that is. One held breath? An ant's afternoon? It was brief, I can promise that much, for although it's been many years now since my children ruled my life, a mother recalls the measure of the silences. I never had more than five minutes peace unbroken. I was that woman on the stream bank, of course. Orleanna Price, Southern Baptist by marriage, mother of children living and dead. That one time and no other the okapi came to the stream, and I was the only one to see it.[19]

In this opening to her novel, Kingsolver explores a multi-layered symbol for her main character's bewilderment at the mystery and beauty of the environment around her, tied into her own essential helplessness, says Maass. "Part of what makes [Kingsolver's] symbols poetic is that all of them emerge from the natural world around her characters," he adds.[6] Nature's symbols are powerful archetypes that reveal compelling story. These symbols abound in Kingsolver's novel that explores the relationships of five women with their environment and the rigid ignorance of their patriarch, Nathan Price. The garden, Maass tells us, provides many examples of this. Price has planted his seeds in a flat, not accounting for the torrential afternoon downpours, which wash away his garden in a flash. Later, the poisonwood tree in their yard gives

Price a horrid rash, suggesting that he is messing with a place he does not understand or respect. How each of the women interacts with her environment over time provides a deeply felt and metaphoric revelation of how she relates to others and to herself—all reflecting her personal journey in the story. [6]

As the quote indicates, Orleanna Price experienced a turning point through discovery. In this example the discovery occurred through a sudden encounter with a natural element. Moments of discovery and emotional turning points associated with environment need not only be encountered in person. In Cixin Liu's *The Three Body Problem*, main protagonist Ye Wenjie is already cynical about human nature from the violence and destruction of the Cultural Revolution. Yet, it is a contraband copy of Rachel Carson's book *Silent Spring* and its revelations that set in motion the pivotal shift in her life trajectory:

> *More than four decades later, in her last moments, Ye Wenjie would recall the influence* Silent Spring *had on her life. The book dealt only with a limited subject: the negative environmental effects of excessive pesticide use. But the perspective taken by the author shook Ye to the core. The use of pesticides had seemed to Ye just a normal, proper—or, at least, neutral—act, but Carson's book allowed Ye to see that, from Nature's perspective, their use was indistinguishable from the Cultural Revolution, and equally destructive to our world. If this was so, then how many other acts of humankind that had seemed normal or even righteous were, in reality, evil?*

> *As she continued to mull over these thoughts, a deduction made her shudder: Is it possible that the relationship between humanity and evil is similar to the relationship between the ocean and an iceberg floating on its surface? Both the ocean and the iceberg are made of the same material. That the iceberg seems separate is only because it is in a different form. In reality, it is but a part of the vast ocean … It was impossible to expect a moral awakening from humankind itself, just like it was impossible to expect humans to lift off the earth by pulling up on their own hair. To achieve moral awakening required a force outside the human race.*

> *This thought determined the entire direction of Ye's life.*[18]

In my near-future speculative novel *A Diary in the Age of Water*, cynical limnologist Lynna sees everything in her life through limnological metaphors, ironically predicting her own future:

> *An oligotrophic lake is basically a young lake. Still immature and undeveloped, an oligotrophic lake often displays a rugged untamed beauty. An oligotrophic lakes hungers for the stuff of life. Sediments from incoming riv-*

ers slowly feed it with dissolved nutrients and particulate organic matter. Detritus and associated microbes slowly seed the lake. Phytoplankton eventually flourish, food for zooplankton and fish. The shores then gradually slide and fill, as does the very bottom. Deltas form and macrophytes colonize the shallows. Birds bring in more creatures. And so on. Succession is the engine of destiny and trophic status its shibboleth.

As Nature tames the unruly lake over time, one thing replaces another. As a lake undergoes its natural succession from oligotrophic to highly productive eutrophic lake, its beauty mellows and it surrenders to the complexities of destiny. Minimalism yields to a baroque richness that, in turn, heralds extinction. The lake shrinks to a swamp then buries itself under a meadow.

We hold ourselves apart from our profligate nature. But we aren't unique. We are more part of Nature than we admit. Using the thread of epigenetics and horizontal gene transfer, Nature stitches in us a moving tapestry of terrible irony. The irony lies in our conviction that we were made in the inimitable divine image of God. That we are special. Yet over a third of the human population is secular—atheists and agnostics—who do not believe in God. Or anything, for that matter.

Water flows endlessly through us, whether we're devout Catholics or empty vessels with no purpose. Water makes no distinction. It flows through us even after we bury ourselves.[20]

In the following excerpt from *Brokeback Mountain*, Annie Proulx uses a mix of senses—but mostly smell—in an evocative description of two shirts to symbolize a love loss:

The shirt seemed heavy until he saw there was another shirt inside it, the sleeves carefully worked down inside Jack's sleeves. It was his own plaid shirt, lost, he'd thought, long ago in some damn laundry, his dirty shirt, the pocket ripped, buttons missing, stolen by Jack and hidden here inside Jack's own shirt, the pair like two skins, one inside the other, two in one. He pressed his face into the fabric and breathed in slowly through his mouth and nose, hoping for the faintest smoke and mountain sage and salty sweet stink of Jack, but there was no real scent, only the memory of it, the imagined power of Brokeback Mountain of which nothing was left but what he held in his hands.[21]

In Bong Joon-Ho's 2013 motion picture *Snowpiercer*—about a train career-

ing the world with the remains of humanity—place and destiny are welded
together in tight metaphor. The train is the world. This dark surrealistic allegory examines all iterations of place in a class struggle between the front and tail ends of the train. In an early scene, one of the ruling class, Minister Mason, evokes her own metaphors to remind the lower class of their place and destiny:

> *"Order is the barrier that holds back the flood of death. We must all of us on this train of life remain in our allotted station ... Would you wear a shoe on your head? Of course you wouldn't wear a shoe on your head. A shoe doesn't belong on your head. A shoe belongs on your foot. A hat belongs on your head. I am a hat. You are a shoe. I belong on the head. You belong on the foot. Yes? So it is.*

> *"In the beginning, order was proscribed by your ticket: First Class, Economy, and freeloaders like you. Eternal order is prescribed by the sacred engine: all things flow from the sacred engine, all things in their place, all passengers in their section, all water flowing, all heat rising, pays homage to the sacred engine, in its own particular preordained position. So it is. Now, as in the beginning, I belong to the front. You belong to the tail.*

> *"When the foot seeks the place of the head, the sacred line is crossed. Know your place. Keep your place. Be a shoe."*

In my short story *The Way of Water*, water's connection with love flows throughout the story:

> *They met in the lobby of a shabby downtown Toronto hotel. Hilda barely knew what she looked like but when Hanna entered the lobby through the front doors, Hilda knew every bit of her. Hanna swept in like a stray summer rainstorm, beaming with the self-conscious optimism of someone who recognized a twin sister. She reminded Hilda of her first boyfriend, clutching flowers in one hand and chocolate in the other. When their eyes met, Hilda knew. For an instant, she knew all of Hanna. For an instant, she'd glimpsed eternity. What she didn't know then was that it was love.*

> *Love flowed like water, gliding into backwaters and lagoons with ease, filling every swale and mire. Connecting, looking for home. Easing from crystal to liquid to vapour then back, water recognized its hydrophilic likeness, and its complement. Before the inevitable decoherence, remnants of the entanglement lingered like a quantum vapour, infusing everything. Hilda always knew where and when to find Hanna on Oracle, as though water inhabited*

the machine and told her. Water even whispered to her when her wandering friend was about to return from the dark abyss and land unannounced on her doorstep.[22]

In a world of severe water scarcity through climate catastrophe and geopolitical oppression, the bond of these two girls—to each other through water and with water—is like the shifting covalent bond of a complex molecule, a bond that fuses a relationship of paradox linked to the paradoxical properties of water. Just as two water drops join, the two women find each other in the wasteland of intrigue. Hilda's relationship with Hanna—as with water—is both complex and shifting according to the bonds they make and break.

3.2.3 Place as Allegory

An allegory is a complete narrative whose images and material things represent an abstract idea or theme such as a political system, religious practice or figure, or a philosophical viewpoint. The entire narrative is a metaphor in which all components are symbolic. Most fairy tales, folk tales and myths are allegories. Examples include: Edmund Spencer's *Faerie Queen*; Mary Shelley's *Frankenstein*; and *Beowulf*.

The narrative of allegory is a fractal nest of symbolic names, places and things, that contribute key elements to the story (e.g., Luke Skywalker and Han Solo in *Star Wars*; Gabriel Oak in *Far From the Madding Crowd*; John Savage of *Stanger in a Strange Land*; Darwin Mall in *Darwin's Paradox*; Middle Earth in *Lord of the Rings*; Lilliput in *Gulliver's Travels*). Setting and place in allegory symbolizes the theme being explored (e.g. Orwell's farm in *Animal Farm* represents a totalitarian world of oppression; the road in John Bunyan's *Pilgrim's Progress* represents the journey of humankind; the island in William Golding's *Lord of the Flies* represents the world at war). As an aside, the science of place names, geographical names or **toponyms** (derived from a topographic feature) is called **toponymy**. The city of Montreal, for instance, is a toponym (named after *le mont Royal*). Toponyms often come through the local vernacular. Given their link to cultural identity, such place names can provide a significant symbolic role in story.

In **Animal Farm**, George Orwell uses animals to describe the revolution against a totalitarian regime (e.g. the overthrow of the last Russian Csar and the Communist Revolution of Russia). The animals embrace archetypes to symbolize the actions and thoughts of various sectors within that world. The pigs are the leaders of the revolution; Mr. Jones represents the ruling despot who is overthrown; the horse Boxer is the ever-loyal and unquestioning labor class.

John Bunyan's **The Pilgrim's Progress**, published in 1678, tells the story of a narrator who falls asleep and dreams of a man named Christian fleeing the City of Destruction while bearing a heavy burden (e.g., symbolizing his own sins) on his back. A character named Evangelist shows Christian the way to Celestial City, a perilous journey through the Slough (swamp) as characters called Mr. Worldly Wiseman and Hypocrisy try to lead him astray.

In *Lord of the Flies*, William Golding explores the conflict in humanity between the impulse toward civilization and the impulse toward savagery. The symbols of the island, the ocean, the *conch shell*, Piggy's glasses, and the Lord of the Flies, or the Beast, represent central ideas that reinforce this main theme. Each character has recognizable symbolic significance: Ralph represents civilization and democracy; Piggy represents intellect and rationalism; Jack represents self-interested savagery and dictatorship; and Simon (the outsider in so many ways) represents altruistic purity.

Many of Golding's potent symbols to power his allegory come from the natural world. These include the use of smoke, fire, and snakes to invoke the imaginary beast (that exists within each of them). The scar left from the plane crash that destroys this natural paradise symbolizes our savage and destructive nature.

Allegories may also be powerful as satires. The social commentary of satires expose and criticize corruption and foolhardiness of societies, groups or even individuals through humor, irony and even ridicule. *Gulliver's Travels* by Jonathan Swift is a good example of satire and parody. Swift targets politics, religion and western culture through satire. Aspects of place, landscape and setting are wonderfully used to feature his commentary. Another excellent example of political satire and use of place and setting with embedded character is found in Lewis Carroll's *Alice's Adventures in Wonderland*.

Excellent examples of satires with less obvious allegorical structure (but it's there) can be found in the genre of science fiction—a highly metaphorical literature that makes prime use of place and setting with archetypal characters to satirize an aspect of society. *Brave New World* by Aldous Huxley is a satirical response to his observation of humans' addiction to (sexual) pleasure and vulnerability to mind control and the dumbing of civilization in the 1930s. George Orwell's *Nineteen Eight-Four* satirizes humanity's vulnerability to fascism, based on his perception of humans' sense of fear and helplessness under powerful governments and their oppressive surveillance. Margaret Atwood's *The Handmaid's Tale* satirizes a society in which a woman struggles in a fundamentalist Christian dictatorship where women are forced into a system of sexual slavery for the ruling patriarchy. Other examples include: *Stanger in a Strange Land* by Robert Heinlein; *The Dispossessed* by Ursula K. Le Guin; *The Time Machine* by H. G. Wells; *The Hunger Games* by Suzanne Collins. Each of these stories examines the world of the day and provides critical commentary through premise, place and character. In each of these stories, place and set-

134   ting help define premise and theme (e.g., what is being satirized.)

3.2.4 Inside Places

Good examples of informative interior settings can be found in *The Glass Menagerie*, Scott Fitzgerald's *The Great Gatsby* and Mary Gordon's *The Important Houses*. In Gordon's story, "we get a marvelous sense of character despite the fact that we never meet any of the people," says Russo. The contents provide a revealing portrait of its vacant owner:

> ...*every object in her house belonged to the Old World. Nothing was easy; everything required maintenance of a complicated and specialized sort* ...[23]

I vividly recall the opening scene of the 1974 film version of Scott Fitzgerald's *The Great Gatsby*: the camera slowly pans a sweeping view of both the opulent interior and state of abandonment of Gatsby's house. Encompassed within a few moments, a man's entire life is revealed.

In Margaret Atwood's *The Handmaid's Tale*, her main character Offred introduces her room with details of dark foreshadowing:

> *A chair, a table, a lamp. Above, on the white ceiling, a relief ornament in the shape of a wreath and in the centre of it a blank space, plastered over, like the place in a face where the eye has been taken out. There must have been a chandelier once. They've removed anything you could tie a rope to.*[16]

Every word heightens tension, creates a foreboding, and teases curiosity.

In her description of a bookstore in *Harry Potter and The Philosopher's Stone*, J.K. Rowling creates a sense of the ordered chaos of her magical world:

> *They bought Harry's school books in a shop called Flourish and Blotts where the shelves were stacked to the ceiling with books as large as paving stones bound in leather; books the size of postage stamps in covers of silk.*[24]

In Tennessee Williams's *The Glass Menagerie*, Tom Wingfield—tasked with supporting his poor family and yearning to escape—describes his apartment from his position on the fire escape:

> *The Wingfield apartment is in the rear of the building, one of those vast hive-*

like conglomerations of cellular living-units that flower as warty growths in overcrowded urban centers of lower middle-class population and are symptomatic of the impulse of this largest and fundamentally enslaved section of American society to avoid fluidity and differentiation and to exist and function as one interfused mass of automatism.[25]

The fire escape, where he has positioned himself, symbolizes his yearning to escape poverty.

3.2.5 Outside Places

"The relationship between character and her exterior setting is more mysterious," says Russo, because your character doesn't "own" a landscape or a street or a neighborhood.[4] Each setting highlights different aspects of your character, based on how they relate to it and their ability or need to control it.

In Barbara Kingsolver's *Flight Behavior*, main character Dellarobia Turnbow's relationship with the migrating monarch butterfly symbolizes her transformative journey. The reader senses an often pivotal moment whenever she is with the butterflies. This following scene close to the end of the book is, therefore, revealing on several levels:

The density of the butterflies in the air now gave her a sense of being underwater, plunged into a deep pond among bright fishes.[26]

In *Oliver Twist*, Charles Dickens describes the bustling centre of 19th Century London with vivid detail that draws on all the senses:

The public-houses, with gas-lights burning inside, were already open. By degrees, other shops began to be unclosed, and a few scattered people were met with. Then, came straggling groups of labourers going to their work; then, men and women with fish-baskets on their heads; donkey-carts laden with vegetables; chaise-carts filled with livestock or whole carcasses of meat; milk-women with pails; an unbroken concourse of people trudging out with various supplies to the eastern suburbs of the town. As they approached the City, the noise and traffic gradually increased; when they threaded the streets between Shoreditch and Smithfield, it had swelled into a roar of sound and bustle.[27]

136   In his thriller *In the Miso Soup*, Ryu Murakami describes Tokyo as only someone who has experienced it can:

> *It was still early in the evening when we emerged onto a street in Tsukiji, near the fish market. ... Wooden bait-and-tackle shops with disintegrating roofs and broken signs stood next to shiny new convenience stores, and futuristic highrise apartment complexes rose skyward on either side of narrow, retro streets lined with wholesalers of dried fish.*[28]

Murakami captures the gritty paradox of this modern city by highlighting the chaotic juxtaposition of old decrepit and new clean.

EXERCISE 4: METAPHOR TO ENHANCE MEANING OF PLACE

1.   Compare a place to the following: a prison; a stranger; a lover; an animal; a memory; a smell. What physical and emotional connotations do you get?

2.   The house _____ like _____. Fill in the blanks based on these different potential relationships of the house with the POV character: a) where she grew up; b) where her mother died; c) a place she can't afford.

3.   Take a piece of your own writing and find all the metaphors and similes. Highlight them then interrogate them. What purpose are they fulfilling? Are they necessary?

_____
_____
_____
_____
_____
_____
_____
_____
_____
_____
_____

Reference: "The Fiction Writer: Get Published, Write Now!" (Starfire World Syndicate) by Nina Munteanu, 2009.

3.3 PLACE AND CULTURE

Both the power and possible limitation of metaphor is that its efficacy and comprehension often relies on cultural knowledge. Because metaphor uses vernacular tied to culture, writers can make use of metaphor to illuminate important aspects of a culture or world. Writers can enhance or illuminate difference in cultures or people through their use (and misuse) of metaphors when characters of different cultures meet and communicate verbally and through body language. Such collisions of culture can create misunderstandings and foment conflict—the stuff of story.

In Frank Herbert's *Dune*, water is a precious currency used among its native Fremen. Without water one dies, after all. When Stilgar, the Fremen leader, first meets the Duke's party, he spits on the polished table. The Duke's men surge to their feet with insult. But one of the Duke's men, aware of the true nature of this gesture as a token of respect, prevents a scrap by cutting in: "We thank you, Stilgar, for the gift of your body's moisture. We accept it in the spirit with which it is given," says the Duke's man. He then, in turn, spits on the table. When he later agrees to serve with the Fremen, Stilgar pronounces quite literally, "your water is ours," indicating that their tribes are now one.[50]

3.3.1 Place and Language

The Splintered Universe: In my trilogy *The Splintered Universe*, I created an entire lexicon based on the alien cultures in the trilogy. Some terms arose from intra- and inter-cultural perceptions and relationships. Other terms came from various technologies and their use (or misuse).

For example, the expression, "Don't be a creon," arises from the general perception that those from the planet Creon are lazy, lack good judgement and imagination (as in, *"We don't permit shapeshifters here, creon."*).

The term "jag" refers to the act of straying off the space-time stream of faster-than-light travel and often accompanied by dangerous ship stress. Most pilots don't live past their jagging experience. The term has been adopted beyond the space pilot community and is used colloquially to indicate a serious misjudgment (as in *"he jags up all the time"*). "Jagging" is also used as an expletive to describe a person, concept or action that lacks sense, is inappropriate or causes harm, embarrassment or discomfort (as in, *"He's jagging with your mind"* or *"she's so jagging stupid"*). "Jagged" is often used to refer to a serious error or bad circumstance (as in, *"we're jagged."*).

A blenoid is a ferocious dog-like animal with three sets of razor sharp teeth, massive head, three eyes and tough red hide that lives in the desert of Upsilon

2 in the Epsilon Endari system. Blenoids are considered dull-witted, mad and violent creatures. The term is used to describe a person with these traits (as in "*Have you gone blenoid?*")

Hedon is a mildly euphoric recreational drug that is smoked and produces a pungent yellow smoke. Chronic use of the drug is known to interfere with cognitive abilities. The term is used colloquially to indicate incredulity on hyperbole or something considered unrealistic (as in "*You must be blowing hedon.*")

Quintle is a dark energy particle found in everything. Its destructive energy is discharged from a weapon known as a Q-gun that resonates with matter to dematerialize an object. The term is used colloquially to express something of importance (as in, "*Who gives a quintle about spice?*")

The Expanse: The TV series *The Expanse*, based on novels by James S.A. Corey, is set 200 years in the future when humanity has colonized the moon, Mars and the Asteroid Belt to mine minerals and water. Humanity has split three ways culturally, ethnically and even biologically: Earth is currently run by the United Nations; Mars is an independent state, devoted to terraforming with high technology; and the Belt contains a diverse mix of mining colonies, settlers, workers and entrepreneurs. Belters' physiology differ from their Earth or Mars cousins, given their existence in low gravity. Subtle but powerful differences between the Belter culture, Earthers and Martians (all human) includes language. Belters use a creole that's a mix of several Earth languages that were spoken by the original human settlers in the Belt colonies. The language resembles a Caribbean twang and cadence with words containing a mix of slang English, Chinese, French, Zulu, Arabic, Dutch, Russian, German, Spanish, Polish and others. For instance, "Inyalowda" means inner or non-belter. "Sa-sa" means to know. "Copin" means friend. Language is not just an interesting texture to the differing cultures portrayed in *The Expanse*; language adds to the nuanced tensions, attitudes and misunderstandings among them.

Exercise 5: Linking Metaphor with Alien Cultures

1.   *Go through your WIP and/or your glossary of "alien" and "world" terms and characters and list at least five of them below in column A.*

2.   *Find examples in your WIP (or create them) of metaphors used in narrative or dialogue that make use of the term to highlight culture and values.*

A. Alien or World Term	B. Example of Metaphor using the Term

3.4 PLACE AND FIRST IMPRESSIONS

Openings (of a book or chapter or even paragraph) create tone and colour. More importantly they promise of what's to come. When combined with place, we glimpse what lies at the heart of the story and seize the guiding rope dangled before us.

3.4.1 First Impressions of the Canadian Forest

Annie Proulx opens her novel *Barkskins* with a scene in which René Sel and fellow barkskins (woodcutters) arrive from France in the late seventeenth century to the still pristine wilderness of Canada to settle, trade and accumulate wealth:

> *In twilight they passed bloody Tadoossac, Kébec and Trois-Rivières and near dawn moored at a remote riverbank settlement ... Mosquitoes covered their hands and necks like fur. A man with yellow eyebrows pointed them at a rain-dark house. Mud, rain, biting insects and the odor of willows made the first impression of New France. The second impression was of dark vast forest, inimical wildness.*[29]

The opening combines subtle to obvious images of an "unwelcoming" wilderness—as dark behemoth—and foreshadows the forest's eventual destruction by settlers intent on conquering Nature. Proulx's 300-year saga starts with the arrival of the Europeans in Canada's pristine forest and ends with a largely decimated forest under the veil of global warming.

Within the first ten pages we gain a rich and potent collage of first impressions by the settlers of "the moody darkness" of the New France forest, previously only seen by the "*sauvages.*" The barkskins "tramped up the muddy path toward a line of black mist ... In a few hours the sodden leaf mold gave way to pine duff. Fallen needles muted their passage, the interlaced branches absorbed their panting breaths ... evergreens larger than cathedrals, cloud-piercing spruce and hemlock. The monstrous deciduous trees stood distant from each other, but overhead their leaf-choked branches merged into a false sky, dark and savage ...They walked on through the dim woods, climbing over mossy humps, passing under branches drooping like funeral swags," hearing pines hissing in the wind," and crossing "snarling water," and "swarms of mosquitoes in such millions that their shrill keening was the sound of the woods."[29]

These bleak impressions of a harsh environment crawling with pests such as *bébites* and *moustiques* underlie the combative mindset of the settlers to conquer and seize what they can of a presumed infinite resource. By page seventeen, we know that mindset well. René asks why they must cut so much forest when it would be easier to use the many adequate clearings to build their houses and settlements. Trépagny fulminates: "Easier? Yes, easier, but we are here to clear the forest, to subdue this evil wilderness." He further explains the concept of property ownership that is based on strips of surveyable land parcels—an application of the enclosure system. For them, the vast Canadian boreal forest was never-ending and for the taking: "It is the forest of the world. It is infinite. It twists around as a snake swallows its own tail and has no end and no beginning,"[29] Trépagny claims.

Ever mindful of the importance of place, Proulx even includes subtle reference to it when first describing her main characters. Main character, René Sel is illiterate but must sign a contract to ratify his indenture with the seigneur:

> *At his turn René made not only an X but the letter R—marred by a spatter of ink from the quill—a letter which he had learned in childhood from the old priest who said it was the beginning of René, his name. But the priest had died of winter starvation before he could teach him the succeeding letters.*[29]

Of the seigneur, Monsieur Trépagny, she conveys much in her simple description of his gait: "He did not so much walk as hurl himself along on his varied legs, one limber, one stiff."[29]

3.4.2 First Impressions of Trees, Cities, Fire & Water

Richard Powers starts his eco-fiction novel *The Overstory* about the destruction of the forests with this opening:

> *First there was nothing. Then there was everything.*

> *Then, in a park above a western city after dusk, the air is raining messages. A woman sits on the ground, leaning against a pine. Its bark presses hard against her back, as hard as life. Its needles scent the air and a force hums in the heart of the wood. Her ears tune down to the lowest frequencies. The tree is saying things, in words before words.*[30]

This strongly personified opening lures the reader into the existentialism

of Power's story: of trees with spirit, soul, and timeless societies. The opening 143
reveals a grand story of fractal layers from the tree spirits down to the human avatars.

George Orwell's dystopian novel *Nineteen Eighty Four* opens with:

> *It was a bright cold day in April, and the clocks were striking thirteen. Winston Smith, his chin nuzzled into his breast in an effort to escape the vile wind, slipped quickly through the glass doors of Victory Mansions, though not quickly enough to prevent a swirl of gritty dust from entering along with him.*[31]

The cold dirty wind of the April day symbolizes the oppressive political and social environment of Winston's miserable world. Of course, Winston will not be quick enough to escape the vile wind that pursues his rebellion and ultimate entrapment.

In the opening of my eco-science fiction novel *Darwin's Paradox*, the protagonist, who has been exiled to the outer wasteland, dreams longingly of her AI partner and the inner city where she grew up:

> *Julie walks SAM's crystal matrix, gazing at the shimmering of purple and green logic along the passageways. She imagines herself a creature of coloured light, a pilgrim like Dante, who wanders SAM's vast and ordered crystal landscape in search of home. SAM used to "live" in her head back in Icaria. Her A.I. partner...her best friend...This must be a dream then, she thinks.*[32]

Symbols hint at her yearning for the order and community of the city from which she had to flee, suggesting unfinished business in a place she still considers home.

In his science fiction dystopian novel *Fahrenheit 451*, about censorship and suppression of creativity, Ray Bradbury opens with:

> *It was a pleasure to burn.*

> *It was a special pleasure to see things eaten, to see things blackened and changed. With the brass nozzle in his fists, with this great python spitting its venomous kerosene upon the world, the blood pounded in his head, and his hands were the hands of some amazing conductor playing all the symphonies of blazing and burning to bring down the tatters and charcoal ruins of history. With his symbolic helmet numbered 451 on his solid head, and his eyes all orange flame with the thought of what came next, he flicked the*

igniter and the house jumped up in a gorging fire that burned the evening sky red and yellow and black. He strode in a swarm of fireflies. He wanted above all, like the old joke, to shove a marshmallow on a stick in the furnace, while the flapping pigeon-winged books died on the porch and lawn of the house. While the books went up in sparkling whirls and blew away on a wind turned dark with burning.

Montag grinned the fierce grin of all men singed and driven back by flame.

He knew that when he returned to the firehouse, he might wink at himself, a minstrel man, burnt-corked, in the mirror. Later, going to sleep, he would feel the fiery smile gripped by his face muscles, in the dark.[33]

This powerful opening foreshadows a complex journey for fireman Montag, who betrays a yearning for more and shows potential for change. Fire is a strong symbol of creative destruction; fire creates in its destruction the opportunity for renewal and the germination of seeds in Nature. In referencing himself to music and other creative pursuits, Montag betrays a clever spirit and strong urge for original thought and creativity—something the ordered society wishes to suppress and something which foreshadows his conflict and journey.

My short story *The Way of Water*—about a young woman struggling in near-future Toronto under the wave of water shortage—begins with water:

She imagines its coolness gliding down her throat. Wet with a lingering aftertaste of fish and mud. She imagines its deep voice resonating through her in primal notes; echoes from when the dinosaurs quenched their throats in the Triassic swamps.

Water is a shape shifter.

It changes yet stays the same, shifting its face with the climate. It wanders the earth like a gypsy, stealing from where it is needed and giving whimsically where it isn't wanted.

Dizzy and shivering in the blistering heat, Hilda shuffles forward with the snaking line of people in the dusty square in front of University College where her mother used to teach. The sun beats down, crawling on her skin like an insect. She's been standing for an hour in the queue for the public water tap. Her belly aches in deep waves, curling her body forward.[22]

Hilda is dying of thirst two metres from a water source. She recognizes the irony of water—this anomalous, steadfast yet moving substance that baffles and confuses as it comforts and nourishes. Hilda's fate is tightly woven with water, whose fate at the vagaries of geopolitical intrigue, corporate technology and greed is elusive and ironic. As with water, Hilda's fate will challenge her concept of existentialism.

3.5 PLACE AND EMOTION

Place may amplify a character's emotions or contradict them, depending on the circumstance of your character, her mood, disposition, tendencies and observational skills. And the kind of story you're telling. Either way, setting provides an "emotional landscape" upon which a character's own temperament may play counterpoint or may resonate in a wonderful symphony. Always think of the less obvious; think of contrast and how you can increase tension and emphasize the character's situation.

For instance, if your character has just moved east from the west and is homesick, the setting can act as her ally by commiserating and sharing her misery in weeping rain. Or the setting may provide an otherwise cheerful setting of bright azure sky and brilliant fall colors that plays the role of villain, its empty crispness mocking her sadness and her ache for the sultry smells of home: even the weather doesn't share her misery; she is utterly alone.

POV characters bring their mood to a scene. The action that unfolds provides cues to the character's sentiments. Sometimes, the action or event can trigger a dramatic change to a character's perspective. This is the case in Lynda La Plante's crime novel *Above Suspicion*, when DS Anna Travis discovers that a stranger has been in her flat after she's just been assigned to help solve her first murder case:

> *Reaching for the bedside lamp, she stopped and withdrew her hand. The photograph of her father had been turned out to face the room. She touched it every night before she went to sleep. It was always facing towards her, towards the bed, not away from it. … In the darkness, what had felt safe before now felt frightening: the way the dressing-table mirror reflected the street-light through the curtains and the sight of the wardrobe door left slightly ajar.*[34]

3.5.1 Place and Point-Of-View

New York agent and writing coach, Donald Maass tells us that "when point-of-view is done well, place and perception are inextricably entwined. A place is filtered not only through the person, but through the person's age, social station, personality, and where they are in their life's development."[6]

Differing perceptions of the same place by different characters is superbly depicted in Thomas Hardy's *Return of the Native*. The perception of Egdon Heath ranges among its characters based on their relationship with it. Upon his return from Paris, Clym Yeobright (the native) embraces the heath to work the land as a furze-cutter. He loses most of his eyesight yet finds joy in his monotonous labour and the microscopic vision of the small animals and insects surrounding him as he works—effectively becoming:

> *A brown spot in the midst of an expanse of live-green gorse, and nothing more.*[35]

Clym romanticizes the heath as renewing and fresh and nonjudgmental in contrast to the "flashy" and "effeminate" Paris. Says Clym of the bleak heath:

> *To my mind it is most exhilarating and strengthening, and soothing. I would rather live on these hills than anywhere else in the world.* [35]

In contrast, Eustacia Vye—who had not succeeded in escaping the heath— maintains a very different relationship, one of a trapped prisoner, ever yearning to escape the barren confines of this wild dark tract of land. Of Egdon, she passionately declares, "Tis my cross, my shame, and will be my death!"

Hardy superlatively uses metaphor and symbols to show us these diametrically opposed relationships through a myriad of often subtle point-of-view observation and experience. The irony of Eustacia Vye was that she was a true creature of the heath, one in the same with Edgon. Her wish to escape might as well have been a wish to escape herself. Unconventional and considered a witch by the simple heath folk, Eustacia more resembled a pagan goddess, a goddess of the night, of Egdon in "the shady splendor of her beauty", her keeper. Egdon created her:

> *Eustacia Vye was the raw material of a divinity. On Olympus she would have done well with a little preparation. She had the passions and instincts which made a model goddess, that is, those which make not a model woman.*[35]

In the opening scene, one of the heath folk spots her solitary figure on
Rainbarrow, a hill associated with the Celts who are as old as Egdon Heath.
Showing a perfect unity with her surroundings, she stands as queen of the
heathland:

> Such a perfect, delicate and necessary finish did the figure give to the dark
> pile of hills that it seemed to be the only obvious justification of their outline.
> Without it, there was the dome without the lantern; with it the architectural
> demands of the mass were satisfied. The scene was strangely homogenous,
> in that the vale, the upland, the barrow, and the figure above it amounted
> only to unity.[35]

3.5.2 Place and Time

"Our perception of place changes as we change," Maass writes. "The difference between a town as remembered from long ago and how it seems now
is the difference between who we once were and who we are now. The same is
true of characters in fiction. Take them anywhere and show us how they feel
about the place, or how that place makes them feel, and you will reveal to us
volumes about their inner frozenness, or growth."[6]

In his novel *Brideshead Revisited* (1945), Evelyn Waugh creates a strong sense
of history through setting as protagonist Charles Ryder visits his friend's family mansion before and after World War II. The mansion—once illustrious and
grand—now takes on a ghostly, nostalgic character after damage and neglect
impose their changes.

Julian Barnes tells us that Canadian short story writer Alice Munro—win-
ner of the Nobel Prize—can move characters through time in a way that no
other writer can. "You are not aware that time is passing, only that it has
passed—in this, the reader resembles the characters, who also find that time
has passed and that their lives have been changed, without their quite understanding how, when, and why."

Linn Ullmann, author and daughter of Ingmar Bergman and actress Liv
Ullmann, whose "home" shifted often, felt herself resonating with the following passage in Munro's story *Face*:

> Something had happened here. In your life there are a few places, or maybe
> only one place, where something has happened. And then there are the other
> places, which are just other places.

The story enacts a strange love story centred on a boy who has a wine-colored birthmark over half his face. As a child, he makes friends with a girl about his age. Twice, she imitates his face—once, using red paint, and again later in a more permanent, devastating way. "She does this out of love, or a destructive thing that love can sometimes be: "I love you so much that I want to *be* you," Ullman shares.[36]

At the time, the gesture wounds the boy, and his family interprets it as an act of mocking cruelty. The two children are no longer permitted to see each other. It's only as an adult, when he learns of her second attempt to look like him by using a razor to cut his same mark on her face—that he comes to realize that the exchange in the basement was "a crucial moment of his life; even though he didn't realize it at the time, it may have been the closest he ever came to having his marred face looked upon honestly but without reproach, with something like love. But by the end of the story, we sense that this is what matters most to this character, as he looks back. After the revelation at the funeral, he decides not to sell the house where he grew up, where the exchange in the basement happened, as he had planned. Instead, he lives inside it for the rest of his life."[36]

That childhood house remains his reference point, the point of greatest significance, where something happened. "Those precious few settings where something *happened* are where meaning resides—they contain the story, they *are* the story," says Ullman. "Yes, I think that, to Alice Munro, story *is* place—the two are that deeply connected. You do not have a story of a life without an actual place. You can't separate one from the other."[36]

Ullman suggests that this is why Munro is "intensely local in her fiction, like many other great writers (Faulkner, Joyce, and Proust come straight to mind). Munro's stories unfold in remote places in Canada ... but in these geographically small places, whole worlds play out. The best writers provide a sense of events unfolding in this specific place, a place that informs and feeds the characters and events. What comes first: the place or the story? The story or the place? With great fiction, it can be impossible to distinguish."[36]

Exercise 6: Psychology of Place #2: Character on a Journey

1.   *Choose a main POV character in your story in a pivotal moment in their journey (a high moment, turning point, climax). Describe the place. How does the place make your character feel? Use as many senses as possible. Use metaphor, personification, etc. to describe mood, tone, feel with the place.*

_____

_____

_____

2.   *Move the story into the future (enough to have that POV character in a different stage in their journey) and have that character return to the same place. Describe the place again through that character's POV. How is it the same? How is it different? Use things that are obvious and things that are almost imperceptible.*

_____

_____

_____

3.   *Move the story to a while before that original pivotal moment in #1; describe that place then.*

_____

_____

_____

This exercise is adapted from Writing the Breakout Novel Workbook by Donald Maas. In the workbook Maass shares: "many participants like to use the paragraph they wrote in Step [2]. There is something powerful about returning to a place of significant action and discovering how it feels different. Did you ever return to a childhood home and find that it looked smaller to you?...By the same token, your protagonist will never feel the same way twice about a particular place."[6]

3.6 PLACE THROUGH THE SENSES

We have five major senses and several minor ones we aren't even consciously aware of. The major ones include sight, hearing, smell, touch, and taste. Other senses include: balance (equilibrioception), proprioception (knowing which parts of the body are where); kinaesthesia (sense of movement); and chronoception (sense of passing time). Yet others include intuition, sense of frequency (infrasound), and the "other."

In the April 2000 issue of *Fiction Writer* Janet Fitch, author of *White Oleander*, tells us that we are biologically and psychologically designed "for intense experience in a richly sensual world. But we find ourselves in a senses-depleted world, a world limited largely to visuals, and ersatz ones at that." She suggests that our readers are starving for sensual information. "For fiction writers, the senses are not only a window onto external reality, but also the gateway into the inner realms."[3]

Readers don't just "watch" a character in a book; they enter the character's body and "feel".

How do writers satisfy the readers' need to experience the senses fully? Description, yes. But how cold is cold? What does snow really smell like? What color is that sunset? How do you describe the taste of wine to a teetotaler?

Literal description is insufficient. To have the sense sink in and linger with the reader, it should be linked to the emotions and memories of the character experiencing it. By doing this, you are achieving several things at the same time: describing the sense as the character is experiencing it—emotionally; revealing additional information on the character through his/her reaction; and creating a more compelling link for the reader's own experience of the sense.

Senses can be explored by writers through metaphor, linking the sense to memories, using synesthesia (cross-sensory metaphor), linking the sense psychologically to an emotion or attitude, and relating that sense in a different way (e.g., describing a visual scene from the point of view of a painter or photographer—painting with light).

How a sense is interpreted by your protagonist relies on her emotional state, memories associated with that sense and her attitude.

Using baby powder as an example, Fitch suggests that you can "describe it literally: sweet, chalky, talcy, dusty, sneezy; or you can use synesthesia: smells pastel, smells tender. Then move to the psychological element. Take an attitude on that smell: insipid, cloying, stultifying, like diaper rash, airless. Try a different attitude: sad, lost, vulnerable, hopeless." This is a sense-impression based on a memory or emotional experience and pinned on that smell to create an entire sensation. What this does is reveal a great deal about the character in a seamless and powerful way, while establishing a rich setting to the story.[3]

3.6.1 Sense of Smell

The sense of smell was no doubt one of the first senses to evolve in living creatures; it told us what was safe to eat and whether danger lurked in the bushes nearby. Smell also affects behavior, such as finding a mate, synchronizing menstrual cycles, and communicating with the other animals in your group. Dr. Karl tells us that "women can tell (by the smell of swabs taken from the armpit) who has been watching happy or sad movies (men are not so good at this). A breast-feeding baby can differentiate the smell of his or her mother, from any other nursing mother. Dogs and horses can smell fear in humans."[3]

Taste and smell appear to linger most in memory and yet are often neglected by writers. According to the California Institute of Technology, smell is generally considered the sense tied most closely to human memory. Smell profoundly influences people's ability to recall past events and experiences. "A smell from your distant past can unleash a flood of memories that are so intense and striking that they seem real," says Dr. Karl (Kruszelnicki), author of *Great Moments in Science*. "This kind of memory, where an unexpected re-encounter with a scent from the distant past brings back a rush of memories, is called a 'Proustian Memory'."[3] In *Remembrance of Things Past*, Marcel Proust writes:

> When from a long-distant past nothing subsists, after the people are dead, after the things are broken and scattered, taste and smell alone, more fragile but more enduring, more immaterial, more persistent, more faithful, remain poised a long time, like souls.[37]

In this excerpt of *The Florist's Daughter* by Patricia Hampl, fragrance permeates with meaning:

> The flower shop was here and it was my father's domain, but it was also marvelously other, this place heavy with the drowsy scent of velvet-petaled roses and Provencal freesias in the middle of winter, the damp-earth spring fragrance of just-watered azaleas and cyclamen all mixed up with the headachey smell of bitter chocolate.[38]

In John Steinbeck's *East of Eden,* his main character recalls the following memories, through several evocative smells:

> *I remember my childhood names for grasses and secret flowers. I remember where a toad may live and what time the birds awaken in the summer — and what trees and seasons smelled like — how people looked and walked and smelled even. The memory of odors is very rich.*[39]

3.6.2 Place, Sense and Theme

A good example of using a cacophony of senses in literature to draw the reader right into the place is the following excerpt from Charles Dickens' *Hard Times:*

> *It was a town of red brick, or of brick that would have been red if the smoke and ashes had allowed it; but as matters stood, it was a town of unnatural red and black … It had a black canal in it, and a river that ran purple with ill-smelling dye, and vast piles of building full of windows where there was a rattling and a trembling all day long, and where the piston of the steam-engine worked monotonously up and down, like the head of an elephant in a state of melancholy madness.*[40]

In the same vein, in this scene from David Mitchell's novel *Number9dream,* a young boy—in Tokyo for the first time to find his missing father— collides with the claustrophobic closeness of the crowded inner city. The senses are evoked less directly. They are evoked more through imagery than literal description, linked through theme:

> *Tokyo is so up close you cannot always see it. No distances. Everything is over your head — dentists, kindergartens, dance studios. Even the roads and walkways are up on murky stilts. Venice with the water drained away.*[41]

The vicissitudes of weather and shifting moods of the city impact the boy's senses and ultimately foreshadow the struggles of his inner journey. In the excerpt below, the boy describes the same place after a typhoon had just struck:

> *One hour later and the Kita Street/Omekaido Avenue intersection is a churning confluence of lawless rivers. The rain is incredible. Even on Yakushima,*

we never get rain this heavy. The Holiday atmosphere has died, and the customers are doom-laden … Outside … a family of six huddles on a taxy roof. A baby wails and will not shut up.[41]

EXERCISE 7: Writing Sensually to Connect with Place

1.   *Think of a childhood memory that inspires powerful emotions. Describe it from as many senses as you can remember. Include the setting / place in your sensual description. What role did it play in making the experience memorable?*

2.   *List at least ten of your favorite smells. Use at least two of them in a scene of a story you are working on.*

3.   *Take one of them and describe it from the POV of several people with different emotional states and/or cultural backgrounds.*

_____
_____
_____
_____
_____
_____
_____
_____

Reference: *"The Fiction Writer: Get Published, Write Now!"* (Starfire World Syndicate) by Nina Munteanu, 2009.

3.7 PLACE THROUGH SYNESTHESIA

"A person with synesthesia might hear and taste her husband's voice as buttery golden brown, feel the flavor of food on her fingertips, sense the letter J as shimmering magenta or the number 5 as emerald green," says the introduction to David Eagleman and Richard Cytowic's 2009 book *Wednesday Is Indigo Blue*.[42]

In a strange and compelling May 2008 article in *Wired Magazine* entitled "Poetry Comes from Our Tree-Climbing Ancestors,"[43] Brandon Kelm asks where synesthesia comes from:

"Perhaps [synesthetes] are under the influence of hallucinogenic drugs ... Or maybe they're simply good with metaphors," he suggests irreverently. Kelm is actually pretty close to the truth, according to neuroscientist V.S. Ramachandran, who stressed that "what appears as metaphor is a literal sensory experience for synesthetes." This may explain why synesthesia is eight times more common among poets, artists, novelists and women than the general population. According to Eagleman and Cytowic, one in twenty people experiences synesthesia in a palpable form. [42]

According to Ramachandran, synesthesia developed to help our ancestors climb trees. "Doing so requires a vision-informed mental map of the branches before us," says Kelm, "as well as a touch-informed mental map of our limbs' positions. Somehow these have to correlate. Which is quite a trick, when you think about it. Once early primates pulled off that feat of abstraction, it wasn't long – evolutionarily speaking — before we were drawing on cave walls and whispering sweet nothings and holding Shakespeare revivals," Kelm adds pithily.[43]

According to Lakoff and Johnson, "[t]he essence of metaphor is understanding and experiencing one kind of thing in terms of another". However, "... metaphor is not just a matter of language, that is, of mere words. ... [O]n the contrary, human *thought processes* are largely metaphorical" (emphasis in original).[44]

We use synesthetic metaphors all the time, without thinking about it. Examples of cross-sensory (synesthetic) metaphors include: "loud shirt," "bitter wind" or "prickly laugh," "dark sounds" and "sweet smells." Many of these cross-sensory terms have been so often used to become cliché.

I first made intentional use of synesthesic metaphors in my space thriller trilogy *The Splintered Universe*. The main protagonist was the human galactic detective Rhea Hawke, who as a young girl had been tecked with the ability to smell emotions. The premise opened an entire suite of delicious possibilities to describe feelings and emotions through metaphoric imagery and cross-senses

156 (another reason I so love the genre of science fiction). In the following scene from Book 1 of the trilogy, *Outer Diverse*, Rhea goes against her first rule of engagement and lets a man into her life:

> *"Rhea, stay with me, here," Serge whispered into my hair with sudden excitement. "Move in. Stay." I smelled his enticing fragrance of strawberries and musk and knew what I wanted to say.*
>
> *"I'll think about it."[8]*

In the next scene, Rhea challenges new boyfriend, Serge, whose past she knows nothing about and he responds:

> *His face flushed and he smiled carelessly. "I must have dreamt it," he said, emitting a burst of confusing aromas, a complex mixture of sweet meadow flowers, fishy smell of a lake, and the musk of bog and cottonwoods.[8]*

Having determined that Serge is not an innocent bystander but a calculating spy, Rhea chases him in the scene below to haul him into the precinct:

> *Then I spotted Serge. He'd run to the far end of the room.*
>
> *Upon hearing me enter, he'd turned and met my gaze head on.*
>
> *"Rhea!" he shouted, obviously feigning delighted surprise.*
>
> *I knew he'd recognized me earlier during my pursuit. I'd smelled his spike of excitement. Now I felt him emit yet another smell, a rather pleasant mixture of fermenting fruit and young wine, and felt a thrill surge through me in response. I didn't show it and pointed my MEC steadily at his chest with my lips pursed in venomous resolution.* "A hunting dog will eventually lose its life on the mountain — *old Chinese proverb."* [8]

Cytowic and Eagleman argue that perception is already multisensory, though for most of us its multiple dimensions exist beyond the reach of consciousness. Reality, they point out, is more subjective than most people realize. Synesthesia is a window on the mind and brain; highlighting the amazing differences in the way people see the world. "The difference between synesthetic and nonsynesthetic brains is not whether cross talk exists" Cytowic and

Eagleman note "but rather its degree." [42]
    How about that tingly feeling you get when you hear music you like, or the fact that you salivate when you see salty food? Synesthesia.

3.8 PLACE AS ENVIRONMENTAL FORCE

Environmental forces—such as weather, climate, forests, mountains, water systems—convey the mood and tone of both story and character. These environmental forces are not just part of the scenery. To a writer, they are devices used in plot, theme and premise. They may also be a compelling character, particularly in eco-fiction, climate-fiction, and speculative fiction. Dystopian fiction often explores a violent world of contrast between the affluent and vulnerable poor that often portrays the aftermath of economic and environmental collapse (e.g., *Maddaddam Trilogy, The Windup Girl, Snowpiercer, Interstellar, Mad Max*). In any fiction genre it is important to get the science right. Readers of fiction with strong environmental components, however, expect to learn as much from the potential reality as from the real science upon which the premise depends.

3.8.1 Weather & Storms

Weather as described in story can provide powerful and compelling imagery. As a force of Nature, the ocean storm scenes from *The Life of Pi, The Old Man and the Sea, Mutiny on the Bounty* grip the reader. More subtle scenes of weather can however be equally compelling. The key is to link them to the POV character. Having character interact with environment as character will compel the reader in a meaningful way. This does two things: it creates the drama of a natural force of interest itself; more impactful is that it provides important information on the character through their interaction with it.

In Margaret Miles's *A Mischief in the Snow*, Captain Edmund Montagu—finally on his way home to his neglected beloved as he returns from a covert mission in Boston in 1766—encounters a snow storm in the countryside:

Edmund Montagu reined in his horse for perhaps the hundredth time, wondering how he had ever gotten himself into such a situation. Once he regained the road, he would find he village of Bracebridge. The builders had made enough cuts through the low hills to indicate where it might be, but

*he'd seen none of them for half an hour due to the snow—now, the increas-
ing gloom had turned to night. There was no point in going back. The wind
continued to hurl sheets of icy snow at the horse's tail. Because his lantern il-
luminated nothing more than what whirled around him, he'd begun to feel as
though he walked through an endless box, whose dull sides never changed.*[45]

The storm does far more than provide dramatic tension in a difficult journey. It reflects Montagu's inner conflict on the loss of his son and tardy home-
coming and creates an opportunity to confront the stormy nature of his decisions, his intolerance, stubbornness, pride and fear of showing weakness.

As a writer, be mindful not to overdo the use of weather as metaphor. Some
uses have become cliché (e.g., the dark storm of impending doom). Avoid the
obvious. Be creative. Be subtle. Use contrast. And remember to show rather
than tell. In an article for *Articlesbase*, Mark Walton suggests that one focus on
the changing light, textures, sounds and smells when considering any phenomenon to help convey story. Link these to the sub-text of the POV character's journey. When you're doing your research, ensure that you get your facts
straight; don't place a hurricane in a location it never occurs, unless it's meant
to be an oddity.[46]

3.8.2 Climate (Change)

Climate and its associated environment provides compelling and informative setting to story. As we read in Part I, climate does not occur in isolation
but in a two-way interchange between it and its environment. As example,
trees create rain and forests affect the global water cycle and climate through
carbon sink or loss.

A story set on the coast of an ocean will read differently than a story set
inland where sea water does not dominate the environment. From obvious to
subtle, elements of a coastal climate will imbue aspects of story and inform the
movements of its characters. Influences may include metaphoric and sensual
elements of ocean water and air to the physical attributes of the actual coast-
line. Is a character afraid of water and at the same time attracted to it? Can
they swim? Does the vast open sea free them or make them fearful? Given the
many symbolic qualities of water and the ocean as a vast body of water, the
possibilities for metaphoric revelation are endless.

In Annie Proulx's *Shipping News*, protagonist Quoyle returns to Newfoundland on the stormy Atlantic coast, where he chooses to write about boats and
water—despite being extremely fearful of water and storms (he can't swim).
Ironically, it is here, in this harsh and unforgiving place where Quoyle finds

the warmth of companionship and overcomes his many personal fears to accept himself and dare to hope.

For if Jack Buggit could escape from the pickle jar, if a bird with a broken neck could fly away, what else might be possible? Water may be older than light, diamonds crack in hot goat's blood, mountaintops give off cold fire, forests appear in mid-ocean, it may happen that a crab is caught with the shadow of a hand on its back, and that the wind be imprisoned in a bit of knotted string. And it may be that love sometimes occurs without pain or misery.[12]

Climate change has provided a strong premise for climate fiction from Emmi Itäranta's *Memory of Water* and Margaret Atwood's *Year of the Flood* to Kim Stanley Robinson's *New York 2140* and my own *A Diary in the Age of Water*.

Paolo Bacigalupi—who explores a near-future of water scarcity resulting from climate change and corporate greed and mismanagement—opens his speculative thriller *The Water Knife* with a strong water metaphor.

There were stories in sweat. The sweat of a woman bent double in an onion field, working fourteen hours under the hot sun, was different from the sweat of a man as he approached a checkpoint in Mexico, praying to La Santa Muerte that the federales weren't on the payroll of the enemies he was fleeing...Sweat was a body's history, compressed into jewels, beaded on the brow, staining shirts with salt. It told you everything about how a person had ended up in the right place at the wrong time, and whether they would survive another day.[47]

Bacigalupi's *The Water Knife* is set in a near-future drought-stricken American southwest, where corrupt state-corporations have supplanted the foundering national government. Where water is the new gold—to barter, steal, and murder for. Corporations have formed militias and shut down borders to climate refugees, fomenting an ecology of poverty and tragedy. Massive resorts—arcadias—constructed across the parched landscape, flaunt their water-wealth in the face of exploited workers and gross ecological disparity. Water is controlled by corrupt gangsters and "water knives" who cleverly navigate the mercurial nature of water rights in a world where "haves" hydrate and "have nots" die of thirst.

My novel *A Diary in the Age of Water* features the memoir of a Canadian limnologist, swept up in climate catastrophe and severe water shortage, resulting from water diversion by China and the United States. Limnologist Lynna laments Canada's lack of political stamina in deterring the Americans from taking all its water.

In the struggle for resources, there are always takers and there are always givers. When it comes to Canada, it's obvious which one we are. The USA, now basically run by China, cheerfully mines Canada's rain, along with its surface water, groundwater, ice and other resources. And Canada helps it along.

We are so darn polite.

This spring, CanadaCorp shut off all the house taps and forced us to buy water from the public iTaps. No one knows about the cistern and rainwater collection system I installed in my house. I'm sure that someone will revoke that right eventually. There is no free water.

The Water Management Authority is the umbrella organization for CanadaCorp and their policies are skewed towards USA's interests, not Canada's. And USA's policies are skewed towards China's interests. What does China want? Well, that's obvious. Particularly since the Tengger Desert, now the size of Bulgaria, has swept across Northern China. The encroaching desert with its intense sandstorms have eaten Beijing, scattering climate refugees to northern Mongolia.

I'm counting the days for Canada ...

Should Hilde and I be learning Mandarin and Cantonese?...[20]

3.8.3 The Desert of "The English Patient"

Michael Ondaatje's *The English Patient* uses the desert setting and the hot winds to evoke mood, tension, and theme; the setting ultimately paints an evocative picture of a character on a journey:

The desert could not be claimed or owned—it was a piece of cloth carried by winds, never held down by stones, and given a hundred shifting names long before Canterbury existed, long before battles and treaties quilted Europe and the East.[48]

Reflecting the properties of the desert, the main character—a map maker—refuses to be tied down in his roaming life. Intense, moody, and misunderstood by most, the map maker ironically seeks love but cannot hold it. Love, like the desert sands, slips through his fingers even as he clings to its shifting fabric.

3.8.4 The Wind of "Chocolat"

Wind serves as a strong metaphor to evoke theme and the vagaries of character in the opening of Joanne Harris's *Chocolat*:

> *We came on the wind of the carnival. A warm wind for February, laden with the hot greasy scents of frying pancakes and sausages and powdery-sweet waffles cooked on the hot plate right there by the roadside.* [49]

Like the wind that brings her to the small parochial community, Vianne yearns to settle but fears the consequences; she feels the pull of motion and new adventure. Her carefree spirit and deep connection to sensual pleasures eventually evoke the key conflict in the town that will trigger her own inner conflict of "belonging" and staying.

3.8.5 The Worms of "Dune"

The immense sandworms of Frank Herbert's *Dune* are strong archetypes of Nature—large and graceful creatures whose movements in the vast desert sands resemble the elegant whales of our oceans:

> *It came from their right with an uncaring majesty that could not be ignored. A twisting burrow-mound of sand cut through the dunes within their field of vision. The mound lifted in front, dusting away like a bow wave in water.* [50]

Misunderstood, except by the indigenous Fremen, the giant sandworms are targeted as a dangerous nuisance by the colonists—when, in fact, they are closely tied to the ecological cycles of the desert planet through water and spice.

3.9 CONNECTING CHARACTER WITH ENVIRONMENT

Strong relationships and linkages can be forged in story between a major character and an aspect of their environment (e.g., home/place, animal/pet, minor character as avatar/spokesperson for environment [e.g. often indigenous people]). In these examples the environmental aspect serves as symbol and metaphoric connection to theme. They can illuminate through the subtext of metaphor a core aspect of the main character and their journey: the *grounding nature* of the land of Tara for Scarlet O'Hara in *Gone With the Wind*; the white pine forests for the Mi'kmaq in *Barkskins*; The animals for Beatrix Potter of the Susan Wittig Albert series.

3.9.1 The Mi'kmaq & the White Pine Forest of "Barkskins"

Annie Proulx's *Barkskins* chronicles two immigrants who arrive in Canada in 1693 (René Sel and Charles Duquet) and their descendants over 300 years of deforestation of North America; a saga that starts with the arrival of the Europeans in pristine forest and ends with a largely decimated forest under the veil of global warming. "Barkskins" (woodcutters) are, in fact indentured servants who were brought from the Paris slums to the wilds of New France to clear the land, build and settle. Sel is forced to marry a native woman and their descendants live trapped between two cultures; Duquet runs away to become a fur trader and builds a timber empire.

The Mi'kmaq are interwoven with the land and the forest. Missionary Pere Crème, who studies language makes this observation of the natives and the forest:

> *He saw they were so tightly knitted into the natural world that their language could only reflect the union and that neither could be separated from the other. They seemed to believe they had grown from this place as trees grow from the soil, as new stones emerge aboveground in spring. He thought the central word for this tenet, weji-sqalia'timk, deserved an entire dictionary to itself.* [29]

In a letter to his sister Marguerite, he writes of the Mi'kmaq:

*One of the most curious of their attributes is their manner of regarding
Trees, Plants, all manner of Fish, the Moose and the Bear and others as their
Equals. Many of their tales tell of Women who marry Otters or Birds, or
Men who change into Bears until it pleases them to become Men again. In
the forest they speak of Toads and Beetles as acquaintances. Sometimes I feel
it is they who are teaching me... To them Trees are Persons. In vain I tell them
that Trees are for the uses of Men to build Houses and Ships.*[29]

The foreshadowing of doom for the magnificent forests is cast by the shadow of how settlers treat the Mi'kmaq people. The fate of the forests and the
Mi'kmaq are inextricably linked through settler disrespect for anything indigenous and a fierce hunger for "more" of the forests and lands. Ensnared by
settler greed, the Mi'kmaq lose their own culture and their links to the natural
world erode with grave consequence. In a pivotal scene, Noë, a Mi'kmaw descendent of René Sel, grows enraged when she sees a telltale change in her
brothers:

*The offshore wind had shifted slightly but carried the fading clatter of boots
on rock. They were wearing boots instead of moccasins. Noë knew what that
meant but denied it ... The men should be setting out to hunt moose, but
because of the boots she knew they were going to work for the French logger.*[29]

Achille, another Mi'kmaw descendent of René Sel, observes as he signs up
with a French logger:

*Men were chopping pine in hundreds of places. The big softwoods fell. New
seedlings burst up on cutover ground, but now there was a break in the
density of the woodland, and as new trees sprouted the species succession
shifted a little in each cutover tract. The forest began to alter in small ways.
It still lived but it was not what it had been. The forest was a grand resource
and it was both the enemy and wealth. Achille felt it was the same with the
Mi'kmaq; the white settlers used them and took them down.*[29]

From the opening of the novel, the natives are called sauvage just as Nature is considered an "evil wilderness." Both are to be subdued and controlled. Both are treated as less than what they are by the white settlers, who
truly wish only to use them as resource or tool. Sosep, a descendent of René
Sel tells his brother:

...we suffer advances from both French and English. The French see us as soldiers to fight for them, our woman good only for fucking. The priests see us as bounty for their God as we might see beaver skins. They do not see us as worthy people ... They do not understand that we are allies of the French king, but not his subjects ... Now the British greedily claim even more land than the French king gave that was not his to give.[29]

The great pines of the Gatineau forest are treated like the Mi'kmaq:

The Gatineau forest was noisy, echoing with ax blows and the rushing crackle of falling timber, with shouted warnings and orders. The axmen cut the great pines, but only a few in each plot were suitable for squaring. The rest were left to rot on the ground ... unwanted trees lay prostrate, severed branches everywhere, heaps of bark and mountains of chips ... There were so many trees, what did it matter? Maine men were used to waste—it was usual—but this was beyond anything even they had seen.

In the Penobscot settlement, the trees fell, tracks inched through the forests, only one or two then seven, then webs of trails that over the decades widened into roads. The roads were muddy, sometimes like batter, sometimes thick and clutching until late summer; when they metamorphosed into choking dust so fine it hung in the air long after a horse and carriage passed, settling on the grass as the English people settled on the land ... Fields of wheat and hay took the land, these fields enclosed by linked stumps, the root wads of the forest that had once stood there turned on their edges to bar the whiteman's cows and sheep.[29]

When Duke and Sons discovers the giant eastern white pine forest in Michigan off the Saginaw Trail, Lavinia Duke surveys her new acquisition with pure greed:

The endless procession of huge trees aroused a new sensation in Lavina—a powerful sense of ownership: they were her trees, she could cause these giants to fall and be devoured by the saws. She regarded their monolithic forms with scorn ... And the little birds that rested in them, her birds, her squirrels and porcupines, all of it.[29]

There is never enough ...

3.9.2 Rhea Hawke & the Blenoids of
"The Splintered Universe" Trilogy

The *Splintered Universe Trilogy* is a science fiction action-adventure that follows Galactic Guardian Rhea Hawke—a cynical and angry human—on her quest for the truth behind the massacre of a mysterious religious sect. What she finds is compassion and the truth about herself—with the help of a ferocious predator of the Upsilon 3 desert, the blenoid.

Background:
Rhea Hawke is a troubled, highly prejudiced and angry human detective in an all-alien force of Eosians. Despite her quest to make the world a better place, she is very disconnected from that world. Her reputation on the force is as a ruthless killer, an anti-social loner with no compassion. The rumor that she sold-out her partner—an alien—is borne out by her known anti-alien sentiments. One Eosian alien on the force created a cruel limerick about her: "Rhea, scare ya, wouldn't you cry? She kissed the baldies and made them die."

The blenoids are dog-like desert creatures with three sets of razor teeth and a reputation for their ferocious mad temperament; they are known to attack, tear up and eat anything, even their own kind. Blenoids are hunted for their meat and considered dull-witted, often loners and not socially organized. The myth surrounding blenoids is that they will attack anything, no matter what its size and tear it to shreds. They are known to rip one another apart in a frenzy of aroused anger or if they sense any weakness—natural selection at its cruelest. Given their reputation, a vernacular has emerged among the galactic community that uses them for various expletives for wild, dim-witted violent action: e.g., "have you gone blenoid? You can't do that!"; "You blenoid-shitting me?" "They don't give a blenoid's ass about you ... They'll feed you to the blenoids." "Don't lead me on a wild blenoid chase."

Metaphoric Connection:
In Book Two, *Inner Diverse*, Rhea has the opportunity in the wild to discover the blenoid's true nature. She has learned to shapeshift into one, which permits her to observe a group of hunting blenoids disgorge their hunted portions; each ate its equal share of the total catch, leaving disgorged meat for the ones that had been less successful:

> *Had I chanced on an anomaly? I dismissed it as unlikely; their behaviour was so ingrained. Then I remembered how the blenoids in Ka's compound had behaved. It was only during a confined feeding frenzy that blenoids truly acted like the mad creatures they'd been called. I concluded that while*

blenoids were vicious predators of other species, they only turned that viciousness on one another when placed in unnatural circumstances such as captivity. They were, in fact, an intelligent animal with a social order, oddly based on altruism. It was the exact opposite of what everyone thought a blenoid was. Reputations are often spread from a single truth wrongly interpreted and aggrandized to larger-than-life proportions ... I both rejoiced in [my discovery] and felt a kind of sadness for the blenoid who had been so maligned and misunderstood.[51]

Rhea finds compassion for the plight of the blenoid as she personally experiences how these misunderstood creatures are cruelly treated by hunters who have brought them to near extinction. She resonates with their lack of voice; this is subtly reflected in the loss of her own voice after travelling the hot expanse of the desert. When faced with the summary execution of her companion, her parched throat prevents her from stopping it.

EXERCISE 8: Connecting a Main Character with a Minor Character (mirrored plotlines)

1. **A.** *Choose one of the following: 1) minor character of interest; 2) a place; 3) a development. Ensure that your selection experiences change or movement during the course of the story.*
B. *Map the "journey" of your main protagonist alongside the minor character's journey.*
C. *Draw a connecting line between the stage of each journey, if they interact and influence the other in some way. Summarize what that is on the connecting line.*

2. *How does the interaction (e.g., conflict, learning, empathy, etc.) reflect the journey of the other character? If there is no interaction, explore how one reflects the other without it.*

Protagonist:	Minor character:

By increasing the linkages between your main character and his/her environment (including all other characters, setting and world, and circumstances), you provide a richer, deeper, more meaningful and ultimately more interesting platform for story.

3.10 SACRED PLACES

What makes a place sacred?

T.H. McLuhan describes sacred places as "landscapes of the holy, as centres of inspiration where human consciousness is temporarily set free … [to experience] a re-entry into a state of wholeness—an introduction to your true origins … [These places are] paths to the very heart of human existence."[52] Is this not the ultimate destiny of the hero's journey toward wholeness?

Scholars agree that sacred places are almost always ancient, holy, and living repositories of sacred images and eternal truths that resonate with the human spirit. They are often mysterious and without clear origin or original purpose—like the megalithic stones of Carnac in Brittany or the King's chamber in the Great Pyramid. What is sacred to one may not be sacred to another, however. Different cultures imbue different spiritual values on things. In the 13th century, the desecration of pagan sacred sites along the Baltic Sea by the Teutonic Order was enacted by the Christian knights with no guilt or remorse; they did not consider them sacred—or important.

Given that the origin of the word *sacred* (holy) comes from "whole," sacred landscapes and natural phenomena are ideal settings for strong metaphor and connection to deeper layers of story.

In *The Spirit of Place*, D.H. Lawrence tells us that:

> *Every great locality has its own pure daimon [attendant spirit], and is conveyed at last into perfected life … Every great locality expresses itself perfectly, in its own flowers, its own birds and beasts, lastly its own men, with their perfected works. Mountains convey themselves in unutterable expressed perfection in the blue gentian flower and in the edelweiss flower, so soft, yet shaped like snow-crystals. The very strata of the earth come to a point of perfect, unutterable concentration in the inherent sapphires and emeralds. It is so with all worlds and all places of the world.*[53]

Author Kathleen Norris recounts how an improbable landscape and contradiction in the *Plains of Dakota* open a window to sacredness:

> *A person is forced inward by the sparseness of what is outward and visible in all the land and sky. The beauty of the Plains is like that of an icon; it does not give an inch of sentiment or romance. The flow of the land, with its odd twists and buttes, is like the flow of Gregorian chant that rises and falls beyond melody, beyond reason or human expectation, but perfectly. Maybe*

seeing the Plains is like seeing an icon; what seems stern and almost empty
is merely open, a door into some simple and holy state.[54]

Scholar and ecologist Thomas Berry writes of his discovery when a young boy of an obscure meadow in the Appalachians that provided a moment of clarity and inspiration which he took with him in his remaining life:

> *It was an early afternoon in May when I first looked down over the scene and saw the meadow. The field was covered with lilies rising above the thick grass. A magic moment, this experience gave to my life something. I know not what, that seems to explain my life at a more profound level than almost any other experience that I can remember. It was not only the lilies. It was the singing of the crickets and the woodlands in the distance and the clouds in the clear sky. It was not something conscious that happened just then. I went on about my life as any young person might do. Perhaps it was not simply this moment that made such a deep impression upon me. Perhaps it was a sensitivity that was developed throughout my childhood. Yet as the years pass this moment returns to me.*[55]

Novelist Gretel Ehrlich reflects on how we may recognize the nature of sacred landscape:

> *The ways in which we come to know a landscape are preliterate. "A sense of place" implies a sensory knowledge. It mounts up in our minds, empires of smells and sounds, textures and sights held fast by memory, flooding back again and again in such urgent, pungent ways so as to let us reenter those places. A river slits its neck for us; the eerie sound a sandhill crane makes comes into our human throats as song; in the mountain fastness of granite cracks, a pine tree grows ... All during our lives, in any and every place we live or visit, the sacramental landscape unrolls before us. It is our text. It is public and private, social and wild, political and aesthetic. To see—that is, to discover—is not an act of interpretation, of transfixing with preconceived ideas what is before us; rather, it is an act of surrender.*[56]

In this passage from his essay *Walking*, Henry David Thoreau wrote:

> *When I would recreate myself, I seek the darkest wood, the thickest and most interminable and, to the citizen, most dismal swamp. I enter a swamp as a sacred place—a sanctum sanctorum. There is the strength, the marrow of*

Nature. The wild-wood covers the virgin mould—and the same soil is good for men and trees.[57]

3.11 TIPS FOR SETTING & PLACE IN STORY

The following tips summarize key points to look for when describing place and setting in your story:

- *Don't tack setting in*: make it an integral part of the story. By linking place to theme, the story resonates with deeper meaning
- *Don't describe setting all at once* in the beginning: work it in slowly throughout the story
- *Describe selectively* and with purpose: do this through integration in scene rather than exposition
- *Be specific*: soft pink rose, not flower; beat up Chevy, not car; old clapboard cottage, not house
- *Use metaphors*, similes, personification to describe setting; this ensures meaningful description rather than literal description
- *Use the senses* like sight, sound, smell, taste, feel
- Don't tell, *show*: don't say the time is the 1940s; show the cars, radios, dresses. Don't tell the reader it's raining; show them by describing the dripping trees
- *Compare and contrast* settings: relate these to the POV characters

FOUR ... Three Case Studies

4.1 THOMAS HARDY'S EGDON HEATH

Perhaps best known for his melancholic stories of fatalistic, ironic tyrannies, Victorian author Thomas Hardy wrote with a tender and poetic sensibility about Nature, and particularly the heath where he grew up. All of Hardy's writings embody a strong sense of place. Nature—like his omniscient narrative form—lies beyond the scope of humanity: vast, amoral, existentialist and unfathomed by humanity; and yet, inextricably linked to the feckless actions of its humans. Egdon Heath in *Return of the Native* remains one of Hardy's most enduring characters and best examples of the power of place in story.

Hardy opens the novel with a compelling sensual description of his main character:

A Saturday afternoon in November was approaching the time of twilight, and the vast tract of un-enclosed wild known as Egdon Heath embrowned itself moment by moment. Overhead the hollow stretch of whitish cloud shutting out the sky was as a tent which had the whole heath for its floor ... It could best be felt when it could not clearly be seen, its complete effect and explanation lying in this and the succeeding hours before the next dawn: then, and only then, did it tell its true tale ... the somber stretch of rounds and hollows seemed to rise and meet the evening gloom in pure sympathy, the heath exhaling darkness as rapidly as the heavens precipitated it. And so the obscurity in the air and the obscurity in the land closed together in a black fraternization ... The place became full of a watchful intentness now; for when other things sank brooding to sleep, the heath appeared slowly to awake and listen. Every night its Titanic form seemed to await something; but it had waited thus, unmoved, during so many centuries, through the crisis of so many things, that it could only be imagined to await one last crisis—the final overthrow.[35]

Every verb, adjective, adverb and noun personifies. The heath is not simply there; it moves and shivers with attitude and intention. It is alive. Further down the page, Hardy hints at human perception: "Egdon appealed to a subtler and scarcer instinct, to a more recently learned emotion than that which responds to the sort of beauty called charming and fair ... The untameable Ishmaelitish thing that Egdon now was it always had been. Civilization was its enemy, and ever since the beginning of vegetation its soil had worn the same antique brown dress, the natural and invariable garment of the particular formation. In its venerable one coat lay a certain vein of satire of human vanity in clothes."[35] Hardy then hints at ominous foreshadowing: "Singularly colossal and mysterious in its swarthy monotony, [Egdon] ... had a lonely face, suggesting tragic possibilities."

Egdon Heath is a metaphoric black hole from which no light escapes. None of Hardy's characters escape the embrace of this behemoth. Dark, swarthy and associated with the night: "The face of the heath by its mere complexion added half an hour to evening; it could in like manner retard the dawn, sadden noon, anticipate the frowning storms scarcely generated, and intensify the opacity of a moonless midnight to a cause of shaking dread." Each character is touched by its brooding grip and each feels its power differently: hapless Wildeve; idealist Clym; desperate Eustacia and suffering Thomasin.

In the following passage, Thomas Hardy reveals Egdon's subtle minutiae as the wind plays on its surfaces in a dark symphony:

The wind, indeed, seemed made for the scene, as the scene seemed made for the hour. Part of its tone was quite special; what was heard there could be heard nowhere else. Gusts in innumerable series followed each other from the northwest, and when each one of them raced past the sound of its progress resolved into three. Treble, tenor, and bass notes were to be found therein. The general ricochet of the whole over pits and prominences had the gravest pitch of the chime. Next there could be heard the baritone buzz of a holly tree. Below these in force, above them in pitch, a dwindled voice strove hard at a husky tune, which was the peculiar local sound alluded to. Thinner and less immediately traceable than the other two, it was far more impressive than either. In it lay what may be called the linguistic peculiarity of the heath ... Throughout the blowing of these plaintive November winds that note bore a great resemblance to the ruins of human song, which remain to the throat of fourscore and ten. It was a worn whisper, dry and papery, and it brushed so distinctly across the ear that, by the accustomed, the material minutiae in which it originated could be realized as by touch. It was the united products of infinitesimal vegetable causes, and these were neither stems, leaves, fruit, blades, prickles, lichen, nor moss. They were the mummied heath bells of the

past summer, originally tender and purple, now washed colourless by Mich-
aelmas rains, and dried to dead skins by October suns.[35]

The power of Egdon Heath is best revealed through Eustacia Vye, its trapped soul—and errant mistress. She who roams Egdon's hills in the darkest hours, surveilling it with royal disdain.

Ironically, Eustacia best represents Egdon's soul, despite her passion for escape. She too is dark, difficult and mysterious—and indifferent to the heath dwellers. Holding herself superior like a pagan goddess, she—like the brooding heath—is a highly sensual creature, with animal-like sensibilities.

She had pagan eyes of nocturnal mysteries, and their light, as it came and went and came again was hampered by their oppressive lids and lashes; and these the under lid was much fuller than it usually is with English women."
... Her hair "closed over her forehead like nightfall extinguishing the western glow ... Her nerves extended into those tresses, and her temper could always be softened by stroking them down. When her hair was brushed she could instantly sink into stillness and look like the Sphinx. If, in passing under one of the Egdon banks, any of its thick skeins were caught, as sometimes were, by a prickly tuft of the large Elex Europoeus—which will act as a sort of hairbrush—she would go back a few steps, and pass against it a second time ... The mouth seemed formed less to speak than to quiver, less to quiver than to kiss. Some might have added, less to kiss than to curl ... So fine were the lines of her lips that, though full, each corner of her mouth was as clearly cut as the point of a s spear. The keenness of corner was only blunted when she was given over to sudden fits of gloom, one of the phases of the night side of sentiment which she knew too well for her years.

Her presence brought memories of such things as Bourbon roses, rubies, and tropical midnight; her moods recalled lotus-eaters and the march in Athalie; her motions, the ebb and flow of the sea; her voice, the viola. In a dim light, and with a slight rearrangement of her hair, her general figure might have stood for that of either of the higher female deities. The new moon behind her head, an old helmet upon it, a diadem of accidental dewdrops round her brow, would have been adjuncts sufficient to strike the note of Artemis, Athena, or Hera respectively, with as close an approximation to the antique as that which passes muster on many respected canvases.[35]

The superstitious women of the heath, like Susan Nunsuch, believe her a witch:

Egdon was her Hades, and since coming there she had imbibed much of what was dark in its tone, though inwardly and eternally unreconciled thereto. Her appearance accorded well with this smoldering rebelliousness, and the shady splendour of her beauty was the real surface of the sad and stifled warmth within her. A true Tartarean dignity sat upon her brow, and not factitiously or with marks of constraint, for it had grown in her with years.[35]

Her relationship with Egdon was more like a lover's. She was its reluctant queen, ensnared among its barbs and always looking romantically afar.

To dwell on a heath without studying its meanings was like wedding a foreigner without learning his tongue. The subtle beauties of the heath were lost to Eustacia; she only caught its vapours. An environment which would have made a contented woman a poet, a suffering woman a devotee, a pious woman a psalmist, even a giddy woman thoughtful, made a rebellious woman saturnine.[35]

"To be loved to madness—such was her great desire. Love was to her the one cordial which could drive away the eating loneliness of her days. And she seemed to long for the abstraction called passionate love more than for any particular lover."

Perhaps on some level, Eustacia comes to represent both the plight of women and of Nature; throughout the novel and to its conclusion, she remains caught between competing forces—fate and free will, love and hate, the past and the present, the countryside and the city. Such complexity is reflected in the heath, which has the simultaneous capacity for beauty and horror and whose wild face is slowly being encroached and changed by the settlers.

Eustacia can no more escape the heath than herself: a woman indentured to her male counterparts, who truly determine her station and movements. Women during the Victorian times of Hardy's story were certainly not given the same breadth of movement, choice and autonomy as men. This is reflected in Clyn's ability to freely move in and out of the heath but Eustacia's desperate dependence on her male suiters Clym and Wyldeve for her movements. In the end, there's no contest between the two human males—mere shadows to the virile heath—and the powerful behemoth Egdon. Her fate is sealed.

4.2 FRANK HERBERT'S DESERT

Frank Herbert's *Dune* chronicles the journey of young Paul Atreides, Duke Leto's son, who according to the indigenous Fremen prophesy will eventually bring them freedom from their enslavement by the colonialists—The Harkonens—and allow them to live unfettered on the planet Arrakis, known as Dune. But, as the title of the book clearly reveals, this story is about place—a harsh desert planet whose 800 kph sandblasting winds could flay your flesh—and the power struggle between those who covet its arcane treasures and those who wish only to live free from slavery. Place—and its powerful symbols of desert, water and spice—lies at the heart of this epic story about taking, giving and sharing. When he thinks of Dune, the newly placed Duke Atreides uses water metaphors: "He sighed, glanced back at the dry landscape where the flowers were gone now—trampled by the dew gatherers, wilted under the early sun."[50]

The Atreides family have come from water-rich Caladan at the command of the Emperor to take over the spice mining operation on Arrakis (Dune) from the Harkonens, colonialist predators who refuse to relinquish their fief because they covet the spice for themselves. Called mélange, the cinnamon-scented spice is found only on this desolate desert planet and is the most prized substance in the universe; it extends life, expands consciousness, and is vital to space travel. Aside from acquiring spice, the Harkonens care little for the planet and less for its native population, who they consider a nuisance and wish to exterminate. In their oppression of the native Fremen, the Harkonens reflect an oppression of the desert and its very ecology—and a misunderstanding of Arrakis's intricate connections to well-being and to spice. Despite the desert belt and the south polar regions being marked by the colonists as uninhabitable—due to storms and giant worms—Fremen inhabit them.

Paul—who early on shows an arcane understanding of the desert—will form a bridge with not only the indigenous Fremen but with the planet. When he first sets out into the desert, wearing the Fremen stillsuit—which keeps him hydrated by recycling his body moisture—Paul intuitively puts the suit on correctly; he needs no adjustment, prompting the question from the planetary ecologist: "You've worn a stillsuit before?" No, says Paul, who seems to wear it like a second skin—as though born to it. When he first encounters a worm up close, he is thrilled more than frightened:

> ...*a silver-gray curve broached from the desert, sending rivers of sand and dust cascading all around. It lifted higher, resolved into a giant, questing mouth. It was a round, black hole with edges glistening in the moonlight. The mouth snaked toward the narrow crack where Paul and Jessica huddled.*

Cinnamon yelled in their nostrils. Moonlight flashed from crystal teeth. Back and forth the great mouth wove ... Paul felt a kind of elation ... The landscape had undergone a profound shifting.[50]

Paul quickly intuits the intimate connection of the native Fremen with the huge 400-metre long desert sandworms that roam the desert, attracted by vibration and sound and upon which the Fremen ride like dragons; he also makes the connection of the giant worms (called *shai-hulud*) to the cinnamon-scented spice *mélange*, recognizing that the worms are "guarding" the spice deposits from interlopers as they look for prey. His greatest discovery is that *Mélange* is a byproduct of the life cycle of the giant sandworms, which created and maintain the desert and require the arid climate for their survival.

It begins with the ancient sandswimmers (sandtrout associated with a previous water environment) that blocked off water to create a desert "ocean" with waves of sand dunes; these give way to the giant sandworms (*shai-hulud*) for which water is poisonous. Fremen lure the giant worms to scatter spice for the sand plankton upon which the worms feed. The plankton, in turn, grow and burrow to become "Little Makers" (half-plant-half-animal precursors of the Arrakis sandworm). The flat and leathery Little Makers (also called "sandtrout" or "water stealers") block off water "into fertile pockets within the porous lower strata" and are capable of forming living cisterns of water. The sandtrout attracts water to it and its excretions, when flooded with incoming water, forms a pre-spice mass—a fungusoid wild growth of gases—which rise from deep underground to eventually "blow" on the surface. With exposure to sun and air, the mass becomes mélange. The sandtrout die in the millions with each "spice blow" and the few survivors hibernate as semi-dormant cysts, emerging six years later as small sandworms—to eventually become the colossal sandworms to whom water is poisonous. Fremen breed the small worms and drown stunted worms to make the awareness-spectrum narcotic they call Water of Life. The digestive factory of a giant sandworm with high concentrations of aldehydes and acids gives off a cinnamon aroma and is responsible for creating high amounts of oxygen.

The subtle connections of the desert planet with the drama of *Dune* is most apparent in the actions, language and thoughts of the Imperial ecologist-planetologist, Kynes—who rejects his Imperial duties to "go native." Self-professed "steward of the sands," he is the voice of the desert and, by extension, the voice of its native people, the Fremen. As with all Fremen, Kynes embraces the Fremen saying: "polish comes from the cities, wisdom from the desert." He understands the role that water plays as part of a delicate balance of giving, taking and sharing. "It is said in the desert that possession of water in great amount can inflict a man with fatal carelessness,"[50] says Kynes to a presumptuous water-shipper. Calling it a rule of ecology, Kynes says, "the struggle between life elements is the struggle for the free energy of a system." He may have well been talking about the struggling Fremen or the desert habitat equally threatened by excessive mining and destruction. "The highest function of ecology is understanding consequences," he later thinks to himself as he is dying in the desert, abandoned there without water or protection by the Harkonens.

Dune is just as much about what it lacks (water) as it is about what it contains (desert and spice).

The planet, says Kynes, "demands a special attitude toward water. You are aware of water at all times. You waste nothing that contains moisture."[50] This water-centricity includes a strange ceremony enacted by the Fremen to retrieve the water of their dead to reuse. "A dead man, surely, no longer requires that water." When she sheds tears on hearing of the death of her mate, Jessica thinks in hurt anger, "What a stupid waste of a body's water." Just like a Fremen. When Paul cries over a useless killing, the Fremen are inordinately impressed with his choice to give away his water. For the Fremen, success in battle is not measured in blood spilled but in "water spilled." When they speak of a place where a person belongs, they describe it as "the place of his water." [50]

Reacting to the Duke's almost cavalier attitude to the environment of Arrakis, Kynes coldly states, "You never talk of likelihoods on Arrakis. You speak only of possibilities."[49] And the possibilities are endless. They all have to do with the harsh desert climate, its treacherous sands and the huge sandworms that grow up to 450 metres in the deep desert. As if conspiring with the worms against intruders who don't belong, the sands themselves hide an arsenal of subversive weapons. Compacted sand called "drum sand" starts to drum at the slightest step—bringing the worms. A depression of centuries-settled sand so vast that it contains currents and tides is called a "tidal dust basin." Unwary intruders who stray into these are swallowed up. Though not described in the book, one can easily deduce that their flailing attempts to escape also attract this great sand predator.

Through its harsh complexity, the desert planet asserts great power on its inhabitants' core identity: "Arrakis makes us moral and ethical," says the Duke not long before he is betrayed and killed. He adds, "On Caladin, we ruled with sea and air power … Here, we must scrabble for desert power."[50] Much of that means water, understanding the desert ecology, the nature of the sands, the role of the sandworms, and the native Fremen who ride them. Fremen respect the giant worms that dominate the dunes; but Fremen fear the uncontrollable vicissitudes of the wind and its companion, the flaying sand.

Like true indigenous peoples, the Freman embrace their environment as part of them. This is reflected in how they view themselves—as a single "or-

178 ganism" bound by water. The Fremen say, "A man's flesh is his own; the water belongs to the tribe." This is remarkably demonstrated in their custom of sharing their water. After a skirmish in which many of the Duke's men are wounded, one of the men asks Stilgar, a Fremen leader, if his party can help their wounded. Stilgar responds, "What do your wounded say? Are there those among them who can see the water need of your tribe." The Duke's man doesn't understand that Stilgar is suggesting a water decision. Stilgar tries to clarify: "How many of your wounded would you spend ... Your wounded know you have no water. Both wounded and unwounded must look to the tribe's future." He is implying, of course, that some could sacrifice their water for the tribe. "Let our tribes be joined" through the bond of water, says Stilgar. Once bonded through water-sharing, the two "tribes" are now one tribe—literally. In the same manner, wild Fremen are not adverse to ambushing unsuspecting travelers and killing them for their water.

Following the treacherous attack of the Harkonnens, Paul and his mother flee directly into a deadly sandstorm—Paul maneuvers their vehicle into a vortex that snatches it and spews it up and out like a grain of drifting sand. "Paul looked down, saw the dust-defined pillar of hot wind that had disgorged them, saw the dying storm trailing away like a dry river into the desert." His mother concludes: "We faced it and did not resist. The storm passed through us and around us. It's gone, but we remain."[50] This is because on some level Paul *is the storm.*

"The desert stretched out like a static ocean." The open desert "lay there full of moon-silvered waves—shadows of angles that lapsed into curves and, in the distance, lifted to the misted gray blur of another escarpment." [50] When a sandworm approaches them, they hear a hissing and see a twisting burrow-mound of sand cut through the dunes with the mound lifted in front and dusting away like a bow wave: "It came from their right with an uncaring majesty that could not be ignored." [50]

Paul gradually pieces the ecology of planet and Fremen together, recognizing their ambitious attempts to create a balance of desert and vegetation by creating great water reservoirs. The plan is to restore some of the original wetlands of Arrakis while maintaining significant desert for the worms.

When the desert triggers Paul's last stage in his transition into the force he is destined to become—and he discovers that he is a Harkonnen—he realizes his terrible purpose on this desert planet and likens himself ironically to a seed. "He suddenly saw how fertile was the ground into which he had fallen, and with this realization, the terrible purpose filled him, creeping through the empty place within, threatening to choke him with grief." [50]

To ensure his leadership of the Fremen as Paul-Muad'Dib, Paul must learn to ride the worm: "Its great teeth within the cavern-circle of its mouth spread like some enormous flower. The spice odor from it dominated the air." This one, Stilgar tells him is an "old man of the desert." Paul must "have proper respect for such a one." The worm loomed, its cresting front segments throwing a sand-wave sweeping across his knees. The wave lifted his feet, then he planted his hooks and leapt and maneuvered himself up the worm. To become *mudir* of the sandride. And in that same moment, as a curry-toned sandstorm crests the horizon, Paul visualizes another storm and his terrible purpose related to it: "The turmoil comes and if I'm not where I can unravel it, the thing will run wild." [50]

Paul is the storm. He is the storm of change: for both the incumbent Harkonens, who refuse to give up their power and the spice, and the indigenous Fremen, who have their own plans to reclaim part of the desert planet for their subsistence.

When describing spice, Paul reveals the double-edged quality of this elixir: "A poison—so subtle, so insidious … so irreversible. It won't even kill you unless you stop taking it. We can't leave Arrakis unless we take part of Arrakis with us." [50]

The novel's use of Islamic mysticism and connections to ancient Sufism—in which the opium trade played a central part in political intrigue between the British Empire, Russia and other stakeholders—weaves religion into the core of its political intrigue. On some level, Paul is Arrakis. His development from Duke-heir to Paul Muad'Dib ("One Who Points the Way")— religious leader of all Fremen and of the planet Arrakis (and eventually of the universe as Emperor in the later books)—follows the dialectic of living in ecological symbiosis with nature as part of a larger cycle of cosmic forces.

4.3 RICHARD POWER'S TREES

Richard Powers's *The Overstory* follows the life-stories of nine characters and their journey with trees. At its heart is the pivotal life of botanist Patricia Westerford, who will inspire a movement.

Patricia Westerford—whose work resembles that of UBC's Suzanne Simard—is a shy introvert who discovers that trees communicate, learn, trade goods and services—and have intelligence. When she shares her discovery, she is ridiculed by her peers and loses her position at the university. Just as with Lynn Margulis and her theory of endosymbiosis, Westerford is finally validated—but not before she almost kills herself with a deadly stew of *Amanita bisporigera*, a foreshadowing of her destiny. Patricia Westerford is the archetypal 'mother tree', the metaphoric *Tachigali versicolor*, who ultimately brings the tangle of narratives together through meaning. Westerford writes in her book *The Secret Forest*:

> There are no individuals in a forest, no separable events. The bird and the branch it sits on are a joint thing. A third or more of the food a big tree makes may go to feed other organisms. Even different kinds of trees form partnerships. Cut down a birch, and a nearby Douglas fir may suffer ... Fungi mine stone to supply their trees with minerals. They hunt springtails, which they feed to their hosts. Trees, for their part, store extra sugar in their fungi's synapses, to dole out to the sick and shaded and wounded. A forest takes care of itself, even as it builds the local climate it needs to survive.[30]

Born in 1950 with a severe hearing problem, Patricia grows up close to her naturalist father; she is close to deaf and yet she will learn to hear the arcane silences of trees. Patricia nurtures a strong connection to the American Beech, her father's favourite tree: "Best tree you could ever want to see," he tells her. "If you see a trunk carved full of letters, it's a beech. People can't help writing all over that smooth gray surface. God love 'em. They want to watch their lettered hearts growing bigger, year after year," He says. The beech is a social tree. The beech's smooth trunk more resembles stone than wood and its parchment-coloured leaves ride out the winter—*marcescent*—shining out against the neighbouring bare hardwoods like a cheerful exhortation. Like she will eventually. "What happened to them," she asks as they walk through a clearing once covered in dark beech forest. "We did," he says. On her fourteenth birthday, her father gives her a copy of Ovid's *Metamorphosis*, whose first line predicts her own journey of transformation: *Let me sing to you now, about how people turn into other things.* This change proves far more than metaphoric in nature as she finds her calling—and challenge—at Purdue University to study forest ecology and her heart's mind migrates from beech and maple to spruce and Douglas-fir.

Like the *marcescent* beech, Patricia finds herself asynchronous with the rest of the forestry department at Purdue, in fact with the entire forestry discipline in the country. She disagrees with their edict of needing to "clean the forest of snags and wind throw to improve forest health." She disagrees with their use of terms like *thrifty young forests and decadent old forests, mean annual increment and economic maturity*—not ecological but economic terms based on exploitation and human utility.

Her early conviction that these silent trees are social creatures, sets her on a singular path that will push the boundaries of doctrine and a hegemony of human utility. Patricia assiduously sets out to prove her premise of social trees and in so doing, *becomes* the forest. "She works all day in the woods, her back crawling with chiggers, her scalp with ticks, her mouth filled with leaf duff, her eyes with pollen, cobwebs like scarves around her face, bracelets of poison ivy, her knees gouged by cinders, her nose lined with spores, the backs of her thighs bitten Braille by wasps, and her heart as happy as the day is generous." [30] Like Ovid, she is becoming.

Her intuition is vindicated when her experiments prove that trees communicate with one another. "Her maples are *signaling*. They're linked together in an airborne network, sharing an immune system across acres of woodland. These brainless, stationary trunks are protecting each other." The conclusion to her radical paper incites: "The biochemical behaviour of individual trees may make sense only when we see them as members of a community." The press goes crazy. She is invited to speak at conferences. Then the axe comes down; the old guard mocks her research; leading dendrologists claim her methods are flawed. She's a woman, a girl with ridiculous notions of intelligent trees. Her university doesn't renew her contract. Her career is dead.

She loses herself in the forest. "She tramps the winter trails, feeling the thick, sticky horse chestnut buds with her frozen fingers. The understory fills up with tracks like longhand accusations scribbled on the snow. She listens to the forest, to the chatter that has always sustained her. But all she can hear is the deafening wisdom of crowds." She even tries suicide through deadly mushrooms. But something stops her: "*Not this. Come with. Fear nothing.*" Is it the forest talking to her? She transforms into a creature of the forest. One day, she glimpses herself in a service station mirror: "She looks marvelously weathered, old beyond her years. She has gone to seed. Soon she'll start to scare people. Well, she has always scared people. Angry people who hated wildness took away her career. Frightened people mocked her for saying that trees send messages to each other. She forgives them all."[30]

Patricia observes how these motionless trees are actually migrating: "immortal stands of aspen retreating before the latest two-mile-thick glaciers, then following them back north again." She too is migrating. Her journey takes her to the giant trees of the west coast, where she is overwhelmed by their massive size, dense biomass and profligate nature.

> "Clicks and chatter disturb the cathedral hush. The air is so twilight-green she feels like she's underwater. It rains particles—spore clouds, broken webs and mammal dander, skeletonized mites, bits of insect frass and bird feather ... Everything climbs over everything else, fighting for scraps of light. If she holds still too long, vines will overrun her ... The earth gives beneath her like a shot mattress ... Death is everywhere, oppressive and beautiful ... The prodigious forest pulls her along, past the trunk of an immense western red cedar ... whose girth rivals the height of an eastern dogwood."[30]

Humbled and compelled to address the giant tree, Patricia follows the indigenous peoples before her and thanks the tree and the forest for everything.
   During the decade she hides in the deep forest, forestry research catches
up and an enclave of like-minded foresters invite her into their research camp
to continue her work. That's when "Patricia gives herself to Douglas-firs. Ar-
row-straight, untapering, soaring up a hundred feet before the first branch."
Yet these independent-looking behemoths tell a very different story beneath
the obvious, in their roots. Just as Patricia secretly yearns for humanity, these
trees yearn for one another.

> When the lateral roots of two Douglas-firs run into each other underground,
> they fuse. Through those self-grafted knots, the two trees join their vascu-
> lar systems together and become one. Networked together underground by
> countless thousands of miles of living fungal threads, her trees feed and heal
> each other, keep their young and sick alive, pool their resources and metab-
> olites into community chests ... Before it dies, a Douglas-fir, half a millen-
> nium old, will send its storehouse of chemicals back down into its roots and
> out through its fungal partners, donating its riches to the community pool
> in a last will and testament. We might well call these ancient benefactors
> giving trees.[30]

   Patricia later thinks: "It will take years for the picture to emerge. There will
be findings, unbelievable truths confirmed by a spreading worldwide web of
researchers in Canada, Europe, Asia, all happily swapping data through faster
and better channels." A living spreading network talking about another living
spreading network. "There are no individuals," Patricia concludes. "There ar-
en't even separate species. Everything in the forest is the forest. Competition is
not separate from endless flavors of cooperation. Trees fight no more than do
the leaves on a single tree ... If trees share their storehouses, then every drop
of red must float on a sea of green."
   When friend Dennis says to her, "You're self-reliant. Like your trees," she
responds without thinking, "But that's just it, Dennis. They aren't self-reliant.
Everything out here is cutting deals with everything else." Then they "cut a
deal" to get married. "She takes his shaking hand in the dark. It feels good,
like a root must feel, when it finds, after centuries, another root to pleach to
underground. There are a hundred thousand species of love, separately invented, each more ingenious than the last and every one of them keeps making things." When Den passes away, she continues to hear him high up in the
Douglas-fir in the middle of a howling storm.
   Patricia sees the forest as if for the first time and it's mostly underground,
unseen: "Mats of mycorrhizal cabling link trees into gigantic, smart commu-

nities spread across hundreds of acres. Together, they form vast trading networks of goods, services, and information." All day and all night long, this almost deaf woman listens to trees. "Her only people are the trees, and her only means of speaking for them are words, those organs of saprophytic latecomers that live off the energy green things make."

Patricia writes a book—*The Secret Forest*—to help bring awareness of humanity with their living partners, the trees. The opening reads:

> *You and the tree in your backyard come from a common ancestor. A billion and a half years ago, the two of you parted ways. But even now, after an immense journey in separate directions, that tree and you still share a quarter of your genes...*[30]

When Patricia writes about "Old Tjikko", a nine thousand-year-old Norway Spruce (*Picea abies*) in Sweden—a clonal tree, regenerated by new trunks, branches and roots over millennia—she collides headlong with humanity's canon of self-serving utility:

> *She works to squeeze the nine-thousand-year saga into ten sentences: a procession of trunks falling and springing back up from the same root. There's the hopeful she's after ... But hope and truth do nothing for humans, without use. In the clumpy clumsy finger-paint of words, she searches for the use of Old Tjikko [oldest living Norway Spruce in the world], up on the barren crest, endlessly dying and resurrecting in every change of climate. His use is to show that the world is not made for our utility. What use are we to the trees? She remembers the Buddha's words: A tree is a wondrous thing that shelters, feeds, and protects all living things. It even offers shade to the axmen who destroy it.*[30]

That is how she ends her book. And with those last words, she seals her fate of becoming. She dives deeper into the depths of scientific heresy to suggest that creatures other than humans are social, intelligent and have intent.

> *Love for trees pours out of her—the grace of them, their supple experimentation, the constant variety and surprise. These slow, deliberate creatures with their elaborate vocabularies, each distinctive, shaping each other, breeding birds, sinking carbon, purifying water, filtering poisons from the ground, stabilizing the microclimate. Join enough living things together, through the air and underground, and you wind up with something that has intention. Forest. A threatened creature.*[30]

Patricia agrees to serve as expert witness in a court case to help an injunction to stop clearcutting a contested area of old growth forest in western Oregon. She moves the judge with her impassioned expert knowledge; but the injunction doesn't hold and the aggressive cut resumes. In her view, extraction "can't ever slow down. The only thing we know how to do is grow. Grow harder; grow faster. More than last year. Growth all the way up the cliff and over." She laments how "the towering, teetering pyramid of large living things is toppling down already, in slow motion, under the huge, swift kick that has dislodged the planetary system. The great cycles of air and water are breaking. The Tree of Life will fall again, collapse into a stump of invertebrates, tough ground cover, and bacteria."

She starts a seed bank. Along with a consortium of four universities, she establishes the Global Seedbed Germplasm Vault. The vault will preserve "those tens of thousands of tree species that will vanish in our lifetimes." She travels the world, collecting rare and undervalued seeds. The reporters ask her why she isn't focusing on plants that will be useful to people, come catastrophe. "She wants to say: *useful is the catastrophe.*" At some point, the pointlessness of her salvage pursuit comes clear to her: "what good [is it] to save a species without all the epiphytes, fungi, pollinators and other symbionts that, in the trenches of the day, give a species its real home?" Then she discovers the woman in the tree—a figure naturally carved on a buttressed tree—and Patricia thinks of Ovid's first line: *let me sing to you now about how people turn into other things.*

She writes another book; about her seeds, about the world's forests. Reminded of the woman in the tree, she writes: "No one sees trees. We see fruit, we see nuts, we see wood, we see shade. We see ornaments or pretty fall foliage. Obstacles blocking the road or wrecking the ski slope. Dark, threatening places that must be cleared. We see branches about to crush our roof. We see a cash crop. But trees—trees are invisible." Like she is:

In a world of perfect utility, we, too, will be forced to vanish.[30]

Despite her growing agoraphobia, Patricia accepts an invitation from Stanford to be a keynote speaker on the role of trees in helping humanity toward a sustainable future. "People need things from her. People mistake her for someone else. People mean to drag her violently back into what people mistakenly call *the world.*"[30] To unbecome ...

"The conference organizers want a keynote from a woman who once wrote a book on the power of woody plants to restore the failing planet. But she wrote that book decades ago, when she was still young enough for courage and the planet still well enough to rally." She reads the invitation several times while listening to the crickets chirp in the night. Her father had taught her how to convert the chirps per minute into degrees Fahrenheit. "For sixty years, the nighttime orchestra all around her has been playing one of those folk dances that keep speeding up until all the players tumble in a heap." They don't want a tree woman to keynote their gathering, she concludes. "They want a master illusionist. A sci-fi novelist. The Lorax. Maybe a colorful faith healer, with epiphytes for hair." A techno-shaman serving dreams of technological solutions of streamlined efficiency that won't upset the "just a little more" highway of success.

In her final moments—as she stands at the podium in the Stanford auditorium to deliver her first and last keynote—Patricia looks past the large crowd assembled there, to the redwood walls "questionably obtained" and rests her gaze on a painting of a "naïve wooden ark with a parade of animals winding up into it." It sparks the opening of her keynote, a sacrificial eulogy to trees that will strike at the very heart of who and what she has become.

"When the world was ending the first time," she begins, "Noah took all the animals, two by two, and loaded them aboard his escape craft for evacuation. But it's a funny thing: he left the plants to die. He failed to take the one thing he needed to rebuild life on land, and concentrated on saving the freeloaders." The crowd laughs, not fully understanding where she's going with this. "The problem was," she continues, "Noah and his kind didn't believe that plants were really alive. No intentions, no vital spark. Just like rocks that happened to get bigger." Then she gets to the point: "A reporter once asked Rockefeller how much is enough. His answer: Just a little bit more. And that's all we want ... just a little bit more." The audience begins to stir restlessly, not clear on her progression. "Just a little more timber. A few more jobs." Now the shifting in the seats, nervous coughs and whispers. "Life is so generous," she builds relentlessly. "And we are so ... *inconsolable*. But nothing I can say will wake the sleepwalk or make this suicide seem real. It can't be real, right? I mean, here we are, all still ..." She takes a turn and lets them regroup from her snare. "You see, a lot of folks think trees are simple things, incapable of doing anything interesting. But there's a tree for every purpose under heaven. Their chemistry is astonishing. Waxes, fats, sugars. Tannins, sterols, gums, and carotenoids. Resin acids, flavonoids, terpenes. Alkaloids, phenols, corky suberins. They're learning to make whatever can be made. And most of what they make we haven't even identified." The crowd relaxes with this apparent trajectory of information. But it's the lag phase of an exponential curve. "At some time over the last four hundred million years, some plant has tried every strategy with a remote chance of working ... Life has a way of talking to the future ... To solve the future, we must save the past. My simple rule of thumb, then, is this: when you cut down a tree, what you make from it should be at least as miraculous as what you cut down." It is at this point that her hearing lapses either due to her hearing aids malfunctioning or her childhood deafness reinstating itself; this, of course, is a signal of her final becoming. She is no longer lecturing with information. She is preparing. Patricia describes the legacy of what outsiders like her have learned about trees despite the naysayers and intellectual bullies: trees communicate, save water, share, heal, synchronize and feed their young. "A forest knows things," she says. They solve problems, make decisions. Fungal synapses. Root plasticity. "Link enough trees together and a forest grows *aware*," she says. If we could only see green. If we could only understand green ... what would green say?

Patricia describes the *Tachigali versicolor tree*—the suicide tree—that flowers only once, before dying. Its once-in-a-lifetime's offspring germinates right away, in the shadow of giants with not enough light to grow. "They're doomed," she says, "unless an old tree falls. The dying mother opens a hole in the canopy, and its rotting trunk enriches the soil for new seedlings." The ultimate parental sacrifice. She asks one last question: *what is the single best thing a person can do for tomorrow's world?* Then responds by ending her life.

Patricia is the Douglas-fir, the *Giving Tree*—the ancient tree that in its last act gives all its secondary metabolites back to the community. Just as each of the other characters finally embraces their trees in their final destiny.

In his review of *The Overstory*, Benjamin Markovits of *The Guardian* wrote, "There is something exhilarating ... in reading a novel whose context is wider than human life. Like *Moby-Dick*, *The Overstory* leaves you with a slightly adjusted frame of reference ... And I found, while reading, that some of what was happening to his characters passed into my conscience, like alcohol into the bloodstream, and left a feeling behind of grief or guilt, even after I put it down." This happens when a story encompasses the epic scope of place as character. Like Hardy's Egdon Heath, Herbert's Dune planet, Power's forests are the main characters of the story. And characters like Patricia Westerford, who embraces the forest through every act and thought, are its avatars.

REFERENCES

PART 1: ECOLOGY

1. Wulf, Andrea. 2015. "The Invention of Nature: Alexander von Humboldt's New World." *Vintage Books*, New York, NY 552pp.
2. Munteanu, Nina. 2016. "Water Is…The Meaning of Water." *Pixl Press*, Vancouver, BC 586pp.
3. Kenkel, N.C. & D.J. Walker. 1993. "Fractals and ecology." *Abstracia Botanica* 17(1-2): 53-70.
4. Wohlleben, Peter. 2015. "The Hidden Life of Trees." *Greystone Books*, Vancouver, BC. 272pp.
5. Mapes, Lynda V. 2017. "Witness Tree." *Bloomsbury*, New York. 224pp.
6. Goldman, Jason G. 2018. "A Scientist Found a Kelp on a Worm in a Hole in the Mud on the Bottom of the Sea." *Hakai Magazine*, November 2, 2018. Online: https://www.hakaimagazine.com/news/a-scientist-found-a-kelp-on-a-worm-in-a-hole-in-the-mud-on-the-bottom-of-the-sea/
7. Ho, Mae-Wan. 2007. "Quantum Jazz: the Tao of Biology." *ISIS Lecture*, Institute of Science in Society.
8. Voeikov, V.L. and E. Del Guidice. 2009. "Water Respiration—The Basis of the Living State." *Water* 1: 52–75.
9. Hubel, Tatjana Y., Julia P. Myatt, Neil R. Jordan, Oliver P. Dewhirst, J. Weldon McNutt & Alan. M. Wilson. 2016. "Energy cost and return for hunting in African wild dogs and cheetahs." *Nature Communication* 7 (11034 [2016])
10. Carbone, Chris, Amber Teacher, and J. Marcus Rowcliffe. 2007. "The Costs of Carnivory." *PLosBiol.* 5(2) DOI: [10.1371/journal.pbio.0050022]
11. Anonymous. 2016. "Strategies dealing with the cuckoo mafia." *Max-Planck Research*, May 17, 2016. Online: https://www.mpg.de/10517426/cuckoo-mafia-host-tolerance
12. Munteanu, Nina. 2020 (due). "A Diary in the Age of Water." *Inanna Publications*, Toronto. 170pp.
13. Simon, Matt. 2017. "Absurd creature of the week: the wasp that lays eggs inside caterpillars and turns them into slaves." *Wired Magazine*, October 17, 2017. Online : https://www.wired.com/2014/10/absurd-creature-week-glyptapanteles-wasp-caterpillar-bodyguard/
14. AccessScienceEditors. 2018. "Trophic cascade in Yellowstone National Park." *Briefing*, August, 2018. DOI: https://doi.org/10.1036/1097-8542.BR0428152

188 15. Lorenz, Konrad. 1977. "Behind the Mirror: A Search for a Natural History of Human Knowledge." *Harcourt Brace Jovanovich*, New York.

16. McCullough, Michael. 2010. "Beyond revenge: the evolution of the forgiveness instinct." *The Journal of Positive Psychology*, p. 97-100.

17. Munteanu, Nina. 2009. "The Fiction Writer: Get Published, Write Now!" *Starfire World Syndicate*, Louisville, KY. 264pp.

18. Hane, Elizabeth N., Steven P. Hamburg, Adelia L. Barber, and Jennifer A. Plaut. 2003. "Phytotoxicity of American beech leaf leachate to sufar maple seedlings in a greenhouse experiment." *Can. J. For. Res.* 33: 814-821.

19. Ball, Philip. 2000. "H2O: A Biography of Water." *Phoenix*, London, UK. 387 pp.

20. Emoto, Masaru. 2005. "The Secret Life of Water." *Atria Books*, New York. 178 pp.

21. Beresford-Kroeger, Diana. 2010. "The Global Forest." *Penguin Books Ltd.* 175pp.

22. Reimchen, T.E. 2001. "Salmon Nutrients, Nitrogen Isotopes and Coastal Forests." *Ecoforestry*. Victoria, British Columbia. Fall, 2001. Online: www.ecoforestry.ca

23. Reimchen, T.E., D. Mathewson, M.D. Hocking, and J. Moran. 2002. "Evidence for Enrichment of Salmon-derived Nutrients in Vegetation, Soil, and Insects in Riparian Zones in Coastal British Columbia." *American Fisheries Society Symposium XX:* 1–12 pp.

24. Vannote, R.L., G.W. Minshall, K.W. Cummins, J.R. Sedell, and C.E. Cushing. 1980. "River Continuum Concept." *Can. J. Fish. Aquat. Sci.* Vol 37: 130-137.

25. Holling, C.S. 1973. "Resilience and Stability of Ecological Systems." *Annual Rev. Ecol. Syst.* 4: 1–23.

26. Holling, C.S. 1977. "Myths of Ecology and Energy." In: "Proceedings, Symposium on Future Strategies for Energy Development." Oak Ridge, Tenn., 20–21 October, 1976. *Oxford University Press*, New York, N.Y.

27. Holling, C.S. 1987. "Simplifying the Complex: The Paradigms of Ecological Function and Structure." *Eur. J. Oper. Rel.* 30: 139–146.

28. Ricci, C. And D. Fontaneto. 2017. "The importance of being a bdelloid: Ecological and evolutionary consequences of dormancy." *Italian Journal of Zoology*, 76:3, 240-249.

29. Robinson, Kelly and Julie Dunning. 2016. "Bacteria and humans have been swapping DNA for millennia". *The Scientist Magazine*, October 1, 2016. Online: https://www.the-scientist.com/?articles.view/articleNo/47125/title/Bacteria-and-Humans-Have-Been-Swapping-DNA-for-Millennia/

30. O'Leary, Denise. 2015. "Horizontal gene transfer: Sorry, Darwin, it's not your evolution anymore." *Evolution News*, August 13, 2015. Online: https://www.evolutionnews.org/201508/horizontal(underscore)gene/

31. Qiu, Huan, Hwan Su Yoon, and Debashish Bhattacharya. 2013. "Algal endosymbionts as vectors of horizontal gene transfer in photosynthetic eukaryotes. " *Frontiers in Plant Science*, 4 : 366.

32. Anonymous. 2015. "Genetically modified people." *The Economist*, March 189 12, 2015. Online: https://www.economist.com/news/science-and-technology/21646197-human-beings-ancestors-have-routinely-stolen-genes-other-species-genetically

33. Williams, Sarah. 2015. "Humans may harbour more than 100 genes from other organisms". *Science*, March 12, 2015. Online: http://www.sciencemag.org/news/2015/03/humans-may-harbor-more-100-genes-other-organisms

34. Munteanu, N. and G.P. Thomas. 2001. "The Role of Disturbance in Lake Evolution and Implications to Restoration and Management." In: *28th ATW Symposium*, Winnipeg, October 2001.

35. Margulis, Lynn. 1981. "Symbiosis in Cell Evolution: Microbial Communities in the Archean and Proterozoic Eons." *W.H. Freeman & Co Ltd.* New York, NY. 419 pp.

36. Mazur, Suzan. 2010. "The Altenberg 16: An Exposé of the Evolution Industry" (Chapter 18: 'Lynn Margulis: Intimacy of Strangers and Natural Selection'). *North Atlantic Books*, Berkeley, California. 376 pp.

37. Campbell, Joseph. 1949. "A Hero with a Thousand Faces." *Pantheon Books.* 432 pp.

38. Sahtouris, Elisabet. 2014. "Ecosophy: Nature's Guide to a Better World." *Kosmos*, Spring/Summer 2014: 4–9.

39. Weinhold, Bob. 2006. "Epigenetics: the science of change." *Environmental Health Perspectives*, 114(3): A160-A167.

40. Libby, Eric and William C. Ratcliff. 2014. "Ratcheting the Evolution of Multicellularity." *Science* 24 October: 426 – 427.

41. Pianka, E.R. 1970. "On r and K selection." *American Naturalist* 104(940): 592–597

42. Ridley, Matt. 1998. "The Origins of Virtue: Human Instincts and the Evolution of Cooperation." *Penguin Books*, London. 304pp.

43. Ehrlich, Paul R. and Peter H. Raven. 1964. "Butterflies and Plants: A study in coevolution." Evolution 18: 586-608.

44. Ryan, Frank. 2011. "Virolution." *Harper Collins Publishers*, London 400pp.

45. Munteanu, Nina. 2007. "Darwin's Paradox." *Dragon Moon Press*, Calgary, AB. 320pp.

46. Ruche, Alain. 2014. "International Cultural Engagement. Part One: Are We at the Tipping Point?" *Kosmos*, Spring/Summer Issue: 55–59.

47. Eisler, Riane. 1988. "The Chalice and the Blade: Our History, Our Future." *Harper*, San Francisco. 261 pp.

48. Kaminski, June. 2013. "Theory: Learning with the Natural World". *First Nations Pedagogy*. Online: http://firstnationspedagogy.com/earth.html

49. Bozzo, Sam. 2008. "Blue Gold," a film based on the book by Maude Barlow and Tony Clarke and narrated by Malcolm McDowell. *Purple Turtle Films*. 90 min. Online: www.bluegold-worldwaterwars.com

190 50. Lovelock, J.E. and L. Margulis. 1974." Atmospheric Homeostasis by and for the Biosphere: the Gaia Hypothesis". Tellus: a bimonthly journal of Geophysics, *Swedish Geophysical Society* 26(1): 2–10.

51. Margulis, Lynn. 1998. "Symbiotic Planet: a New Look at Evolution." *Weidenfeld & Nicolson*, London. 176 pp.

52. Arthur, Brian. 2004. In: Mitchel M. Waldrop (author), "Complexity: The Emerging Science at the Edge of Order and Chaos." *Simon & Schuster Paperbacks*, New York. p. 333.

53. Anonymous. 2014. "The Big Five Mass Extinctions." *Cosmos Magazine*. https://cosmosmagazine.com/palaeontology/big-five-extinctions

54. Fox, Douglas. 2016. "What Sparked the Cambrian Explosion?" *Nature*. 16 February, 2016. Online: https://www.nature.com/news/what-sparked-the-cambrian-explosion-1.19379

55. Narbonne, Guy M., Marc LaFlamme, Carolyn Greentree and Peter Trusler. 2009. "Reconstructing a lost world: Ediacaran rangeomorphs from Spaniard's Bay, Newfoundland." *Journal of Paleontology* 83(4): 503-523.

56. Centre for Biological Diversity. 2018. "The Extinction Crisis." *Centre for Biological Diversity*. Online: https://www.biologicaldiversity.org/programs/biodiversity/elements_of_biodiversity/extinction_crisis/

57. Carrington, Damian. 2018. "Humanity has wiped out 60% of animal populations since 1970, report finds." *The Guardian*, October 30, 2018. Online: https://www.theguardian.com/environment/2018/oct/30/humanity-wiped-out-animals-since-1970-major-report-finds

58. McKirdy, Euan. 2017. "New study suggests insect populations have declined by 75% over 3 decades." *CNN*, October 20, 2017. Online: https://www.cnn.com/2017/10/19/europe/insect-decline-germany/index.html

59. Richmond, Courtney E., Denise L. Breitburg, and Kenneth A. Rose. 2005. "The role of environmental generalist species in ecosystem function." *Ecological Modelling* 188 (2-4): 279-295.

60. Peers, Michael J. L., Daniel H. Thornton, and Dennis L. Murray. 2012. "Reconsidering the Specialist-Generalist Paradigm in Niche Breadth Dynamics: Resources Gradient Selection by Canada Lynx and Bobcat." *PLoS ONE* 7(12): e51488. https://doi.org/10.1371/journal.pone.0051488

61. Peers, Michael J. L., Daniel H. Thornton, and Dennis L. Murray. 2012. "Reconsidering the Specialist-Generalist Paradigm in Niche Breadth Dynamics: Resources Gradient Selection by Canada Lynx and Bobcat." *PLoS ONE* 7(12): e51488. https://doi.org/10.1371/journal.pone.0051488

62. Devictor, Vincent, Joanne Clavel, Romain Julliard, Sebastien Lavergne, David Mouillot, Wilfried Thuiller, Patrick Venail, Sebastien Villeger and Nicolas Mouquet. 2010. "Defining and measuring ecological specialization." *Journal of Applied Ecology* 47: 15-25.

63. Ab Hamid, Suhaila and Che Salmah Md Rawi. 2017. "Appliction of Aquatic

Insects (Ephemeroptera, Plecoptera and Trichoptera) in Water Quality Assess- 191
ment of Malaysian Headwater. *Trop Life Sci Res.* 28(2): 143-162.

64. McLachlan, J. S., Hellmann, J. J., & Schwartz, M. W. 2007. "A framework for debate of assisted migration in an era of climate change." *Conservation Biology*, 21(2), 297-302.

65. Aitken, S. N., Yeaman, S., Holliday, J. A., Wang, T. & Curtis- McLane, S. 2008. "Adaptation, migration or extirpation: climate change outcomes for tree populations." *Evolutionary Applications*, 1(1): 95- 111.

66. Tang, G., Beckage, B., & Smith, B. 2012. "The potential transient dynamics of forests in New England under historical and projected future climate change." *Climatic change*, 114(2), 357-377.

67. Yong, Ed. 2013. "Honey bees can move each other with electric fields." *National Geographic*, March 26, 2013. Online: https://www.nationalgeographic.com/science/phenomena/2013/03/26/honeybees-can-move-each-other-with-electric-fields/

68. Kluger, Jeffrey. 2015. "The Search for Life in the Universe." *Time Books*, NY, New York. 96pp.

69. Encyclopaedia Britannica. 2007. "Cytoplasmic streaming." *The Editors of Encyclopaedia Britannica*. Online: https://www.britannica.com/science/cytoplasmic-streaming

70. Law, Yao-Hua. 2016. "How insect-eating plants persuade insects to pollinate them." *BBC Earth*, October 11, 2016. http://www.bbc.com/earth/story/20161010-how-insect-eating-plants-persuade-insects-to-pollinate-them

71. The Patek Lab. 2013. "Mechanics of Movement: Trap-Jaw Ants." *Patek Lab of Duke University*. Online: https://pateklab.biology.duke.edu/mechanics-movement-trap-jaw-ants

72. Yong, Ed. 2013. "Trees Trap Ants Into Sweet Servitude." *National Geographic*, November 6, 2013. Online: https://news.nationalgeographic.com/news/2013/11/131106-ants-tree-acacia-food-mutualism/

73. Ricci, C. And D. Fontaneto. 2017. "The importance of being a bdelloid: Ecological and evolutionary consequences of dormancy." *Italian Journal of Zoology*, 76:3, 240-249.

74. Cormier, Zoe. Year. "Fish are the sex-switching masters of the animal kingdom." *BBC Earth*. Online : https://ourblueplanet.bbcearth.com/blog/?article=incredible-sex-changing-fish-from-blue-planet

75. Jobling, S. and C.R. Tyler. 2003. "Endocrine disruption in wild freshwater fish." *Pure and Applied Chemistry* 75 (11-12) : 2219-2234.

76. Anhäuser, M. 2007. "The Silent Scream of the Lima Bean." *MaxPlanckResearch* 4. Online: https://www.mpg.de/942876/W001_Biology-Medicine_060_065.pdf

77. Simard, Suzanne. 2016. "How Trees Talk to Each Other." *Ted Talk*, July 22, 2016. Online: https://en.tiny.ted.com/talks/suzanne_simard_how_trees_talk_to_each_other

78. Toomey, Diane. 2016. "Exploring How and Why Trees 'Talk' to Each Other." *Yale Environment 360*, September 1, 2016. Online: https://e360.yale.edu/features/exploring_how_and_why_trees_talk_to_each_other

79. Haskell, David George. 2017. "The Songs of Trees." *Viking*. 304pp.

80. Van Huis, Arnold. 2017. "Cultural significance of termites in sub-Saharan Africa." *J. Ethnobiol. Ethnomed.* 13:8.

81. Cell Press. 2018. "4,000-year-old termite mounds found in Brazil are visible from space." Science Daily, November 20, 2018. Online: https://www.sciencedaily.com/releases/2018/11/181120073648.htm

82. Jouquet, Pascal, Saran Traoré, Chutinan Choosai, Christian Hartmann, David Bignell. 2011. "Influence of termites on ecosystem functioning. Ecosystem services provided by termites." *European Journal of Soil Biology* 47: 215-222. Online: https://esanalysis.colmex.mx/Sorted%20Papers/2011/2011%20BFA%20FRA%20GBR%20THA%20VNM%20-Biodiv%20Phys.pdf

83. Yong, Ed. 2010. "Evolutionary arms race turns ants into babysitters for Alcon blue butterflies." *National Geographic*, October 16, 2010. Online : http://phenomena.nationalgeographic.com/2010/10/16/evolutionary-arms-race-turns-ants-into-babysitters-for-alcon-blue-butterflies/

84. Brahic, Catherine. 2008. "Parasitic butterflies fool ants with smell." *New Scientist*, January 3, 2008. Online: https://www.newscientist.com/article/dn13139-parasitic-butterflies-fool-ants-with-smell/

85. Futureblind. 2011. "Generalists vs. Specialists (And the Specialist's Dilemma)." *Futureblind*, July 29, 2011. Online: https://futureblind.com/2011/07/29/generalists-vs-specialists-and-the-specialists-dilemma/

86. Munteanu, Nina. 2012. "Inner Diverse", Book 2 of The Splintered Universe Trilogy. *Pixl Press*. 344pp.

87. Thompson, J.N. 2005. "The geographic mosaic of coevolution." *University of Chicago Press*, Chicago, IL.

88. Bronstein, J.L. 1994. "Our current understand of mutualism." *Quarterly Review of Biology* 69(1): 31-51.

89. Grens, Kerry. 2019. "Not One, Not Two, But Three Fungi Present in Lichen." *The Scientist*, January 17, 2019. Online: https://www.the-scientist.com/news-opinion/not-one--not-two--but-three-fungi-present-in-lichen-65333

90. Ryan, Frank, M.D. 1997. Virus X: Tracking the New Killer Plagues. *Little, Brown and Company*, New York, N.Y. 430pp.

91. Van Loon J. 2000. Parasite politics: on the significance of symbiosis and assemblage in theorizing community formations. In: Pierson C and Tormey S (eds.), *Politics at the Edge* (London, UK: Political Studies Association)

92. Frazer, Jennifer. 2015. "Root Fungi Can Turn Pine Trees Into Carnivores—or at Least Accomplices." *Scientific American*, May 12, 2015. Online: https://blogs.scientificamerican.com/artful-amoeba/root-fungi-can-turn-pine-trees-into-carnivores-8212-or-at-least-accomplices/

93. Villarreal LP, Defilippis VR, and Gottlieb KA. 2000. Acute and persistent viral life strategies and their relationship to emerging diseases. *Virology* 272:1-6. Online: http://birdfluexposed.com/resources/Villarreal1.pdf

94. Knapton, Sarah. 2017. "Fish 'could be as intelligent as primates', scientists predict, as Blue Planet II footage shows collaboration with octopus to hunt." *The Telegraph*, November 11, 2017. Online: https://www.telegraph.co.uk/science/2017/11/11/octopus-fish-join-forces-hunt-prey-filming-first-blue-planet/

95. Sánchez-Andrea, Irene, Nuria Rodríguez, Ricardo Amils, and José Luis Sanz. 2011. "Microbial diversity in anaerobic sediments at Rio Tinto, a naturally acidic environment with a high heavy metal content. *Appl Environ Microbio* 77(17): 6085-6093.

96. Ledford, Heidi. 2007. "Hungry fungi chomp on radiation." *Nature*, June 4, 2007. Online: https://www.nature.com/news/2007/070521/full/news070521-5.html

97. Finstad, Kari, Alexander j. Probst, Brian C. Thomas, Gary L. Andersen, Cecilia Demergasso, Alex Echeverria, Ronald G. Amundson, and Jillian F. Banfield. 2017. "Microbial community structure and the persistence of cyanobacterial populations in salt crusts of the hyperarid Atacama Desert from genome-resolved metageneomics." *Front. Microbio.* July 28, 2017.

PART 2: STORY

1. MacLellan, Lila. 2017. "We've become masters of telling anecdotes, and terrible at telling our friends real stories." *Quartz*, May 28, 2017. Online: https://qz.com/991735/weve-become-masters-of-telling-anecdotes-and-terrible-at-telling-our-friends-real-stories/

2. Munteanu, Nina. 2016. "Water Is... The Meaning of Water." *Pixl Press*, Vancouver, BC 586pp.

3. Munteanu, Nina. 2009. "The Fiction Writer: Get Published, Write Now!" *Starfire World Syndicate*, Louisville, KY. 264pp.

4. Scott Card, Orson. 2010. "The 4 Story Structures that Dominate Novels." *Writers Digest Magazine*. August 24, 2010. Online: https://www.writersdigest.com/writing-articles/by-writing-goal/write-first-chapter-get-started/4-story-structures-that-dominate-novels

5. Russo, Richard. 1999. "Location, Location, Location: Depicting Character Through Place" In: *Fiction Writer*. April, 1999.

6. Maass, Donald. 2004. "Writing the Breakout Novel Workbook." *Writer's Digest Books*, Cincinnati, Ohio. 230pp.

7. Herbert, Frank. 1969. "Interview with Professor Willis E. McNelly." Online: http://www.sinanvural.com/seksek/inien/tvd/tvd2.htm

8. Munteanu, Nina. 2011. "Outer Diverse" Book 1 of The Splintered Universe Trilogy. *Pixl Press*, Vancouver, BC. 324pp.

194   9. Bacigalupi, Paolo. 2009 (2015). "The Windup Girl." *Night Shade Books*, New York, NY. 466pp.

10. Gurgu, Costi. 2017. "Recipearium." *White Cat Publications*, Melvindale, MI. 301pp.

11. Dibell, Ansen. 1999. "Plot (Elements of Fiction Plotting)." *Writer's Digest Books*, Cincinnati, Ohio. 170pp.

12. Proulx, Annie. 1994. "The Shipping News." *Simon and Schuster*, New York, N.Y. 352pp.

13. Bradbury, Ray. 1950. "The Martian Chronicles." *Doubleday*, New York, NY. 222pp.

14. Itäranta, Emmi. 2014. "Memory of Water." *HarperCollins*, New York, NY. 266pp.

15. Atwood, Margaret. 2005. "The Penelopiad." *Knopf*, Toronto. 216pp.

16. Atwood, Margaret. 1985. "The Handmaid's Tale." *McClelland and Stewart*, Toronto. 311pp.

17. Nolan, E. Martin. "Still Point." *Invisible Publishing*, Halifax. 97pp.

18. Liu, Cixin. Year. "The Three Body Problem." *Tor Books*. 400pp.

19. Kingsolver, Barbara. 1996. "The Poisonwood Bible." *Harper*, New York, NY. 546pp.

20. Munteanu, Nina. 2020 (due). "A Diary in the Age of Water." *Inanna Publications*, Toronto.

21. Proulx, Annie. 1997. "Brokeback Mountain." *The New Yorker*, NY.

22. Munteanu, Nina. 2016. "The Way of Water / La natura dell'acqua." Translated by Fiorella Moscatello. *Future Fiction / Mincioni Edizione*, Rome, Italy. 114pp.

23. Gordon, Mary. 1992. "The Important Houses." *The New Yorker*, N.Y.

24. Rowling, J.k.. 1997. "Harry Potter and the Philosopher's Stone." *Bloomsbury*, UK. 223pp.

25. Williams, Tennessee. (1944) 2009. "The Glass Menagerie." *Penguin Books*.

26. Kingsolver, Barbara. 2012. "Flight Behavior." *HarperCollins*, New York, N.Y. 600pp.

27. Dickens, Charles. 1839. "Oliver Twist." *Richard Bentley*, London, England.

28. Murakami, Ryu. 1997. "In the Miso Soup." Translated by Ralph McCarthy. *Yomiuri Shimbun*, Tokyo. 192pp.

29. Proulx, Annie. 2016. "Barkskins." *Simon and Schuster*, New York. 736pp.

30. Powers, Richard. 2018. "The Overstory." *W.W. Norton & Company*, New York, N.Y. 512pp.

31. Orwell, George. 1949. "Nineteen Eighty Four." *Secker & Warburg*, London, UK. 328pp.

32. Munteanu, Nina. 2007. "Darwin's Paradox." *Dragon Moon Press*, Calgary. 320pp.

33. Bradbury, Ray. 1953. "Fahrenheit 451." *Ballantine Books*, New York, N.Y. 158pp.

34. La Plante, Lynda. 2006. "Above Suspicion." *Simon and Schuster*, London, UK. 400pp.

35. Hardy, Thomas. 1878 (2001). The Return of the Native. *Belgravia*, London (Modern Library, London). 448pp.

36. Ullmann, Linn. Year. REF Linn Ullman. 2014. "Before You Can Write a Good   195
    Plot, You Need to Write a Good Place." *The Atlantic*, April 23, 2014. Online:
    https://www.theatlantic.com/entertainment/archive/2014/04/why-every-
    good-story-needs-a-good-setting/361110/
37. Proust, Marcel. 1913. "Remembrance of Things Past." *Grasset and Gallimard*,
    France. 4,215pp.
38. Hampl, Patricia. 2007 (2009). "The Florist's Daughter." *Houghton Mifflin Har-
    court*. 240pp.
39. Steinbeck, John. 1952. "East of Eden." *Viking Press*, New York, N.Y. 608pp.
40. Dickens, Charles. 1854. "Hard Times." *Bradbury and Evans*, London, UK.
41. Mitchell, David. 2001. "Number9dream." *Sceptre*, London, UK. 418pp.
42. Eagleman, David and Richard Cytowic. 2009. "Wednesday Is Indigo Blue: Dis-
    covering the Brain of Synesthesia." *MIT Press*, Cambridge, MA. 320pp.
43. Kelm, Brandon. 2008. "Poetry Comes from Our Tree-Climbing Ancestors."
    Wired Magazine, May 2008.
44. Lakoff, George and Mark Johnson. 1980. "Metaphors We Live By." *University
    of Chicago Press*, Chicago, IL. 242pp.
45. Miles, Margaret. 2001. "A Mischief in the Snow." *Bantam Books*, New York, NY.
    322pp.
46. Walton, Mark. 2008. "One Mistake To Avoid In Setting The Scene In Your Nov-
    el, Is To Overlook The Weather". In: *Articlesbase*, http://www.articlesbase.
    com/writing- articles/one-mistake-to-avoid-in-setting
47. Bacigalupi, Paolo. 2015. "The Water Knife." *Alfred A. Knopf*, New York, N.Y.
    371pp.
48. Ondaatje, Michael. 1992. "The English Patient." *McClelland and Stewart*,
    Toronto. 320pp.
49. Harris, Joanne. 1999. "Chocolat." *Doubleday*, London, UK. 394pp.
50. Herbert, Frank. 1965. "Dune." *Chilton Books*. 412pp.
51. Munteanu, Nina. 2013. "Inner Diverse," Book 2 of the Splintered Universe
    Trilogy. *Pixl Press*, Vancouver. 344pp.
52. McLuhan, T.C. 1996. "Cathedrals of the Spirit." *HarperPerennial*, Toronto.
    306pp.
53. Lawrence, D.H. 1964. "Studies in Classic American Literature." *The Viking
    Press*, New York. p. 30.
54. Norris, Kathleen. 1993. "Dakota: A Spiritual Geography." *Houghton Mifflin
    Company*, Boston. p.157.
55. Berry, Thomas. (1996). "The Meadow Across the Creek." Unpublished manu-
    script, In: *McLuhan*, T.C. "Cathedrals of the Spirit." *HarperPerrennial*, Toronto.
56. Ehrlich, Gretel. 1987. "Landscape." In: Constance Sullivan, ed. "The Legacy of
    Light." *Alfred A. Knopf*, New York. pp. 20-21.
57. Thoreau, Henry David. 1980. "Walking." T*he Natural History Essays*. Peregrine
    Smith, Salt Lake City. p. 116

CONTRIBUTORS

Author: Nina Munteanu, M.Sc., R.P.Bio., is a Canadian ecologist / limnologist and author of over a dozen non-fiction books, novels and short stories. She consulted in the aquatic sciences as senior scientist for over twenty years and conducted aquatic research at the University of Victoria and Concordia University. Nina teaches writing at the University of Toronto and George Brown College in Toronto, Canada. (ninamunteanu.ca; TheMeaningOfWater.com).

Editor: Merridy Cox, B.Sc., MMsl, is a Toronto-based editor and photographer, specializing in technical and scientific works and the natural sciences. An amateur field naturalist, Merridy is managing editor of Lyrical Leaf Publishing and has published two e-books, Shapes of Swan and Edwardian Pets and How to Keep Them. Her poetry and photography have appeared in several anthologies. (www.englishmanual.wordpress.com).

Layout/Cover Design: Costi Gurgu is an Art Director with Superpixel Design (superpix- eldesign.com) and RootPM (http://rootpm.com). He has worked for Playboy Magazine, the French fashion magazine Madame Figaro, the women lifestyle magazine, Tabu, Investment Executive and many other publications and publishing houses (http://illustration.costigurgu. com). He is also an awarded speculative fiction writer (costigurgu.com).

Cover Illustration: Anne Moody is a plant ecologist and artist, living in central British Columbia. She is a member of the Federation of Canadian Artists, Canada's oldest artistic organization. The Federation of Canadian Artists is a not-for-profit organization dedicated to the promotion and professional development of artists, and services for art collectors. Leaders of the organization have included Group of Seven painter, Lawren Harris. Anne has been drawing and painting since childhood. "I consider myself a realist, strongly tempted by abstract elements wrapped in a story."

The Cover Story

As an ecologist, I am keenly aware of the effects of climate change and its resultant effects on our environments. This is evident in sea level rises in coastal marshes (that have been my passion and profession for over 40 years), as well as in the increased risk of fires in the forested environs I now live in.

Within our family of ecologists, daughter Lisa has been involved in fire control efforts in the forests of interior BC. At the end of a long day, she took some stunning photos of firefighters. I, in turn, captured one of these scenes in a painting entitled "Everyday Hero". At the end of his day, the exhausted firefighter looks up at yet another tree bursting into flames (candling) in front of him.

We were surrounded by fires last summer and owe immeasurable thanks to the multitude of firefighters and support personnel who put their safety on the line to save livestock and wildlife, the homes, dreams and lives of residents as well as the local economy. Thank-you doesn't say enough!

—Anne Moody, Vanderhoof, B.C., April 25, 2019

ACKNOWLEDGMENTS

No work of writing is done in isolation. This is particularly true in non-fiction works that make use of much research, observation, discussion and other wonderful interaction. My heartfelt thanks go to the team that helped put this guidebook together: editor Merridy Cox; cover design artist, UX designer and art director Costi Gurgu; artist painter Anne Moody; and director of Pixl Press Anne Voûte for the magic of production. All contributed to making this a book the best it could be.

Much research and discussion went into putting together Part 1, Ecology. This section represents over twenty years of my work as a scientist and environmental consultant in the field of ecology and limnology. Time spent zooming in boats on the Pacific Ocean, clamoring over talus slopes of mine sites to collect water samples, and 24-hour monitoring of a working river; time spent in class or in a bar, debating theory and dogma. There are simply too many people to thank for this unique knowledge, experience, and perspective: you know who you are. Some include Edward J. Maly, Margaret, both Annes, Doina, among so many others. I reviewed many scientific papers, textbooks and articles by expert ecologists and other scientists—most of which are cited in the reference section.

I thank my students and colleagues at the University of Toronto and George Brown College for discussions and insight. These helped me in my discussions in Part 2, Story, and helped me refine my writing exercises into something more practical and useful.

All these helped make this book possible and made it a better book. Any errors, omissions or transgressions are my sole responsibility.

Nina Munteanu   **Writing Guides**

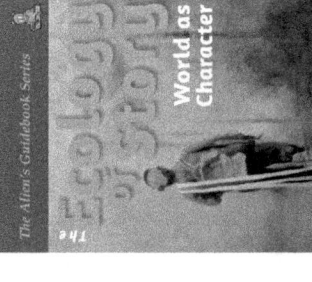

The Alien's Guidebook Series

The Fiction Writer
Get Published, Write Now!
by Nina Munteanu
Starfire World Syndicate / Pixl Press
ISBN 978-0982378304
Published May 8, 2009
Trade Paperback 266p
Digital ebook

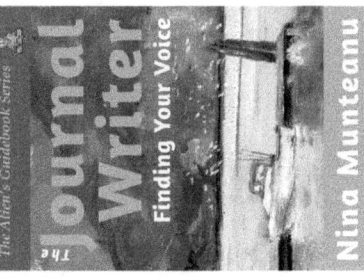

The Alien's Guidebook Series

The Journal Writer
Finding Your Voice
by Nina Munteanu
Pixl Press
ISBN 978-0981163604
Published March 25, 2013
Trade Paperback 172p
Digital ebook

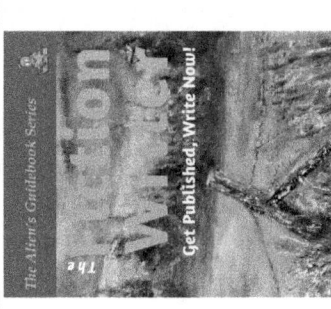

The Alien's Guidebook Series

The Ecology of Story
World as Character
by Nina Munteanu
Pixl Press
ISBN 978-0981101231
Upcoming Spring 2019
in Trade Paperback & Digital ebook

"...Like the good Doctor's Tardis, *The Fiction Writer* is larger than it appears. ...Get *Get Published, Write Now!* right now."
—**DAVID MERCHANT**, UNIVERSITY COMPOSITION INSTRUCTOR

"Good writing is good writing, and Munteanu has worked hard to provide a guidebook that shows exactly how to achieve that result. Highly recommended!"
—**SHERRY D. RAMSAY**, THE SCRIPTORIUM

"Has become my writing bible."
—**CARINA BURNS**, AUTHOR OF *THE SYRIAN JEWELRY BOX*

"As important a tool as your laptop or your pen."
—**CATHI URBONAS**, HALIFAX WRITER

"Those of us who teach creative writing are constantly searching for that perfect resource that will not only instruct, but also inspire our students . . . Nina Munteanu's book is . . . the quintessential guidebook for the soon-to-be-published."
—**SUSAN MCLEMORE**, HIGH SCHOOL WRITING INSTRUCTOR

"I'm thoroughly enjoying the book, and even learning a thing or two!"
—**ROBERT J. SAWYER**, HUGO AWARD-WINNING AUTHOR OF *WAKE*.